THE CASTLE EXPLORER'S GUIDE

THE CASTLE
EXPLORER'S GUIDE

FRANK BOTTOMLEY
Illustrated by Connie Green

KAYE & WARD
LONDON

First published in Great Britain by
Kaye & Ward Ltd.
21 New Street, London EC2M 4NT
1979

ISBN 0 7182 1216 9   (cased)
ISBN 0 7182 1219 3 (paper)

Printed and bound in Great Britain by
Fakenham Press Limited, Fakenham, Norfolk

FOR MICHAEL
WHO SUGGESTED THE IDEA AND
HELPED IN ITS EXECUTION

Micklegate Bar with 'defenders', York City Walls

Scenes from a Tournament

USING THIS BOOK

The book is divided into two sections: a Glossary (pages 1-201) which covers all aspects of castles – purpose, planning, construction, castle life, terminology. The entries are in alphabetical order for easy reference. If an architectural aspect of a castle is not known by name, check the Plan over page; which identifies most features common to castles. The illustrations will also help in the identification if a particular item is not known by name.

The second section is a Gazeteer (pages 203-249) of all the most notable castles in England, Scotland and Wales, identified by name and giving details of location, date, classification and access.

Timber and Earth Castle

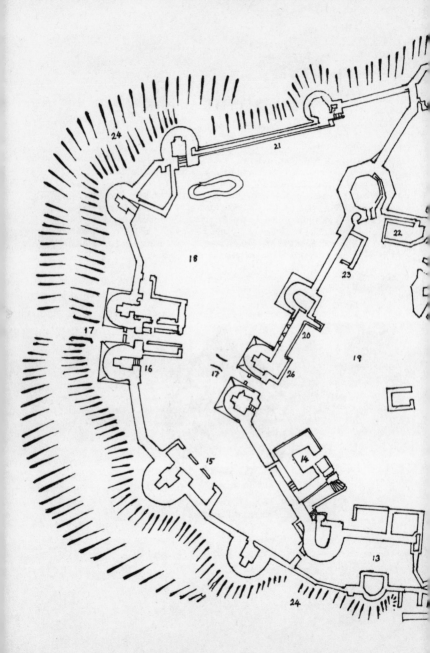

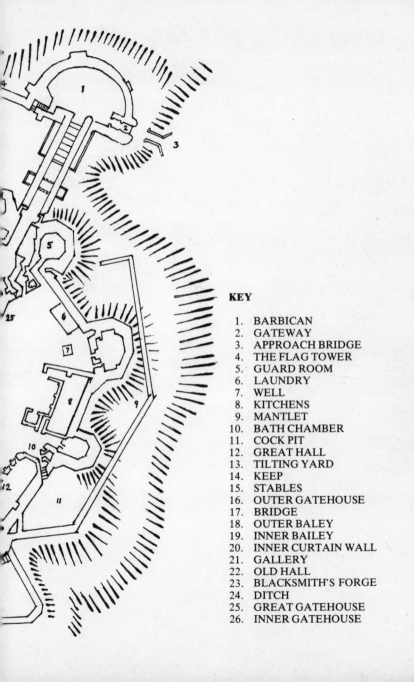

KEY

1. BARBICAN
2. GATEWAY
3. APPROACH BRIDGE
4. THE FLAG TOWER
5. GUARD ROOM
6. LAUNDRY
7. WELL
8. KITCHENS
9. MANTLET
10. BATH CHAMBER
11. COCK PIT
12. GREAT HALL
13. TILTING YARD
14. KEEP
15. STABLES
16. OUTER GATEHOUSE
17. BRIDGE
18. OUTER BALEY
19. INNER BAILEY
20. INNER CURTAIN WALL
21. GALLERY
22. OLD HALL
23. BLACKSMITH'S FORGE
24. DITCH
25. GREAT GATEHOUSE
26. INNER GATEHOUSE

Archer with Short Bow

ABERDEENSHIRE

Probably the richest Scots county for the castle explorer. The following are in the care of the Department of the Environment: Glenbuchat, Huntly, Kildrummy and Tolquhon. Others of interest at Cairnbulg, Craigievar, Drum, Drumminor, Fyvie, Insch, Inverurie, Kinnairds, Kintore, Lumsden (Craig), Midmar, Monymusk, Oyne, Pitcaple, Rosehearty, Terpersie, Turriff (Dalgatie, Towie Barclay) and Udny.

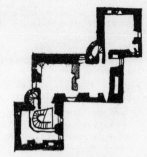

Glenbuchat Z-plan

ACCOUNTS

Sources of knowledge include Pipe Rolls (q.v.) Duchy records, etc. Besides large expenditures on major items such as donjons, walls, barbicans, halls and the like, they also contain such details as payments for huntsmen and dogs, carriage of game to other royal residences (including London), items for the maintenance and replacement of transport, wages and charges, fetters for the prison, parchment for the accounts, planks for a chest to store such accounts, grease for lubricating crane, leather for slings.

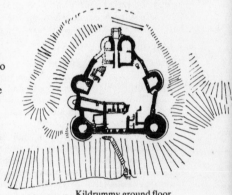

Kildrummy ground floor

ACQUISITION OF CASTLES

The first castles were a reward to William's supporters for their contribution to his success. Subsequently castles were acquired usually by gift, inheritance or marriage, though they could be gained more violently by frontal assault or surrender. During the Anarchy castles changed hands in a number of ways: transferred pledge, sale, loan, trickery (Earl of Chester on a friendly visit to Lincoln siezed arms and expelled his host), or usurpation (Stephen had to eject forcibly his own caretaker from Saffron Walden in 1145).

> 'William gave the custody of castles to some of his bravest Normans, distributing among them vast possessions as inducements to undergo cheerfully the toils and perils of defending them.' (Ordericus Vitalis).

This was only stage one – the lands of Anglo-Saxons defeated and killed at Hastings were distributed among the victors. After the insurrections of 1067, William was more ruthless and confiscated English land on a wide scale, combining thousands of English holdings into less than two hundred great estates called 'honours' (q.v.). Some English tenants retained their lands but were demoted to being sub-tenant to a Norman tenant-in-chief though there were a few English tenants-in-chief at Domesday (1086).

ADULTERINE

Adjective applied to unlicensed castles, especially to those erected during the anarchy (q.v.) of Stephen's reign (1135-1154). Most of these were dismantled during the reign of Henry II. About 1150, it is estimated that there were some 1,115 unlicensed castles.

'And they filled the whole land with these castles. They sorely burdened the unhappy people of the country with forced labour on these castles. And when the castles were made they filled them with devils and wicked men.' (Anglo-Saxon Chronicle, 1137).

In 1155 Henry II resumed castles and other royal property into his own hands and ordered the destruction of unlicensed castles. These seem to have been destroyed as quickly as they were raised and it is unlikely, therefore, that they were stone buildings. Certainly the vast majority must have consisted of earthworks with palisades and wooden buildings within them.

ALLURE

The wall-walk along the top of a curtain (q.v.) to aid its defence; also used of timber walk overhanging the wall face (See Hoarding.)

The overhanging allures at the summit of high walls and towers were a C13 innovation which developed into flying parapets (q.v.) and machicolation (q.v.).

The access to the rampart walk could be by wooden or stone stair parallel to the wall (e.g. Kidwelly) but most often was provided via the mural towers. Harlech is very interesting because, although the vices in the angle-towers communicate with the rampart walk, there is a separate stair for those responsible for guarding the intermediate section entered from the south-east tower.

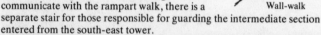
Wall-walk

Wall-walks were often paved with stone slabs (e.g. Warwick). Where this material was scarce the rubble was sometimes covered with lead (grooves for inserting the flashing are discernible at Beaumaris and Conway).

At Conway the allure is continuous, being corbelled out behind the mural towers, but at Beaumaris and Harlech it is continuous except for the gatehouses. Though this system is convenient, defence was improved if the allure was blocked at intervals by towers astride it (see Cavalier Towers) e.g. Bodiam, Caernarvon.

AMENITIES

Even the grim war castles had their softer aspects for they were always homes as well.

Giraldus Cambrensis, churchman, courtier, and man of letters, describes his family castle (Manorbier) in C12 as follows:

'The castle called Maenor Pyrr . . . is distant about three miles from Penroch. It is excellently well defended by turrets and bulwarks, and is situated on the summit of a hill extending on the western side towards the seaport, having on the northern and southern sides a fine fish-pond under its walls, as conspicuous for its grand appearance as for the depth of its waters, and a beautiful orchard on the same side, enclosed on one part by a vineyard and on the other by a wood, remarkable for the projection of its rocks and the height of its hazel trees. On the right hand of the promontory, between the castle and the church, near the site of a very large lake and mill, a rivulet of never-failing water flows through a valley, rendered sandy by the violence of the winds. Towards the west, the Severn sea, bending its course to Ireland, enters a hollow bay at some distance from the castle.'

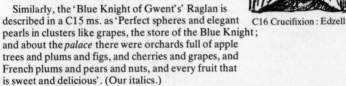

C16 Crucifixion : Edzell

Similarly, the 'Blue Knight of Gwent's' Raglan is described in a C15 ms. as 'Perfect spheres and elegant pearls in clusters like grapes, the store of the Blue Knight; and about the *palace* there were orchards full of apple trees and plums and figs, and cherries and grapes, and French plums and pears and nuts, and every fruit that is sweet and delicious'. (Our italics.)

Amenities were naturally most developed in the royal castles, e.g. at the new castle of Rhuddlan the chamber was 'painted', the queen's room had wood specially imported from Gascony and outside its windows were constructed a fish-pool and a lawn laid with 6,000 turves and protected by a fencing of barrel staves.

Similar provision was made for the queen's arrival at Conway in June 1283 and one of her squires was watering the precious lawn in July. So too in Caernarvon, in time for the royal visit of 12 July 1283, a new lawn was laid. The same castle had a swan's nest specially built in the middle of its mill-pond.

The amenities of royal castles in the early C13 include: a painted chamber at Winchester, a garden outside the bedchamber at Arundel, other gardens at Marlborough and Winchester, together with mews and dovecotes at Nottingham and elsewhere. To these we might add the provision of a park at Nottingham, a chase at Bristol and fish-ponds at Eye, and Newcastle-under-Lyme. There was a vineyard at Warwick in C14.

The fastidious Henry III set new standards in living conditions especially in his favoured palace-castle of Winchester where, among other things, he required a chapel with a tiled floor and a mural painting of Joseph, tiled floors to the royal chambers with 'a painted table' in his bedchamber with the images of 'the guardians of Solomon's bed', repairs to the privy (somewhat of an obsession with this ruler), new shutters for the gallery of the queen's chapel, renovation of the great hall, redecoration and mural paintings, together with furniture in the royal chambers, refurbishing of the queen's chamber including a painted 'Majesty' and gilded images for her oratory. Henry's reign saw an increasing provision of private chambers for officials and servants, some of them panelled in oak ('wainscoted'). Besides providing for the queen's devotions, Henry had an oratory made in his own bedchamber and gave a new marble altar for the castle chapel. He also required that the queen's private chapel was equipped with a rood-beam bearing the customary crucifix and figures of Mary and John and that there should be wall-paintings of St Christopher and St Edward the Confessor.

AMENITIES/OFFICES

The present grim and denuded nature of castles should not obscure the fact that all of them were provided, to a greater or lesser extent, with a variety of amenities and offices which have now disappeared or been obscured. These would not only include water supply often through pipes, drains and sanitary provision in the form of privies, pits and sewers but also special rooms and buildings. These latter usually included buttery (bottlery), pantry (paintry) for supplies of bread and wine, brewhouse and bakehouse (often an annexe to the kitchen). Standard domestic provision included hall, chamber, bower, solar, kitchen, oratory, chapel, together with guest-chamber for royal or other distinguished visitors. There were also workshops (including blacksmith's and carpenter's shops), stores and armoury. Stock fish-ponds were common as were deer-parks (enclosed by ditch and palisade, later replaced by stone wall e.g. Raby, Sudeley).

All castles had prisons, most of them court rooms and some had other administrative offices and repositories for money and goods. The extreme provision was naturally found in royal castles:

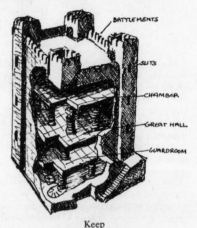

Keep

Hall

4

Edward III's Windsor included bath-houses, the queen's dancing chamber, the king's mews for falcons, a great clock in the keep and a reredos for the chapel which arrived prefabricated in ten carts from Nottingham. (He spent some £50,000 on this, his favourite residence and birthplace, between 1350 and 1377.)

ANARCHY   see also Adulterine, Robber Barons.

The anarchy of Stephen's reign (1135-54) produced literally hundreds of private strongholds. There were over 50 in Cambridgeshire alone.

This was the worst time, but isolated incidents were not unknown at other periods e.g. of Sir John de Somery, builder of Dudley which he owned from 1300 to 1321, it was reported that 'He has obtained such mastery in the county of Stafford that no-one can obtain law or justice therein; that he has made himself more than a king there; that no-one can dwell there unless he buys protection from him either by money or by assisting him in building his castles, and that he attacks people in their own houses with the intention of killing them unless they make fine for his protection.' (Toy, p. 222)

ANGLESEY

Two castle sites in Anglesey are listed: a motte-and-bailey at Aber Lleiniog, and the remarkable Beaumaris. The latter alone would place Anglesey high on a castle-explorer's list.

Beaumaris, Anglesey

ANGUS

Besides royal and mainly C17 Glamis, Angus has the interesting Edzell (DE) and Guthrie, together with the castles of Broughty, Kellie, Glen Cova and Monikie.

APERTURES   see Loops, Windows.

APPEARANCE, EXTERNAL   see also Amenities.

Not only was Caernarvon decorated with a pattern of red and grey stone but also all castles were gay and 'fairy-tale' in their appearance. Their walls were plastered and/or whitewashed (in 1289 there was an expenditure of £3 to a mason for rendering white the top of a tower on the battlements of the outer bailey at Aberstwyth). There were conical roofs on the towers, heraldic pennants fluttering from their highest points and large heraldic shields ('targes') with arms of owner. The illustrations in such a book as the 'Très Riches Heures' are a depiction of reality.

Mars: Decoration Edzell

ARBALEST

Alternative name for crossbow (q.v.); arbalestier (arbalist) is a crossbow-man.

Archer

The arbalest was a development of the primitive Norman crossbow. It was the preferred weapon of Richard I over the old short bow which had been in constant use since Saxon times and long continued as a sporting/hunting weapon. The arbalest surpassed the short bow in both range and penetrative power and up to the mid C13 the corps of arbalestiers was considered the flower of English infantry. About this time the arbalest began to be ousted by the long-bow which was superior in range and power to the primitive crossbow and much superior in its rate of fire. (At Crècy in 1346 the Genoese crossbow-men, allegedly the best in Europe, were shot down in scores while engaged in the cumbrous process of winding up their arbalests.)

Arbalest is also the name given to the large bow, mounted on a stand, which cast heavy darts or lances. The crossbow may be regarded as a portable and individual form developed from this large engine.

Arbalester

ARCHER   see also Arrow, Bow, Butts.

Archers provided the predominant arm in castle garrisons (q.v.) as they did among their besiegers.

An Act of 1466 stated:

'Every Englishman, and Irishman dwelling with Englishmen and speaking English, being between sixteen and sixty years of age, is commanded to provide himself with an English bow of his own length, and one fist mele, at least, between the nocks, twelve shafts of a length of three quarters of the Standard (which would be about 28½) with a bodkin or war-point'.

At the beginning of C15 Caernarvon had 80 archers, Conway 50, Harlech 30, Beaumaris 140, as part of their garrisons.

Archer (C14)

ARDRES

There is a contemporary description of the timber hall of this early C12 castle in Flanders:

'The first storey was on the surface of the ground where there were cellars and granaries and great boxes, tuns, casks and other domestic utensils.
In the storey above were the dwellings and common-rooms of the residents, in which were the larders, the rooms of the bakers and butlers, and the great chamber in which the lord and his wife slept. Adjoining this was a private room, the dormitory of the waiting-maids and children. In the inner part of the great chamber was a certain private room where at early dawn or in the evening or during sickness or at a time of blood-letting or for warming the

maids and weaned children, they used to have a fire.

In the upper storey of the house were garret rooms, in which on the one side the sons (when they wished it) and on the other side, the daughters (because they were obliged) of the lord of the house used to sleep. In this storey also the watchman and the servants appointed to keep the house took their sleep at some time or other.

High up on the east side of the house, in a convenient place, was the chapel which was made like unto the tabernacle of Solomon in its ceiling and painting.

There were stairs and passages from storey to storey, from the house into the kitchen, from room to room, and again from the house into the loggia, where they used to sit in conversation for recreation, and again from the loggia into the oratory.'

ARGYLL

Possesses the interesting Castle Sween, two castles in Kilmartin of which one (Carnasserie) is DE., and others such as Dunollie, Dunstaffnage, Finlaggan, Innellan, Kilchurn, Mingary and Toward.

ARMOURY

One of the uses of a castle was as a weapon-store or armoury, as the Tower of London still is. In the reign of Henry III some siege-engines seem to have been kept there. The same king ordered 15,000 crossbow bolts from the armoury at Corfe for his siege of Bedford. The armoury at Bedford seems to have been in the outer bailey for when this was taken by the king's forces they captured hauberks, suits of mail and crossbows.

Pole, Arms

In 1322/3 in the face of Scottish invasion, the new Constable of Pickering (his predecessor had been captured by the Scots) was instructed to repair the buildings, construct a drawbridge and add to his armament a springald with a hundred bolts, eight crossbows with 1,000 bolts and 40 lances.

Arms (Knight)

ARMS

The quality and costliness of arms and armour indicated and reflected the economic and social status of their wearer (see Knight) e.g.

Peasant – buckler and pick or other agricultural implement, no defensive armour.

Small farmer – leather jerkin with spear or bow.

More important farmer – padded and quilted

Side Arms

body-armour, steel helmet, bow and sword.

Men-at-arms and squires – mounted with
lance, sword and shield and at least
half-armour.

Knight – heavy charger and full armour
('cap-a-pie') and a variety of shock
weapons (q.v.)

Martel De Fer. Battle Axe

The variety of arms available to the 'ordinary citizen' at the end of the C15 are vividly indicated by the records of the Sanctuary at Durham. They include daggers and a variety of staves (the most frequent), the baselard and the bastard-sword, several kinds of axe, lances and many types of 'bills'. Other weapons mentioned were 'pychyng' staffs or forks and 'wood-knives'. It will be noticed that there is no clear line of demarcation among common folk between weapons and everyday utensils.

Though personal arms varied according to rank, taste and period, the sword, bow, spear and axe persisted throughout the Middle Ages.

Maces

ARROW

Of different designs according to their purpose. War arrows for the long-bow were of two lengths: flight arrows (37 ins) for high trajectory long-range fire; sturdier sheaf arrows (27 ins) for close-range piercing of mail and occasionally plate armour (if a square hit could be obtained). The warheads were either broad-head (like the 'broad arrow') to use against horses or the bodkin to pierce chain-mail at short range. The arrow shafts were made of ash and their fletchings were goose feathers.

Bill. Glaive

Edward II paid 200 marks for 2,000 sheaves of arrows in 1480 i.e. 13s 4d for 10 sheaves or 1s 4d a sheaf. It is difficult to estimate how many arrows an archer usually carried but the evidence of contemporary illustration is half a dozen as ready ammunition.

Arrows in Quiver

ARTILLERY see also Ballista, Cannon, Catapult, Mangon, Petraria, Siege, Springal, Trebuchet.

Mediaeval war 'engines' are difficult to classify because of inexact nomenclature. There are no survivals but there are a number of contemporary illustrations of greater or less accuracy. These engines may be classified in terms of their energy source, though some composite machines used more than one source of motive power:

Artillery

(a)   Mangon or mangonel (torsion).
(b)   Trebuchet (counterweight).
(c)   Ballista and springal (tension).

Some castles had an important member of the garrison called an artiller who seems to have been responsible for the construction, maintenance and operation of the large war engines. The accounts of Harlech (1286) record the purchase of one oxhide 'for the use of Simon the Artiller' (presumably for the sling of a trebuchet).

Examples of effective use of siege artillery by Henry IV at Alnwick, Berwick, Warkworth (1405); by the future Henry V at Aberystwyth, Harlech (1406) and Warwick on behalf of Edward IV at Bamburgh (1464).

ARTILLERY FORT

Fear of foreign intervention led Henry VIII to construct (often from the robbed masonry of recently dissolved religious houses) a series of coastal defences designed for artillery. They included Calshot, Hurst (Hants.), Lindisfarne (Northd.), Salcombe (Devon), Sandsfoot (Dorset), Southsea (Hants.). The following are listed: Camber, Deal, Pendennis, Portland, St. Mawes, Sandgate, Upnor, Walmer.

ASHLAR   see also Masons, Rubble.

Stone with cut flat surface, usually of regular (i.e. rectangular) shape.

Stones cut with a concave surface were called 'serches' (used for wells, newel stairs etc.). Other specialist cuts were called 'roydes' and 'eschonchons'.

ASSAULT

As direct assaults cost lives, a beleaguered castle was asked to surrender honourably. If it refused, efforts were made to surmount (see Escalade) or breach its defences. Ditches were filled, wooden defences were attacked with fire, axes, hooks and levers. Stone defences were mined or assailed with picks and crowbars. Large siege engines were only used in major assaults – besiegers did not always possess them and they were costly, required specialist operators and time to assemble. A breach was followed by a second call to surrender or truce (q.v.) and if defiance forced the attackers to an all-out assault they were liable, if successful, to execute surviving garrison in retaliation.

ATTACK AND DEFENCE

C12 and C13 warfare tended towards a pattern: resistance in field, retirement behind defence, diversionary attacks and assaults, counter-attack and sortie, search for peripheral weakness and its exploitation, retreat to keep and its storming. If attacks on perimeter or 'last resort' failed, then a sitting-out until starvation brought surrender.

Assault by Escalade

The mediaeval castle developed in response to its assailants who employed strategems (trick, surprise, deceit, betrayal) as well as direct assault. It provided earthwork and timber against the attack of mailed knights, stone against fire, thicker stone against engines, flanking towers against rams and mines, higher walls against escalade and more powerful artillery, round towers against boring and mining, gatehouses against assaults on gate, sally-ports and posterns against concentration, etc.

Attack and Defence

In general, defence maintained ascendancy within limits of morale, loyalty, endurance and supply.

ATTAINDER

Forfeiture of hereditary honours and dignities following conviction for treason or other serious failure in feudal obligations. Could be, and often was, cancelled and rights restored.

AUMBRY

A cupboard recessed into the thickness of the wall. It provided secure storage for valuables. Large aumbries might have been wardrobes because formal clothes were extremely expensive.

AYRSHIRE

The following may be found of some interest: Colmonell, Craigie, Loch Doon, Dundonald, Killochan, Turnberry.

BADGES

It is rewarding to recognise such badges as Richard II's White Hart, Richard III's White Boar, the Talbot's White Swan, Fienne's Alant, Warwick's Bear.

BANFFSHIRE

The county-town has remains of a castle, Balvenie (Dufftown) is DE and there are also Findochty, Glenliver, Keith, Whitehills and a much altered castle at Cullen.

BAILEY (Base-court, Ward)   see also Motte-and-Bailey.

A Norman-French word meaning 'palisaded enclosure'. Apparently first applied to the defended area on the summit of a motte (q.v.), hence Baile Hill, York; Boley Hill, Rochester, Old Bailey, London. Later used of the enclosure of a castle which gave additional space beyond that of the inner strongpoint (motte, mound, keep). Some baileys are so small as to be really an additional protection to the staircase of mound ('keyhole plan'). Larger ones defended the horses and cattle and later provided additional accommodation for the lord and garrison (e.g. hall, kitchens, chapel, workshops). More elaborate castles had outer and inner baileys, and large baileys were sometimes interrupted by a cross-wall whose purpose was to block the free circulation of troops who had invaded the area.

The bailey could take a variety of shapes of which the most popular was a circle or oval. This was easier to lay out than a rectangular shape and obviated the problem of accumulated earth from the corners of ditches. The 'kidney' shape is probably the most common form of a bailey (e.g. Berkhamsted, Ongar, Pickering).

BALLISTA

Artillery engine in the form of a very large bow which discharged heavy arrows or stones. The range was c. 400 yds and it cast a stone weighing between 50 and 60 lbs.

In its earlier form, power was derived from twisted skeins (like mangon) but later from the 'spring' of the bow (see Arbalest). Confusion is caused by the indiscriminate use of this word which can be applied to 'mangonel' (see Mangon) or 'springald' (q.v.)

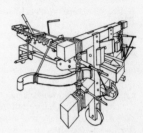

Ballista

In 1211 the tenant of Leaton held his land by the guard-service (see Castle Guard) of appearing, together with his ballista, at Shrewsbury for eight days at his own charge, or for a longer term at the king's expense.

BANNERS   see also Pennants.

Not merely a contribution to colourful pageantry. They located command and provided rallying-points in the confusion of battle. They also identified and marked lordship. The standard flying from the topmost tower of a castle indicated in whose hands it was held. (At the siege of Bedford the rebels hauled up the royal standard on the shattered keep in token of their submission.)

BANQUETS   Cuthbert's Banner (Durham)

Castles are popularly and properly seen as the scene of revels and feasting. For Christmas (1206) at Winchester, King John's orders to the Sheriff of Hampshire included 1,500 chickens, 5,000 eggs, 20 oxen, 100 pigs, 100 sheep. The records are also full of 'endless convoys of good wine rolling towards the royal castle' (Brown 187).

In 1321 the accounts for the first day of a banquet at Conisbrough (September 15th) include:

In bread bought	18d
4 flagons of wine bought	2s
12 flagons of ale bought at Doncaster	18d
16 flagons of ale bought at Conisbrough	16d
Shambles meat (i.e. fresh meat)	2s

Banquet

8 fowls	1s
2 geese	8d
Eggs	3d
Woman's wages fetching ale from Doncaster	1d
Provender for horses	15d

BARBICAN   see also Gatehouse.

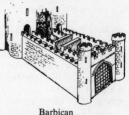

Exterior defence protecting an entrance.
Besides increasing protection at this
necessarily weak point they could shelter a
large assemblage of men preparing a sortie or
cover a retreat. They also confined an
approaching enemy to a narrow front thus
limiting his resources and producing a massed
target. The barbican may be considered as the
application to the whole castle of the principles
which produced the forebuilding of a keep and
thus they show the shift in importance from
the keep to the curtain. They also had the
effect of confusing the enemy (as did the prehistoric earthwork entrances).

Barbican

Originally, they consisted of a simple palisade or an earthwork and were
usually circular or a segment of a circle. Later, they were made of masonry
and usually adopted a rectilinear form e.g. Arundel, Conisbrough,
Scarborough, Warwick, York (Walmgate Bar.) Separate barbicans usually
date from C14 (e.g. Bodiam, Carisbrooke, Lewes.) The most elaborate
development is seen in Edwardian castles (e.g. Beaumaris c.f. Caerphilly) but
the earlier arrangements (e.g. Bamburgh, Conisbrough, Scarborough) show
the basic feature of a projecting gatehouse with a narrow passage linking this
gatehouse to an entrance through the curtain. In the late C13 and C14 the
barbican was an addition to the gatehouse itself (e.g. Alnwick, Kenilworth,
Lewes, Portchester, Warwick).

BAR-HOLE

Horizontal holes behind door at either side to receive
timber bar used as door bolt.

BARMKIN

North of England term for a kind of barbican (with
which it might be cognate), consisting of a large walled
outer ward on the entrance side of the enclosure
containing hall. Often consists of a simple walled
courtyard, without flanking towers or gatehouse,
protecting the entrance of the hall and providing some
sort of cover for animals and harvest. A barmkin might
be seen as a simplified version of motte-and-bailey (q.v.). It was an answer to
insecurity by lesser gentry who had not the means for, or even need of, a great
castle but who occasionally required to protect family and cattle from
marauding Scots (see Pele Tower).

Arms: De Mauley

BARONIAL CASTLES (Private)   see also ownership, Tenure.

Centre of local administration and associated courts, symbol of lordship. In late C12 and afterwards could be a threat to central government and royal power.

Hugh Bigod held four strong castles in East Anglia and this concentration of baronial power led Henry II to build Orford at nearly £1,500 and to the confiscation of all the Bigod castles. Framlingham and Bungay were later restored but demolished after the rebellion of 1173.

Arms: Fitzhugh

Other great baronial strongholds included: Alnwick (Percy), Caerphilly (Clare), Caister (Falstolf), Denbigh (Lacy), Durham (bishop), Kidwelly (Chaworth), Kirby Muxloe (Hastings), Newark (bishop), Tattershall (Cromwell).

BARREL VAULT

A plain vault of uniform cross-section (usually semi-circular).

BARTIZAN   see also Crow's Nest.

Arms: Le Gros (of Skipsea)

Small turret or look-out corbelled out at angle of a tower or on the surface of a wall. The word is etymologically connected with brattice, and such turrets, like the machicolated parapet, are the stone counterpart of the brattices and hoarding of timber which had been applied to fortresses at an earlier date.

Much less common in England than in France, but there are good examples at Lewes and smaller ones at Belsay, Chipchase, Lincoln and York walls.

BASE COURT

The court or ward below the keep or motte (q.v.) and therefore a synonym of bailey (q.v.).

BASEMENT (of Keep).

Not normally a 'dungeon' but a secure storage place for arms and provisions. Often contains the mouth of well.

BASTIDE

Towns developed in France during the Anglo-French wars of the Middle Ages fulfilling a function similar to that of the old 'burh' i.e. a defence and gathering-point for a local community on the border of alien land.

It has also been applied by analogy to Edward's towns and settlements in Wales e.g. Caernarvon, Conway. There are other 'new towns' of this kind in England, planned as a grid where all the streets meet at right-angles and one block is left clear for the church and perhaps another for the market and civic buildings (e.g. Winchelsea).

BASTION

A salient beyond the main body of a fortress designed to cover dead ground, flank curtains and to provide cross-fire. They are usually cased with masonry and they may have an earth or rubble core. The word is usually used of late artillery fortresses e.g. Berwick, but is also used of a solid masonry projection from a wall e.g. Conisbrough.

BASTLE-HOUSE

A 'poor man's pele' i.e. a small stone house with provision for cattle on the ground floor and living quarters with small protected windows on the floor e.g. Akeld, Bellister, Doddington, Neworth, Northd.

Bastle-house, Akeld

BATH

Normally taken in a wooden tub (and in spite of modern myth, there was a lot of bathing in the Middle Ages). The tubs of the rich were often given some privacy by a tent or canopy and a touch of sybaritism by cloth padding. In warm weather, the tub was often placed in the garden and in cold, near the chamber fire. When the lord travelled, the tub often accompanied him together with a bathman to prepare its use (e.g. King John and his bathman William). In some important castles there were permanent bathrooms e.g. Leeds (c. 1291) – a vaulted chamber 23 ft × 17 ft, lined with Reigate stone, to contain 4 ft of

Bath time

water drawn from the lake. Provided with ledge for accessories, recess for bath and a changing room above. At Westminster, Henry III had piped hot and cold water for his bath while Edward III's had bathmats to protect his feet from the cold.

BATTER OR PLINTH   see also Spur.

The angled footing of a wall or tower designed to cause dropped missiles to richochet horizontally. This device also presents deflecting surface to ram or bore enemy projectile thus rendering them less effective. It also provided some protection against mining by offering extra thickness and distributing the weight of the building above (e.g. Caesar's Tower, Warwick; Curtain, Conisbrough; keeps on plinths e.g. Conisbrough, Orford).

BATTERING RAM   see Ram.

BATTLEMENT   see also Crenel, Merlon, Parapet.

Battlements are the distinguishing feature of a castle (i.e. a fortified residence). A licence to crenellate (q.v.) was required from at least the reign of John though it was not always obtained or even sought. The first curtain walls do not seem to have been crenellated and existing battlemented parapets may usually be assigned to a subsequent repair and/or raising of curtain (probably in C13). The battlement provides a

Battering Ram

14

walk on the wall summit (see Allure), a fighting
platform and a defence against escalade (q.v.).
The embrasures were usually from 2 ft 3 ins to
3 ft wide and the breast wall was about 3 ft high.

BEAR   see also Belfry.

A high timber-framed tower from whose summit
archers could harass castle defenders and pick
off engineers working on artillery. There was
one built for the siege of Kenilworth in 1266 but
it was destroyed by catapults within the castle.

BEDFORDSHIRE

Belfry in Action

Apart from the earthworks surviving from the early motte-and-bailey castles,
Bedfordshire has not the remains of a single castle. One can only offer the
derelict fragment of Someries (near Luton) and a selection of earthworks:
Chalgrave, Eaton Socon, Totternoe and Yelden.

BELFRY

A timber tower used in sieges. It seems to
have functioned more as a lookout post or a
firing position to command the walls, towers
or interior of the bailey rather than as a
scaling engine. At the siege of Bedford (q.v.)
the belfry, manned by archers and
crossbow-men, was so effective that the
chronicler reported that no member of the
garrison within the castle could remove his
armour and escape a mortal wound.

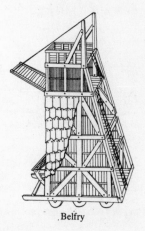

Basically, the belfry was a wooden tower
on wheels which overtopped the point of
assault. It was advanced on wheels or rollers
when the engineers had prepared an
approach for it. It usually had several storeys
gained by scaling ladders fixed at its back and
sometimes the front was furnished with a
wide bridge which could be dropped on the
wall or tower to provide access for the assault
party. It did not always have a bridge and its

.Belfry

early use was to bring light artillery to advantageous position (One used
against Kenilworth (1266) contained 200 archers and 11 catapults.) Because
of its materials it was susceptible to fire and usually protected with raw or
damped hides. It could be provided very quickly when rough wood of
sufficient scanting was available. In some cases it mounted a catapult and
nearly always provided a firing point for archers. Consequently belfries were a
prime target of the besieged who used heavy missiles and incendiaries,
including Greek Fire, against them to shatter or burn them down.

15

BENEFICE

Source of income, commonly land (see Fief), but could include e.g. salaried post, mill-house, rights of toll, market fees, movable chattels, incumbency of church or abbey.

BERKSHIRE

Berkshire is not rich in mediaeval buildings. It has no cathedral, no major monastic remains and, with one exception, no substantial castle. There are a few earthwork remains of motte-and-baileys e.g. Brightwell, Hinton Waldrist, Reading, South Moreton. There is the great C14 gatehouse at Donnington and, of course, Windsor in spite of its Victorian additions and remodelling.

Donnington, Berkshire

BERM

A level terrace or cleared space between the base of a curtain wall and the inner edge of its protective ditch.

BERWICKSHIRE

Has not only lost its county town but most of its castles. Duns is worth mentioning. Greenknowe has ruins of fine town-house and there are remains at Lauder.

BLACKSMITH

A very important craftsman who had to be able to turn his hand to almost anything: forging and sharpening tools and weapons, beating out the dints in armour, making hinges for doors, plates for siege engines, grilles for windows, angle-irons for structures and metalwork for the chapel.

BOLT

A short arrow fired from a crossbow. The head varied according to purpose: practice-firing, bird-shooting, game-hunting or warfare. Battle bolts were of seasoned hardwood about 12 ins long and from ½ in. to 1 in. in diameter. A sharply pointed metal head (pile) was fitted over the shaft and the fletchings were of varnished parchment or thin leather. At a fair range these sharply pointed bolts could pierce most armour except perhaps when striking a glancing blow on a curved surface. To obviate this weakness the quarell (q.v.) was devised.

For the siege of Bedford (q.v.) Henry III ordered 15,000 bolts from the magazines at Corfe and commanded the bailiffs of Northampton to order all the specialist smiths of the town to work day and night to supply an additional 4,000 quarells 'well barbed and well flighted'.

BOMBARDS   see also Cannon.

An account of Wark, Northd. in 1517 describes its keep as being five storeys high 'in each of which there were five great murder-holes, shot with great vaults of stone, except one stage which is of timber, so that great bombards can be shot from each of them'. Bombard was an early form of battering cannon. One was found in the moat of Bodiam and a replica is kept inside the castle.

Bombard

BORE

A beam armed with an iron-spiked head used to attack base of wall. It resembled a battering-ram (q.v.) but it was usually lighter and its head (shaped like a tall pyramid) gnawed into the masonry joints until it could be turned to dislodge individual stones and prepare the way for the pick-men. Particularly effective against salient angles (hence development of round or polygonal towers). Flanking towers, hourds and machicolation were intended to make borers visible and vulnerable.

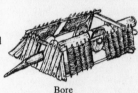

Bore

BOURG

see also Bastide.

An early mediaeval 'new town'. There were C11 plantations at Abergavenny, Carlisle, Pembroke, Rhuddlan.

BOW

There is much indecisive controversy about the relative effectiveness of the long-bow and the crossbow. From the C12 to the end of C15 the crossbow was the favoured weapon except among the English. (The Genoese were the most expert crossbow-men.)

The crossbow seems to have had more penetrating power but no greater range since bolts, unlike arrows, do not 'fly'. The long-bow was light and comfortable while the crossbow was heavy, cumbersome and had more moving parts. The longbow-man could fire five or six arrows while the crossbow-man discharged a single bolt. He could also keep his eye on the foe while re-loading while the crossbow-man could not.

Bowmen

But behind fortifications the crossbow-man seems to have had the advantage. Here he was protected when re-loading and his place at the loop could be taken by a comrade. (Loops seem to have been provided with space for at least two bowmen.) His missile was heavier, it had greater force and a longer effective range.

Ranges: Long-bow 220 yds
   Crossbow 380 yds (Extreme ranges of over ¼ mile have been
   claimed.)

A 'bowshot' as a measure of distance seems to have been between 300 and
400 yds.

BOW, LONG

Appears first among the South Welsh in mid C12
who (according to Gerald de Barri) were able to
penetrate an oak door four fingers thick. By mid
C13 it had become the national English weapon
when all holders of 40s in land, or nine marks in
chattels, were required to provide themselves with
sword, dagger, bow and arrows. The weapon was
practised by all freemen at communal butts (q.v.).
The trained archer of the Hundred Years' War was
able to beat the crossbow-men in range and
penetrating power with a vast superiority in rate of
fire. At a furlong range he could pierce a mailed
knight through breast and back or nail both thighs
to his horse with one shot. This effectiveness
resulted in defensive steps to keep besiegers at a
greater distance.

Long-bow (c. 1250)

   No mediaeval long-bow has survived but careful reconstruction seems to
show that it was characterised by no 'kick'. When drawn 28 ins it pulls 75 lbs
and casts 250 yds. It was made of yew (usually imported) and its dimensions
were 4 ins circumference at its woollen braided hand-grip and 2 ins at the
nocks. The length was proportionate to user: a full-sized bow seems to have
been 5 ft 8 ins but there is some evidence of 6 ft bows. The bow staves arrived
in the rough and were slightly more than 6 ft long before being modified to the
individual's physique. The strings were made of long-fibred hemp. The range
has been variously estimated at an extreme of 400 yds to 500 yds depending
on the strength and skill of the
bowman and wind-force and direction. At 50
or 60 yds, it was extremely accurate and
bowmen could fire six aimed shots a minute
i.e. they could hit gorgets and unprotected
under-arms.

BOW, SHORT

A weapon about 3 ft long which was drawn to
the breast, and not to the ear like the
long-bow. It was the arm of William the
Bastard's archers as well as some of the
English at the Battle of

Short bow: Norman Archer

Hastings but was completely ousted (except for hunting) by the long-bow by
the mid C13.

BOWER

An essential part of mediaeval domestic accommodation. All houses except the very humblest consisted of hall and bower. The bower was the withdrawing-room and sleeping apartment. In large houses, the bower or solar was sometimes known as the great chamber and was reached by a door near one end of the cross-wall behind the dais in the hall. Later usage distinguished the bower as the room of the castellan's wife or 'ladies' apartment'. The new hall at Pickering was rebuilt to provide, inter alia, accommodation for the Countess Alice in 1314 and her bower was an elaborately plastered room with a decorated fireplace.

BRAIE

'An exterior defence of trifling height, protecting the foot of the ramparts, and hindering the enemy's approach'. (Viollet le Duc).

BRATTICE (Bretasch)

A wooden palisade or stockade to provide perimeter defence. Usually made from squared timber (oak), like old-fashioned railway sleepers, planted deep and closely together on top of mound or rampart. Probably secured by horizontal beams at top and bottom and spiked at the top. Some palisades may have been crenellated or loop-holed. The outer edge of the ditch was sometimes protected by quick-set thorn bushes (herrison).

Brattice is also used of a timber tower or projecting wooden gallery (see Hoardings). There are corbels to support such a work over the gatehouse (Constable's Tower) at Leeds, Kent. These brattices were prefabricated for easy assembly and dismantling. They were probably pegged together. In 1221 we hear of a 'bretteche' being moved from Nafferton to Bamburgh and thence to Newcastle where it acted as a temporary replacement for a tower fallen through bad building.

BREACHES

A strong wall or palisade could only be either broken through or surmounted. Theoretically it could also be tunnelled under but there seem to have been no examples of this highly dangerous device with its limited exit. Breaching was perhaps more common and less costly to assaulting forces than escalade (q.v.). A crude, but far from effective, instrument for making a breach was the battering-ram (q.v.). A subtler but slower method used the bore (q.v.)

Breaching Device

which was employed particularly against sharp angles to dislodge single stones. A direct attack on the walls with picks and crow-bars was not unknown though motivation had to be increased by offering cash rewards for the dislodging of a single stone (so Richard I at Acre). The most dreaded device for breaching was the deadly efficient mine (q.v.) against which only rock foundations or a wide, wet moat were adequate defence. Counter-mining was also employed but it might lead, even if successful, to desperate hand-to-hand combats in underground and intrinsically dangerous cavities where the casualties could be ill-spared professionals.

At Alnwick, near the Ravine Tower, variations in the masonry of the outer curtain allegedly mark the site of Bloody Gap, a breach where 300 Scots were said to have been slain in their efforts to carry the breach.

BRECKNOCK

Though there are traces of about a dozen castles, Brecknock cannot be described as a county rich in military architecture. Perhaps the most interesting survival is Tretower. Brecon has fragments of both castle and town walls; other scant remains at Blaen Llynfi, Bronllys, Builth, Hay.

Tretower, Brecknock

BRESSUMER

A beam to support a projection e.g. hoarding.

BRICKS

A Roman material re-discovered in England in C13 but rarely used before C16 e.g. the Dent-de-Lion gatehouse, Garlinge, Kent, (early C15); Fisher Gate, Sandwich (1571). Caister, Herstmonceux, Faulkbourne, Tattershall, have large-scale buildings entirely of brick before the mid C15. Lullingstone gatehouse is c. 1460.

Bricks were frequently robbed from accessible Roman sites and re-used in many castles but there is recent evidence that Saxons and Normans occasionally made their own bricks.

Tattershall (Brick Tower)

BRIDGES, FORTIFIED

Strategic bridges were often directly protected by a castle e.g. Durham, Richmond etc. At Monmouth the bridge itself is fortified with a gatehouse equipped with machicolations and a portcullis. At Warkworth, besides protection from the castle itself, there is a plain rectangular gatehouse for the bridge.

BUCKINGHAMSHIRE

The county is not rich in any kind of mediaeval remains and military architecture is no exception. There are gatehouses at

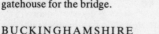
Monmouth Bridge

Long Crendon and Boarstall, but the former is
rather domestic. Not even the earthworks have
been allowed to remain in the county-town but there are survivals of
Castlethorpe, Lavendon, Weston Turville and Whitchurch.

BUILDERS see also Engineers, Professionals.

The Norman invasion of 1066 initiated two centuries of castle-building and
maintenance which took first place amongst the architectural activities of the
Norman and Angevin kings. The greatest castle builder of them all was the
Conqueror himself who, assisted by some of his greatest barons, built about
40 castles. Some of his agents are known: Waldin the Engineer, Radbell the
Artificer, Durand the Carpenter – all of whom acquired substantial
land-holdings for their services in the King's Works. Others acquired
serjeantry for planning ditches, overseeing their construction or keeping the
walls of a castle in repair. Higher in the social scale are great lords like Robert
of Belleme, William Fitzosburn and, above all, Bishop Gundulf of Rochester
who was associated with the two greatest castles – Rochester and the Tower,
buildings whose like had not been seen since the departure of the Romans
seven centuries before. 'These two great towers have no known ancestry' –
they are more than the earliest stone keeps in England, they were
fortress-palaces.

BUILDER BARONS see also Tenure.

Among the names which recur in the history of castles
are the following:- Albemarle, Bigod, Bohun, Bolebec,
Clare, Clifford, De Lacy, Ferrers, Glanville,
Mandeville, Montgomery, Mortimer, Mowbray, Percy,
Plantagenet, Tankerville, Vere.

Bigod

A good deal is known from central records of the
activity of the king and his agents about the royal
castles. We know the names of some of the engineers
and chief master-craftsmen and consequently there is a
tendency to concentrate on this information and give
royal castles an even greater significance than they
rightly possess. But we must remember that throughout
the Middle Ages the baronage was no less active in
castle-building, maintenance and improvement than
was the Crown. Private castles outnumbered royal ones
and not infrequently rivalled them in strength.
(Caerphilly of the Clares not only equals but antedates
the great Edwardian castles.) Nor were some of them
noticeably inferior in their domestic appointments and
comfort.

De Bruce

BUILDING COSTS see also Costs, Transport, Wages.

Details are known e.g. at Flint loopholes in curtain (1281) seem normally to
have cost 6s 3d in mason's wages (though one cost 7s 3d). Revetting 200 ft of
castle ditch (1279) cost £29 3s 0d in wages. The Mote-hall cost £26.13.4
(1283) while the hall and chamber cost £51.1.8 in 1452.

BUILDING PERIODS

There are basically four periods of general castle building:

(a) The Conquest and its consolidation (William I and II).
(b) The Anarchy (Stephen).
(c) The consolidation and updating of original earth and timber building (Henry II).
(d) The strengthening of the borders (Edward I) followed by C13 building in Ireland.

The following are interesting because they represent many periods of construction: Carisbrooke; Chepstow; Dover; Kenilworth; Tower of London; Ludlow; Warkworth. (All D.E.) The following, not in government care, are of similar interest: Alnwick; Caldicot; Saltwood.

BUILDING PROCEDURES

Selection of site; design of castle; marking out; workers' accommodation; temporary defence; digging of ditches, banks and mottes; laying foundations for heavy structures; digging wells; modifying natural site (scarping, cutting rock ditches); arranging supply of necessary materials often over great distances and in some cases involving co-ordination of road, river and sea transport (e.g. Edwardian castles in Wales); assessment of money dues; collection of rents and taxes; keeping accounts; paying workmen and soldiers; building in stone and wood, wattle and daub, thatch and shingle; (trying to keep site defensible from first days, constantly adding to its strength, ensuring that progress did not produce temporary weaknesses); preparation of materials on site and at source – mortar, rubble, free-stone, beams and joists, lead sheets etc. (erection of forges, kilns and shops for making and sharpening tools); constant checking of building for quality and accuracy; assessment of piece-work.

Builders

Building was seasonable and confined to warmer months as frost could crack wet mortar. At season end unfinished building was protected with straw and dung for insulation and to prevent water entering cracks where it might freeze, expand and break down masonry. A small work-force might remain on site during winter for protection and the preparation of materials ready for the return of the major force in spring.

In urgent cases, there are instances of

Engines: Crane

castle-work being pushed on through the winter (no doubt assisted by constant wood fires) and even night-work by candlelight is recorded.

BUILDING RESOURCES

The materials were often local and derived from the rock on which the castle stood, or was to stand, and wood from the surrounding forest. The labour was mainly unskilled, conscripted from dependent manors. The expensive items were metal, carriage and skilled labour. The latter was often recruited from considerable distances as in Edward I's works in Wales e.g. Flint, (July 1277), engaged:

Building Accident
York Glass

970 diggers under the direction of three masters and a knight 330 carpenters under a knight 320 woodmen under a knight 200 masons under one master and a knight
12 smiths
10 charcoal burners

These were organised as four military units and this was only the preparatory work!

BUTESHIRE

Not rich in castles: Rothesay is of considerable interest and Brodick deserves a mention.

BUTLER

Official in charge of large butts and little butts (bottles) i.e. beer and wine. A very responsible and valuable office – a dishonest butler of Henry III acquired 'the wealth of an earl' (see also Sudeley). Departmental head with subsidiary staff which might include brewers, tapsters, cellarers, dispensers, cupbearers and dapifer (man to look after napery) and possibly all having apprentices or boy assistants.

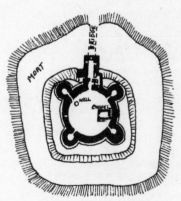

Rothesay (Plan), Buteshire

BUTTERY

'Bottlery' presided over by 'bottler'. A small room between kitchen and hall, usually within 'screens'. Stone buttery-hatches for service survive in Goodrich keep.

BUTTRESS

Thickening of a wall for strength and support, usually tapering towards the top, whereas pilaster (q.v.) is thinner and does not taper. Also an additional strip of masonry to give additional strength and support. Sometimes clasping buttresses at corner of great keeps are of such dimensions as to be able to house spiral staircase (see Vice) within their bulk.

BUTTS

Shooting range for archery practice and/or competitions. Bowmen stood at a fixed mark and usually aimed at 'targes' (round shields) or 'targets' (smaller versions of the same) though other targets were used elsewhere: willow-wand, tethered bird etc.

Butts

CAERNARVON ARCH

Late C13/early C14 architectural feature in which doorway heads are formed of a horizontal lintel supported on two corbels instead of the customary arch. So called because of the prevalence of this feature at Caernarvon Castle.

CAERNARVONSHIRE

Caernarvonshire has not only the magnificent fortress palace of the county town but the almost equally fine Conway with its town walls. If to these are added Criccieth, Dinas Enrys, Dolbadarn, Dolwyddellan and

Caernarvon, Arch

Deganwy there is a roll-call of military architecture which cannot be ignored.

CAITHNESS

Not rich, but perhaps the following are worth mentioning: Halkirk, Scrabster Thurso, Wick.

CAMBRIDGESHIRE

The castle explorer needs some determination in this county. There are slight remains in the county town, Wisbech has vanished under later building but there are traces at Burwell, Castle Camps, Caxton, Ely.

CANNON

Seem to have been introduced in C14 and mentioned in use against the Scots in 1327. An illustration (c. 1327) portrays a four-legged stand supporting a bulbous bottle loaded with a large iron dart. The gunner is firing the charge with a red-hot iron bar (and standing well back!).

Early cannon were inferior in every respect to the great siege-engines: they were slow and small, they were limited in C14 to firing bolts or 'garrots' and they had a very limited range. The weaknesses were due to limited

technology: inability to forge or cast in one
piece or make iron balls. They were probably
as dangerous to their users as to the enemy and
affected the morale of men (and horses) rather
than damaged persons or buildings.
Considerable development in C15 produced
very effective bombards (Mons Meg at
Edinburgh is c. 1460). These terrifying pieces
were given personal names and with
'Newcastle' and 'London', Warwick the
Kingmaker took Bamburgh castle (hitherto
considered impregnable) in 1464. But cannon
were not easily available and the older engines
were in effective use in C16 and after (the
defenders of Pontefract in the Civil War seem
to have used 'petrarii' as well as muskets).

Cannon (c. 1327)

Mons Meg (c. 1460)

CAPHOUSE

Gabled turret, often containing a stair-head.

CARDIGANSHIRE

Not rich in castles, though many fortresses in the Teifi valley were taken and
retaken in C11 and C12. There are scant stone remnants at Aberystwyth and
Cardigan and earthworks at e.g. Abereinon, Blaenporth, Dinerth (not
indexed).

CARMARTHENSHIRE

Sparse remains of castle in county town and at Newcastle Emlyn. Near sea
were Laugharne, Llanstephan and St. Clears. Dramatic and beautiful ruins at
Kidwelly, wild and romantic ones at Carreg Cennen and the castles of the
Vale of Towey: Dryslwyn, Dynevor, Llangattock, Llandovery. (These last are
not indexed, nor are Aber Cowyn, Cenarth Fawr, Llanelly, Llychewin and
Pencader which would be included in an exhaustive list.)

CARPENTERS

One of the most necessary craftsmen in castle-work. Apart from flooring and
roofing, building hourds and brattices, they were also largely responsible for
siege-engines (q.v.). They also made furniture, panelling for rooms and
scaffolding for building operations. One of Edward I's chief carpenters was
Thomas of Haughton who designed woodwork of Queen Eleanor's tomb,
planned siege engines, inspected royal forests and designed a pile-driver.
William Hurley (in the time of Edward III) built, inter alia, the lantern at Ely,
the hall at Caerphilly and a variety of siege-engines.

In C15 a master carpenter at Kirby Muxloe was paid 8d a day. Carpenters
and other skilled craftsmen were called up for the king's works under Edward
I in such numbers that other construction must have been seriously hindered
and Edward III's demands for the glorification of Windsor in the 1350s
resulted in 'almost all the masons and carpenters throughout the whole of
England (being) brought to that building, so that hardly anyone could have
any good

mason or carpenter, except in secret, on account of the king's prohibition'. Throughout the castle period, domestic buildings within the bailey were being constructed of wood. The importance of carpenters is indicated by the vast quantities of timber (q.v.) which they consumed.

Carpenters

When Henry III besieged Bedford (1224), he urgently required carpenters for his siege engines and ordered his constable at Windsor to provide horses for Master Thomas and his fellow carpenters together with their gear 'so that they shall be able to travel to us by day and night as swiftly as they can and not tarry'. Perhaps the most impressive memorial of mediaeval carpenters lies in the rare surviving Great Hall with its marvellous open timber roof composed of trusses and tie-beams, purlins, struts and rafters, braces and wall-posts. The elements were prefabricated on the ground and assembled by pegging together with oak dowels.

CASTELLAN see also Command, Constable.

The resident owner or person in charge of castle (custodian). The great owners included the king, magnates with scattered estates or Marcher Lords responsible for vast frontier areas. In large estates all castles could not have the lord as their castellan so their government was entrusted to a constable.

Castellan

CASTLE

Derived from the Latin 'castellum' a diminutive of 'castrum' and applied to the fortified private houses (as distinct from the communal stronghold) which developed in Europe from C9. The word 'castle' originally applied to the enclosure while the motte (q.v.) within it was called the 'tower'. The castle is a Norman invention and the few in England before 1066 were built by Norman friends of Edward the Confessor. A good modern definition (C. Oman's) is 'a fortified dwelling intended for purposes of residence and defence'. Initially they were designed to

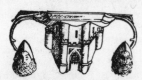

Castles : **Lincoln Misericord**

hold down conquered territory and once their site was chosen, nothing was allowed to interfere with military necessity. On inhabited sites houses were ruthlessly destroyed to clear space for castles e.g. a fifth of York was cleared for fortification and in Lincoln 166 houses were pulled down 'on account of the castle' in the early years of the Conquest. No two castles are alike because of the effect of taste, topography, available materials and resources and the individual genius of designers. This uniqueness is one of the most interesting aspects of castle exploration.

CASTLE GUARD (Castle Ward)

The service due from a tenant with income of £20 per annum to overlord in the form of garrison duty. In a large castle a particular tenant might be entrusted with the defence of a specific tower which, in consequence, might be known by his name. The towers at Dover are all named after the fiefs which provided their knightly garrison. By mid C12 this feudal obligation was being increasingly commuted for a money rent so that castles could be garrisoned by professional soldiers (see Ward Penny).

The manor of Drayton, Bucks., had to contribute two mailed men to Windsor (1085); 171 manors in Kent had obligations in the garrisoning of Dover. Obligation did not always lie to a neighbouring fortress e.g. there were lands in Cambridgeshire which owed service to a castle in Craven. In major castles continuity of service was secured by a system of relays or constabularies e.g. Bury St. Edmunds' Abbey supplied four constabularies to Norwich, each of which served three months.

Other examples: in Shropshire one tenant had to supply a mounted soldier for 40 days while another had to provide a horseman with horse, hauberk, helmet and lance for Oswestry; in 1211 a tenant of Leaton held his land by serving with his ballista for eight days; nearly a century later the same land was held by providing an archer with a bow and three unfeathered arrows for 40 days. (When his term was up the archer had 'to shoot his shafts into three quarters of the said castle (Shrewsbury) and to depart, unless the king wished to detain him'.) The normal length of service seems to have varied from eight to 40 days. In cases of default, distraint was levied first on the goods of the defaulter's serfs and sub-tenants. Commutation was encouraged by the practice of irresponsible sub-tenants who sent unsoldierlike men to do castle-guard.

The obligation of guard-service seems normally to have extended to 20 days in peacetime and in time of war. The complex manning of the Dover towers has been established as follows:

Honour	Fees	Soldiers	Weeks
Avranches	21	21	28
Fulbert	15½	15	20
Arsic	18½	18	24
Peverel	15	14	20
Port	12	12	24
Mamignot	25	23	32
Grevequer	5	5	24
Ada Fitz William	6	6	24

CASTLE WORK

For the lower classes, the most oppressive aspect of Norman castle building was the forced labour by which they were erected and maintained. The

construction of a great mound (perhaps of
100 ft diameter or more) in as little as a week
required a considerable labour force. The
Anglo-Saxon requirement by which men
worked on the communal 'burh' was
re-directed under the Normans to work on the
castles of their overloads. This labour was
organised on a county basis and for work in
London men were impressed from the Home

Castle Work

Counties. Even religious houses had difficulty in gaining exemption from this
general obligation and as late as 1215 the sheriff of Berkshire summoned in
the king's name all the men of his county 'to come without delay to repair the
ditch of our castle and town at Wallingford, as they were accustomed to do in
times past'.

Besides digging, other feudal dues included the maintenance of the palisade
(see Herrison) e.g. certain humble tenants of Bamburgh had to bring a
tree-trunk to the castle every alternate day from Whitsun to 1st August until
in 1280 the obligation was commuted to a total payment of £10 per annum to
the constable. At a higher social level the maintenance of the quarters of the
garrison was the responsibility of the baron whose men performed the service
of castle guard (q.v.). In the anarchy of Stephen's reign, according to the
chronicler, the great lords 'burdened the country with forced labour on their
castles'.

Dunstanburgh masonry shows obvious distinction between the
keep-gatehouse (the work of Master Elias), the frontal wall and towers in
ashlar, and the cliff wall of rubble with clay infilling. This last is clearly
amateurish and is built in sections of about 40 ft length with visible junctions.
It is likely that this work represents a late continuation of the feudal duty of
castle-work carried out by the Embleton tenantry for their lord, Earl Thomas
(on a castle that was not licensed).

Castle work could include: finding wood for
a particular fire-place, serving kitchen with
water, cartage (providing oxen to draw
engines) and attending knights in bailey with
water for washing.

CAT

A long, low timber gallery with longitudinal
roof, sharply pointed and braced with iron to
protect it from descending missiles. So called
from its slow, stealthy approach . This wheeled
shelter protected sappers filling a ditch or
miners digging under masonry. It was brought
into position by rollers and levers or by ropes,
pulleys and winches. Also called 'tortoise' and,
in some French provinces, 'rat'.

Cat

In 1230 the Norsemen broke into Rothesay
by using a cat.

28

CATAPULT (or Scorpion)

An engine for shooting large darts. These projectiles were 6 ft long and very heavy. They could be firebrands and some catapults seem to have thrown small stones. They derived their energy from the 'spring' of a very large and heavy bow.

Catapults effectively defended Kenilworth (1266) when they destroyed a threatening 'bear' (q.v.).

The S.W. tower at Kidwelly is vaulted at all stages and this unusual construction may have been to provide stability for a catapult placed on its roof. (The tower is excellently situated for such an emplacement.) Similarly the N.W. turret of Newcastle keep is multangular (the others are square) probably to provide operational space for a catapult defending the most exposed approach to the castle.

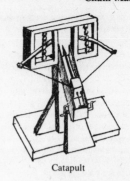

Catapult

CAVALIER TOWER

A square wall-tower astride curtain (popular in C13) which provided additional living space. In the late C13 when domestic buildings began to be laid out against the interior faces of curtain the internal projections of such towers occupied space uneconomically and therefore were cut off flush inside the walls, projecting only towards the field to flank the curtain. At Helmsley the keep is astride the wall and in some places the hall was so placed as to extend into a cavalier tower which then provided a solar.

Cavalier Tower: Mortimers, Ludlow

CESSION

The actual restoration of the king's theoretical right to possess all castles.

CHAIN MAIL

In spite of much discussion and its long use, not much is known for certain about the detailed form and construction of this common defensive armour. It can be said that in C12 and C13 its cost would make it prohibitive to all but the very wealthy in spite of the great quantities which were captured in the

Chain Mail

Crusades. (It was a common object of booty after a battle – see also Hauberk.)

CHAMBER, GREAT (Camera)

A room entered from the upper end of hall which eventually became the nucleus of a range of private apartments. When it was located above the hall (e.g. Conisbrough, Stokesay, Warkworth) it was entered by vice, wooden stair or mural staircase from the hall. It had its own privies and often lavabo and aumbries in the thickness of the wall.

CHAMBER KEEP

A late C12 development where the great hall disappears from the tower accommodation e.g. Bishops Waltham, Brough, Brougham, Chilham, Orford, Peveil.

Conisbrough, Hall, Chamber

CHAPEL

In a religious age, chapels were as important and central to the life of a castle community as of any other. There was usually a chapel in the keep and/or in the bailey where it was sometimes associated with domestic buildings (e.g. Durham, Farnham), or separate from them (e.g. Hastings, Ludlow, Rising, Windsor). It seems to have been the rule that a chapel should have no structure between it and 'heaven' but Newcastle is exceptional with its chapel in the basement of the forebuilding. In spite of military exigencies chapels were orientated as nearly as possible. Many castles had more than one chapel (e.g. Dover, Leeds, Pontefract) and some had within their baileys great cathedral-like collegiate churches e.g. Bridgnorth, Hastings, Leicester, Windsor. The collegiate church of St Mary, Warwick, may have originated in the castle before its removal to a new and more commodious site in the town. Where the castle and parish church stood side by side e.g. Bolton, Earls Barton, Higham Ferrers, the lord and family and the garrison doubtless used the neighbouring church. Nevertheless there are private chapels even when the church is near e.g. Bolton, Ludlow, Warwick.

The chantry movement increased the number of castle chapels e.g. a second chapel at Ludlow, served by two chantry priests, was built in the outer bailey c. 1328 and Elmley had a chantry with eight priests founded in 1308 by one of the Beauchamps.

CHAPELS, LOCATION

In the keep (e.g. Conisbrough, London) or its forebuilding (e.g. Dover, Middleham, Newcastle, Portchester); in gatehouse (e.g. Harlech, Prudhoe, [portcullis chamber]); in towers (e.g. Conway, Kidwelly, Richmond).

Chapel, Conisbrough

CHAPEL ORNAMENT   see also Amenities.

At least as much expenditure was made on the decoration and furniture of a castle chapel as any other chapel. They probably had stained glass and almost certainly wall paintings. They are often the only room in a castle which is carved and vaulted (e.g. Conisbrough, Rising).

Some of the furniture in the form of altars (e.g. Broughton, Chipchase, Nunney) aumbries and piscinas (e.g. Weobley) was 'built in' and their remains are visible. The chapel at Leeds even had a low side window.

The chapel at Farnham (c. 1140) had a crypt, barrel vaulted nave and small chancel while the chapel of St. John in the Tower is a modest sized church.

Chapel, Dover

CHAPLAIN

Chaplains were an early and fundamental appointment to the castle staff. They were even provided for the spiritual welfare of labourers on the site before the castle was built e.g. Kirby Muxloe (1483). The chaplain always seems to have been present in the garrison (among those at Appleby fined in 1176 for facile surrender to the Scots was William, the 'clericus' of Appleby.) He might also act as the local parish priest or as chantry chaplain.

During their three days stay at Newark before advancing to assault Lincoln, King John's forces were prepared for danger of death by confession, absolution and communion.

The chaplain's functions often extended beyond sacerdotal duties e.g. in the early C14 the chaplain at Pickering was given a special allowance for overseeing the building of the new hall. In the early days he may have been the only literate member of the garrison and as such he would function as a 'clerk' i.e. writing and reading letters, keeping accounts etc. In some cases he seems to have been the medical officer or surgeon, like the colourful Philip Porpeis, chaplain of Kenilworth, who mockingly excommunicated the king's forces and the Archbishop of Canterbury in 1264 after he and the rest of the garrison had been excommunicated in earnest. Mention of his extraneous duties must not under-estimate the

Chaplain as Surgeon

chaplain's real spiritual functions to people in
danger of death. His literate function can be
over-estimated in the later Middle Ages when many
castellans were reading knightly romances and their
ladies had their own prayer books. The chapel at
Berkeley had texts from the bible inscribed in
English on its walls translated by its chaplain at the
end of C14. Chaplains obviously varied in status
and the pay of a simple chaplain in the early C13
could be as little as 1d a day. On the other hand, in
the great royal castle at Winchester, Henry III
provided a suite of rooms for the priests and even in
smaller castles the chaplain seems to have had
individual accommodation, usually near the chapel
(e.g. Beverston, Bolton, Conisbrough).

Surgery

CHASES

Slots or grooves above a doorway or in an entrance passage through which the
portcullis descended and which held it in position. Sometimes there are as
many as three sets in a single gatehouse passage e.g. Kidwelly, Pembroke.

CHEMICAL WARFARE

Materials used included super-heated sand which penetrated the joints of
armour and Greek Fire (q.v.). More common materials were boiling water,
animal fat and powdered quick-lime, but there is no evidence for boiling oil or
lead – they were too expensive and rare. There is some evidence for the
existence of arrows in the early C14 where a phial of quick-lime replaced the
barb.

CHEMISE

A protection for the base of a keep or great tower consisting of a wall set a few
yards in advance. Its rampart walk could be attained via a postern and
drawbridge from one of the rooms in the keep. In England a chemise is more
often a feature of C16 artillery forts than of mediaeval castles.

CHESHIRE

The county boasts few castles, though Chester has the remains of one as well
as magnificent walls. Peckforton is included for its unique character. Beeston
and Halton have some masonry remains, while at Aldford and Pulford
earthworks survive as a remainder of a further three royal, and about a dozen
baronial, castles which once existed.

CHIMNEYS

Originally, just an aperture in the centre of the roof to ventilate a brazier
or central hearth. When fireplaces were built against a wall, the earliest
ones had flues (passing straight through the back often ending in two vents
on either side of an external strip-buttress). The windward vent may have

been closed by a damper in heavy wind so that the leeward vent would 'draw' through the assistance of the buttress. Vertical flues in the thickness of the wall are only found in late keeps (e.g. Conisbrough, Scarborough). Chimneys were costly amenities: 30 ft of chimney work at Conway (1285) cost £4.10.0 and the individual chimneys above the Eagle Tower at Caernarvon cost £3 each. The chimney stack over the hall range at St Briavel's has a short spire crowned with the horn of the King's Forester (also Constable) as a finial. Leland remarked (c. 1530): 'One thyng I muche noted in the haulle of Bolton, how chinmeys were conveyed by tunnells made on the syde of the wauls betwixt the lights in the haull: and by this means, and by no Covers is the smoke of the harth in the hawle wonder strangely conveyed'. All traces of these remarkable flues have disappeared. There is a fine chimney at Christchurch and interesting ones at Manorbier. Cylindrical examples at Framlingham (c. 1155) and Grosmont (c. 1330).

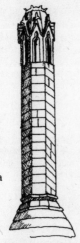

Chimney, Grosmont

CHIVALRY   see also Lady's Favour.

A conscious attempt on the part of the Church to civilise barbarian war-lords and to convert 'might is right' to 'noblesse oblige'. Its efforts were not entirely unsuccessful. Some castles at some times provided shelter and protection for the weak and helpless instead of posing a threat. Royal castles often had an almonry as when Henry III (1241) ordered his constable at Windsor on Good Friday to fill both the great hall and the hall in the keep with poor people and feed them. Perhaps local lords acted similarly and thus originated the tradition of obligation which has long marked the English gentry.

Chevalier

Windsor was a legendary location of the Arthurian Round Table (q.v.) and Edward III revived the tradition on 19th January, 1344, by beginning a fortnight-long Feast of Chivalry marked by tournaments and 'hastiludes'. Five years later on St. George's Day the Order of the Garter was instituted with 26 knights. This was later supplemented by the foundation of a charitable Order of Poor Knights. 'For such valiant soldiers as happened in their old age to fall into poverty and decay' (a kind of Officers' Benevolent Association). Chivalry remained a 'caste' affair and, in spite of the church, its principles tended to be applied only in the treatment of class equals.

Chivalry

CISTERN

In the rare cases where a castle did not have a well within its walls a reserve water supply was maintained in a cistern e.g. Carreg Cennen. Caernarvon had a cistern tower on its south side in addition to the great well tower on the north. Criccieth had a stone-lined cistern in the floor of the gatehouse passage fed by a spring. There was possibly a cistern at the top of Conisbrough keep, probably as part of the defence arrangements.

CLACKMANNONSHIRE

Clackmannon Tower in the county town deserves a mention and Castle Campbell a visit.

Castle Campbell

CLOCK

Towards the end of the Middle Ages the increased luxury of castles sometimes brought the introduction of turret clocks. One survives (1435) at Leeds whose face is decorated with figures of the Crucified, Our Lady and St George. At the beginning of C16, according to Leland, there survived at Bolton 'a very fair clocke cum motu solis el lunae and other Conclusyons.'

COASTAL DEFENCE

The following mediaeval castles (apart from such earlier ones as Dover, Scarborough etc.) were built for coastal defence: Bodiam (1386), Caister (c. 1435), Cooling (1381), Dartmouth (1481), Herstmonceux (1441). To this list could be added the Edwardian castles of Beaumaris, Caernarvon, Conway, Flint etc.

There is a later series, built about 1540, for which see Artillery Fort.

Bodiam

COMMAND

The commanding officer of a castle was usually the constable (q.v.), or castellan, to whom the custody of the castle was entrusted by his lord. The lord himself was rarely present during a siege, probably for the following reasons: it was considered more honourable to fight in the field, he was free to mobilise relief, he was not isolated from great events happening elsewhere and there was less chance of his capture and the consequent and possibly disastrous ransom. In any case the lord was frequently engaged elsewhere: he had other duties and other castles. It was not unknown for his lady to conduct a castle's defence with vigour and success in his absence (see Women, Military Capacity of). In 1174 Odinek de Humfraville, Lord of Prudhoe, spurred his horse Baucan day and night to raise a force for the relief of his castle which was being defended by his constable against the Scots.

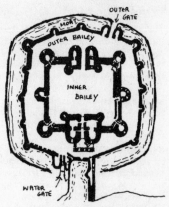

Concentric Plan: Beaumaris

CONCENTRIC PLAN

The final development of castle planning whereby all its defences are united and concentrated against a common front as opposed to the previous 'successive lines of defence' principle. In its perfect form the site on which the castle was built was surrounded by a ditch. The inner scarp of this ditch was crowned (and sometimes partly revetted) by a wall flanked by towers at the angles and, in the largest castles, placed on the intermediate faces. Within this wall,

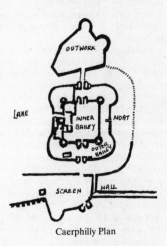

Caerphilly Plan

and only separated from it by a narrow space of open ground, rose a second and much higher wall also flanked at corners and on faces by towers. This inner wall enclosed the main wall and the intermediate space formed the outer ward or 'lists'. There was no keep but entrances were defended by powerful keep-like gatehouses (e.g. Edwardian castles especially Beaumaris and the earlier Caerphilly). This principle was sometimes applied to older fortresses such as Dover and London which were converted to the concentric plan in the time of Henry III. When the site did not lend itself to the full application of concentrism, additions were made according to the basic principle of a unified and aggressive defence e.g. Goodrich, Middleham.

CONSTABLE

The governor or warden of a fortress or castle in the absence of owner and therefore normal in royal establishments. Though he was not the owner he occupied the great chamber as would the lord of a residential castle. It was an important position, sometimes bestowed on a great baron as an honour and some royal castles had hereditary constables. He was responsible in the more or less permanent absence of the owner and had, for instance, to decide whether to hold the castle or surrender it when threatened (e.g. Robert de Stuteville at Wark, in 1173 and 1174).

A notable constable was Hubert de Burgh (Dover 1216) who instructed his men, as he left to pursue the French by sea, 'If I should be taken in the battle rather let me be hanged than surrender this fortress, for it is the key of England'. His salary, from which he provided food for the garrison, was £1,000 a year. (The constable of Pevensey was only paid £22 per year in the early C15.) James of St. George, designer of Edward's great castles in Wales, became first constable of Harlech.

Representative constables looked after their lord's interests and possessions. In the early C14 the constable of Pickering is estimated to have had charge of nearly 3,000 animals whose breeding and well-being played a large part in the life, resources and economy of that castle. Besides being a super gamekeeper the constable could be a kind of royal almoner, as at Windsor in 1241 where he was responsible for feeding the poor on Good Friday. The responsibilities could be dangerous e.g. Gospatric was heavily fined in 1174 for surrending Appleby, and Andrew de Harcla, constable of Carlisle, was executed in 1323 allegedly for treating with the Scots. On the other hand they were expected to use their discretion e.g. 1173 Robert de Vaux repulsed the Scots from Carlisle but in the following year (when they were equipped with siege engines) he asked for a truce.

William Marshall, Constable

Constable's Tower (Gate), Dover

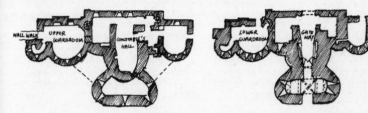

Plan : Constable's Tower, Dover

CONSTABLE'S DUTIES

As an example of dereliction : Richard de Pembridge, constable of Bamburgh in the closing years of Edward III, was accused of allowing the well to be blocked up and its rope and bucket stolen. Furthermore, he had not kept an eye on his underlings. The steward had disposed of beds and furniture to the value of ten marks while his deputy had been negligent in his accounting. Another deputy managed to steal the refectory table, seven stones of lead and the iron frame of a mangonel.

CONSTABLE'S POWERS

Constables of royal castles had extensive powers including toll on goods entering and leaving the town and levies on the townsfolk for the support of the garrison. The constable of Norwich ruled the whole town, and hunting and fishing rights (or claims) were often a subject of dispute with the townsfolk.

Constables also claimed an allowance for the maintenance of prisoners (at the Tower in the reign of Richard II it was 3s 4d a week for yeomen and servants confined with their masters).

The full range of a castle's privileges and powers is seen in the royal castle at Corfe – the head of the Isle of Purbeck. Its constable was Lord Lieutenant and Admiral with power to array the militia, and every tithing (group of ten householders) was bound, in time of war, to provide one member of the garrison at the king's wages for ten days. In addition, many local farms had to supply a set quantity of bushels of wheat or cartloads of hay for the castle. Others owed rents in poultry, salt, cummin, wax, pepper, horseshoes and

Corfe

other payments in kind. One tenantry depended on the holder finding a carpenter when required 'to work about the great tower'. Besides these dues the constable claimed the right to quarry stone and cut timber throughout the Isle, to gather firewood from unenclosed woods, flotsam and jetsam, and a share of all beer brewed in the domain together with cartage for his own wine from the port of Wareham. From any ship putting in at one of his ports he claimed 'prisage' i.e. one tun (252 gallons) or wine from every 20 on board. He also claimed all royal fish (grampuses, porpoises and sturgeons) caught off the coast and all falcons nesting on his lands. He sold licences for sea-fishing and his warreners and gamekeepers punished breaches of the game laws (the gamekeepers were entitled, with notice, to free board and drink for one day each week from every tenant on the Isle.) A tenant could not give a daughter in marriage without the constable's consent.

CORBEL

A stone bracket projecting from a wall to carry gallery, floor, roof-beams etc. A corbel-table is a horizontal row of such projecting stones. A corbelled-out parapet is usually a sign of post-Norman work.

Corbel

CORNWALL

In terms of military architecture, the Duchy's chief interest lies in a group of castles with round keeps: Launceston, Restormel, Trematon. Tintagel must be mentioned because of its site and to complete the picture we have included Carn Brea, Pendennis, Pengersick and St. Mawes.

Trematon, Cornwall, Curtain and Shell-Keep

CORRIDORS

Internal corridors are rare in mediaeval buildings and communication between rooms at ground level was often through timber pent-houses passing along the outer faces of walls (compare cloister-walk in abbeys). There were probably roofed wooden passages across the courtyard from building to building but in all likelihood they were at least partially open at the sides.

COSTS

Royal castles took at least eight per cent of the basic Crown Revenues from 1155 to 1215. 90 castles are mentioned in Henry II's accounts and Dover, Newcastle, Nottingham, Orford, Winchester and Windsor each received over £1,000. (Dover cost nearly £6,500.)

Dover absorbed nearly £7,000 between 1180 and 1191. Henry II spent £428 plus on Chilham, £339 plus on Arundel, £150 plus on Rochester (keep already built), £100 plus on Canterbury and on re-building Wark together with some £1,400 on Welsh castles.

Richard I expended about £250 at York to make good the damage of anti-Jewish riots and £458 plus on Welsh castles.

John spent over £1,000 per annum on 95 castles with heavy expenditure on Corfe, Hanley and Horston (both disappeared), Lancaster (over £500 each) and possibly Norham. He expended over £1,000 each on Kenilworth, Knaresborough and Odiham and well over £2,000 on Scarborough.

Besides heavy expenditure on northern castles John disbursed some £1,700 on Welsh castles. He spent more on Scarborough and Knaresborough than on any other castle.

Edward I's building in Wales came to more than £100,000 (equivalent to far more than £10m). Initial costs were Rhuddlan £9,500, Flint £7,000, Conway £9,000, Caernarvon £20,000, Beaumaris £14,000.

Henry III (or his representatives) spent about £15,000 p.a. throughout his reign (1216-1272) on castles: Dover about £7,500, Welsh castles at least £10,000, York (rebuilding perimeter in stone) over £2,500, Rochester £1,258, Chester £1,717. While the residential castles (Windsor £1,500, Winchester £9,655, Tower £9,683, Marlborough c. £2,000, Bristol £1,759, Gloucester £1,661) had elaborate alterations to bring their halls, chapels and chambers up to Henry's standards of taste and comfort. Their fortifications were not neglected

Dover

though these seem to have been concentrated on castles with which he was familiar (Carlisle, damaged by Scots, was not repaired for 40 years. York was not made an effective fortress until Henry's visit in 1244 which resulted in Clifford's Tower).

COSTS, INDIVIDUAL ITEMS

(Multiply by about 100 to gain a rough estimate of modern equivalent.)

New hall, Pickering (1314)	£341.15.8
Renovation at Pickering and Scarborough (1218-1226)	£667.0.0
'New work round barbican' at Pickering (1224)	£278.16.10½
Completion of gatehouse at Beaumaris (1343) (mason's work £200, carpenters' £80, plumbers' etc. £40)	£320.0.0

At Harlech in 1289 a large drum tower was charged at 45s a foot (thus north-west tower cost nearly £112 while the south-west cost nearly £117). Turrets or 'garrites' cost 12s a foot or £11.8.0 each; fireplace in gatehouse 8s; window 15s; roofing the S.E. tower with wood £22; roofing gatehouse, N.W. and S.W. towers £35.6.8. The cost of lead for these and the kitchen, hall, chapel, and pantry was £10.

To turn to another Welsh castle i.e. Conway (1286) the following costs may be interesting: 7 doorways, corbels in King's chamber and re-making 6 perches of thick walling by well £64; 142 arrow slits at 1s 2d each, £8.5.8; 250 dressed stones (voussoirs) 25s a hundred, £2.12.6; cutting rock by river postern, £10; wall section 48' × 10' × 3' with turrets, £14; outer drawbridge, 34s 7d. The total costs at Conway (including castle, town walls and river works) were about £14,086. The costs of cordage in late C13 were as follows:

Harlech Gatehouse (Reconstruction)

Great cables	£1.0.0. each
Small ropes	4 for 15s
Other ropes	5 for 13s 4d
Small cords (for plumb-bobs and setting courses)	1s

It has been estimated that castle costing falls into something like the following proportions: materials 25 per cent, transport 25 per cent, site-work i.e. finishing and erecting 50 per cent. In spite of the importance and comparatively high salaries of the skilled (master) workmen it is reckoned that over $\frac{1}{5}$ of wages was expended in payments to 'the hodmen with baskets, bags, hand-barrows and tubs, carriers of water in barrels, and watchmen'.

COUNTER-FORT   see also Siege-work.

Besiegers' defence-work.

Hodman with Barrow

COUNTERSCARP

Levelled area on outermost bank of ditch. In earliest castles was probably defended by a herrison (q.v.). The entrance to the earliest keeps rose on a bridge or ladder from the counterscarp of the ditch which ringed the motte.

Counterscarp also describes the outer slope of a ditch as against the scarp which is the slope on the side nearer the castle.

COURTS

Royal justice was often delegated to great vassals who held 'barony courts' in the great hall of their castles. They heard both civil and criminal cases concerned with property, rights, dues and taxes and they often had the explicit 'right of pit and gallows'. (The location of the castle gallows is sometimes known.)

CREASING

The inverted V-shape visible on a wall which marks the pitch of a former roof.

CRENEL   see also Battlements, Parapet.

The embrasure in a parapet between merlons (q.v.).
To 'crenellate' means to 'fortify'. A royal licence
(q.v.) to crenellate was required before a lord could
legally fortify his residence. Records survive of such
licences from the reign of King John and provide
invaluable evidence for dating castles (though they
are not always reliable).

Crenels

The original timber stockades which defended the
earliest castles were probably crenellated. When
wood was replaced by stone wall it was
battlemented and provided with an allure from a
comparatively early date. The form of crenellation
is basically unchanged during C13 to C14 but its
efficacy is improved by increasing the number of crenels and narrowing the
length of the intervening merlons. The apogee of crenellation in England
probably occurs in the double system of parapets on the summit of Caesar's
Tower, Warwick (late C14) – a masterpiece of contemporary military
architecture.

CROSSBOW

Was developed from the larger mounted
'ballista' and in its smaller form came in a
variety of sizes and with various modifications.
(Some seem to have been capable of firing two
bolts (q.v.) at once.)

The primitive crossbow was probably
introduced into England as a military weapon
by the Normans. Their bow was made of wood
and cocked by hand. The arbalist held its
fore-end firmly to the ground with his foot
through the stirrup while pulling back the
string with both hands.

The crossbow became a highly lethal
weapon and was forbidden by the Church. In
spite of this, Richard I who was an expert shot,
encouraged its use. It was perhaps ironical that
he met his death from this weapon, though
some considered it a just retribution for his
defiance of the Church's interdiction of its use
against fellow-Christians.

Crossbow-man

At this date the bow was probably still of
wood but given additional power by a
composite construction using wood, horn,
sinew and glue. During C12 the crossbow was
considerably improved and the wooden bow
was eventually replaced by heavy steel which
required mechanical aid to cock it (windlass,

cranquin or lever). Many of these weapons had a draw-weight of over a quarter of a ton while the heavier siege crossbow could draw over half a ton.

Crossbow strings were made of yarn and greased with tallow.

The East Tower at Warkworth has a huge loop in each of its five outer faces designed for the operation of a crossbow 16 ft long. 'These loops, splayed throughout and fantailed at both top and bottom are the finest examples of cross-loops left in England.' (Thompson, 248) When the crossbow fell out of fashion this tower turned to new uses and signs of its modification are apparent.

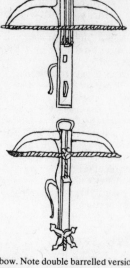

Crossbow. Note double barrelled version

CROSSBOW-MEN

Perhaps the most valuable members of the castle garrison. Because of its deadliness, the crossbow (q.v.) had been (ineffectually) condemned by the Lateran Council of 1139 as a weapon 'hateful to God'. Crossbow-men appear extensively in castles during the reign of John.

There is controversy about the relative effectiveness of the cross and long-bow (and it is perhaps significant that Caernarvon was looped for the long-bow), but there is no doubt that neither was ever rivalled by the hand-gun in the Middle Ages.

For the pay of crossbow-men see Wages. The could vary in social status: of a group of 84 serving King John (c. 1200), 26 travelled with three horses each, 51 with two and seven with one.

CROSS-WALL

An interior wall dividing a keep. It functioned not merely as a partition between rooms but also enabled builders to lay their floors more evenly as timber of a sufficient length to extend across the undivided space was difficult to obtain. They also served a defensive purpose by forming a barrier which divides the tower into two halves. This cross-wall reached from the base to the summit of the keep and it was often central (e.g. Portchester, Rochester, Scarborough). In towers of oblong plan it usually divided them into unequal rectangles (e.g. Middleham, Rising). The cross-wall at Bowes is so eccentric that it divides the keep into large square chambers with a very narrow subsidiary one.

In a square keep the cross-wall is usually opposite the main entrance and parallel with the forebuilding. At Hedingham, Lancaster, Portchester, Scarborough, it is built at right-angles to the forebuilding so that the main entrance is at an end and not a side of the main room (c.f. oblong keep at Rising). The cross-wall at Scarborough ceases at the first floor and at the second floor level is replaced by a transverse arch which throws the rooms into one large chamber (compare Hedingham). On the second floor at Rochester it is broken by two pairs of rounded arches separated by a block which contains the well-shaft.

The cross-wall is not found in all keeps. It is not necessary in small ones (e.g. Clun, Guildford) but even larger keeps dispense with it (e.g. Kenilworth, Richmond, Newcastle). Conversely, some keeps had subsidiary cross-walls (e.g. Rising).

CROW'S NEST

A lofty look-out point. There is a rare example at Warwick, on the wall between Clarence and Guy Towers, allegedly to watch for infringement of curfew in the town below.

Crow's Nest, Warwick

CRUSADES

A considerable influence on castle design (including development of flanking towers and replacement of square or rectangular towers by round or polygonal ones). The Third Crusade brought an increased awareness of the power of siege engines and the dangers of sapping and mining.

CRYPT

The basement of a church or chapel, usually for the preservation of relics. A number of castle chapels had crypts e.g. London Tower, Oxford.

CULVERIN

A C14 small-bore cannon, transitional between hand-gun and full cannon, used for anti-personnel work (as distinct from the bombards which were for battering walls and towers). Some of the gatehouse loops at Bodiam seem to have been designed for culverins. The name is derived from the snake-like handles attached to them. A demi-culverin was even smaller and had a four ins bore.

CUMBERLAND

Cumberland and Westmorland are Marcher counties, indeed in C12 they were part of the Kingdom of Scotland. From the late C13 the North of England was in continuous danger of invasion and border raids and plundering expeditions were endemic. Consequently defence works not only included formal castles but extended to religious houses and smaller domestic structures such as the Vicar's Peles (Lanercost, Croglin), and bastle-houses (Old Vicarage, Denton). This last village seems to have possessed three peles, two bastle-houses and a motte-and-bailey castle (if not two)! The religious college at Kirkoswald had a pele tower among its buildings.

43

Many pele towers are swallowed up in later and grander mansions (e.g. Greystoke). Any attempt at a full list would be beyond the scope of this book and we have contented ourselves with the following: Armathwaite, Askerton, Bewcastle, Carlisle, Cockermouth, Corby, Dacre, Dalston, Egremont, Greystoke, Hayton, Houghton, Irton, Kirkandrews, Kirkoswald, Lammerside, Millom, Muncaster, Maworth, Penrith, Rose, Scaleby, Sowerby, Thistlewood, Triermain.

CURTAIN   see also Height.

Curtain (Conway)

Strictly speaking, the stretch of wall 'hanging' between two towers but often used of the whole wall (including the towers) bounding any portion of a castle. The cross-curtain subdivides the bailey into two wards.

Lofty walls seem to have been the answer to improved siege-engines, especially the trebuchet (q.v.). Raising the walls makes their bases more vulnerable unless the guardians lean out and thus expose themeselves. This problem was solved by hoarding (q.v.) and allures (q.v.) but especially by angle-towers e.g. Carisbrooke, Portchester, and most of all by wall-towers which cover the berm (q.v.) and make attack by mine, pick or ram more hazardous. The following seem to be the earliest curtain walls: Brough (c. 1095), Ludlow (1086), Richmond (1075), Rochester (1087).

Conway

Curtain with rectangular towers at e.g. Framlingham (1190), with rounded towers e.g. Bungay (c. 1294), Criccieth (c. 1220), Dover (c. 1230), Ewloe (c. 1257), Pevensey (c. 1250), Skenfrith (c. 1220), Whitecastle (c. 1220).

DEAD ANGLE, DEAD GROUND

The section of the field into which defenders cannot direct fire without undue exposure of themselves. Fortifications were much concerned with the elimination of such areas e.g. opposite point of square tower, immediately beneath walls.

DECLINE OF CASTLES

It was economics rather than gunpowder that destroyed the castles. The economics of power: money over land, town over country, central over local government; and the economics of cost: castles, like education, became too much for local resources. There were even cheaper military alternatives: cannon fodder was cheaper than knights and more expendable, there was no need for the arbiters of power to risk their own skins any more. Power too had changed geography and the corridors of power were no longer on the Welsh Marches or amid the Northumbrian hills. The form of conspicuous extravagance had changed and power demanded its comforts or, alternatively, status required comfort as a compensation for loss of power. Social gaps had widened and communal life was out of fashion: the great hall became either the servants' hall or a mere vestibule to the private quarters. Even with all this change castles were still good enough for prisoners and as the number of prisoners increased the whole castle was taken over as a prison and up to C19 even new prisons were crenellated.

As fortifications, their obsolescence was hastened by the increasing development of firearms during C14 and after.

As dwelling-houses, increasing luxury led to the great house whose fortifications were only token.

Perhaps too much has been made of the influence of gunpowder – castles put up a prolonged resistance against artillery during the Civil War of C17. More important causes were probably the following: changes in the conduct of war, involving larger armies who decided the issue in the field; the very strength of a castle caused it to be bypassed (many castles have no 'history'); changes in society from feudalism based on land tenure to wealth based on money and trade (with which might be connected the growing importance of towns and their markets); the decline of feudal loyalties and obligations; the growing strength of the monarchy and central

Decline

Early Cannon

government; the effects of the Hundred Years' War; changing alliances so that rebellion became more a matter of principle than of private interest; the rise of middle classes who had never lived in castles, with different values and different notions of 'fame' leading to the decline of military 'virtues'.

DECORATION

Architectural elaboration was introduced from an early period into doorways and windows and the high walls of the great hall may have been lightened by a triforium. At Weobley, Glam. there survives a small window headstop, carved into the likeness of a woman's head, which is a charming and expressive work of art. Stained glass was rare apart from the chapel but not unknown in the halls in the later Middle Ages.

Walls were decorated with tapestries and from the time of Henry III with wall painting. These murals were sometimes abstract (green with gold stars) or consisted of medallions depicting sacred and secular subjects. Later, entire walls were covered with mural paintings (e.g. Longthorpe Tower). Both internally and externally walls were plastered and/or lime-washed so as to give the appearance of an unbroken surface. In 1256 Henry III ordered that his castle of Guildford should have its hall pillars and arches marbled, the great chamber whitewashed and marked out in squares and its ceiling painted green spangled with gold and silver.

In the greater castles, gardens were elaborated into 'pleasaunces' instead of being mere sources of food.

DEDICATIONS OF CASTLE CHAPELS

St Andrew – Dover Oratory
St Clement – Pontefract Chapel
St Dubric – Warwick (C12)
St George – Oxford (c. 1072) of Windsor
St Hilary – Denbigh (c. 1300)
St John the Evangelist – London Tower (C11), Ravensworth (1487), Skipton (before 1512)
St Judoc – Winchester (early C12)
St Lawrence – Warkworth (c. 1400)
St Margaret – Salisbury (C12)
St Martin – Arundel (c. 1200)
St Mary – Prudhoe (c. 1300)
St Mary – Berkeley (before 1364)
St Mary – Portchester (Collegiate Chapel), (c. 1300)
St Mary in Castro – Dover (c. 1300)
St Mary in Castro – Leicester (c. 1200)
St Mary and St George the Martyr – Windsor (1475 or earlier)
St Mary Magdalene – Ludlow (C11)
St Michael – Shrewsbury (1385)
St Nicholas – Arundel (before 1066)
St Nicholas – Marlborough (early C12)
St Nicholas – Carisbrooke (1275)
St Nicholas – Richmond (Robin Hood Tower) (c. 1100)
St Oswald – Bamburgh (c. 1200)
St Peter – Ludlow (1328)

St Peter's Chains – London Tower (C15)
St Thomas of Canterbury – Dover Oratory (C12)
Trinity – Arundel (C14)

'DEFENDERS'

Name given to life-like stone effigies
surmounting the battlements of gatehouses or
towers (e.g. Alnwick, Bothal, Caernarvon,
Chepstow, Hylton, Newcastle (town walls),
Raby, York (walls).

They are thought to be designed to give an
impression of manning, but Hamilton
Thompson remarks that 'An enemy who could
be daunted by the illusion of a rather diminutive
archer or slinger balancing himself upon a
narrow coping must have had very little
experience of warfare'. One may question this,
particularly at night, in the flickering light of a
watch-fire or the half-light of dawn or dusk.

Defender

DEMOLITION

Apart from Cromwellian 'slighting', many
castles were demolished in the Middle Ages:
some by war but perhaps most by Henry II in his
campaign to restore royal power after Anarchy.
Examples of the latter: Benington, Bungay, Framlingham, Saltwood,
Thetford. In some cases the mottes were partly quarried away (e.g. Groby,
Weston Turville) and the defensive timber-work transferred to another site.
In other cases walls or towers were broken rather than completely
demolished. At Owston Ferry there were fines for inadequate demolition.

DENBIGHSHIRE

Apart from remains in the county town, there
are many earthworks often indicated by 'Tomen'
e.g. Tomen y Rhodwydd. Edward I was busy at
Ruthin in 1277 and at Holt and Chirk in 1282/3.
Holt was demolished in C17 and Chirk has been
adjusted for continuous habitation (even if the
Edwardian castle had ever been finished).

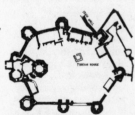

Denbigh (plan)

DERBYSHIRE

Derbyshire is not rich in castles but it has, in Haddon Hall, one of the most
delightful and continuously developing fortified manor-houses in the country,
while ruined South Wingfield 'petrifies the mid C15'. Of true castles there are
remains at Codnor, Mackworth and the romantically sited Peveril. Nothing
much more than the site remains at Bolsover and of Duffield (whose keep
once rivalled Colchester and the White Tower) nothing remains above
ground.

DESIGNERS   see also Engineer.

Specialists in the art of castle
building came from various parts
of feudal society – one of the most
famous was a devout and
emotional Benedictine monk
(Gundulf). Ideas travelled, so that
a feature in one castle could be
copied or improved in another.
Here and there we find real
innovation, a principle well ahead
of its time, but its existence is the
only memorial of its inventor.

Gundulf's St Leonard's, West Malling

DEVON

Exeter has Rougemont and there
are interesting keeps at Gidleigh,
Lydford and Okehampton. Later
than these are the castles at
Powderham and Tiverton.
Compton is later still and we have
rounded off our examples by
including Berry Pomeroy,
Bickleigh, Dartmouth, Hemyock,
Kingswear, Plympton, Salcombe
and Totnes.

DIAPHRAGM

Internal wall running up to full
height of roof-ridge, usually along
the central axis of a long building.

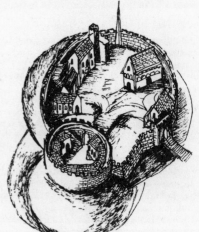

DISTRIBUTION

Remained pretty constant
throughout the history of castles.
They were concentrated on the
borders of the mediaeval
kingdom: the marches of Scotland
and Wales and the S.E. coast
towards France as well as other

Totnes, Devon

vulnerable points on the coast. During Anarchy, castles seem to have been
distributed at about ten mile intervals, at least in some parts of the country e.g.
Cambridgeshire, Leicestershire.

Castles are found in every county of the interior because of their original
purpose of holding the Norman Conquest against local rising. They were
maintained as status symbols and because possessions might still need to be
defended. There was a continuing possibility of civil factions as long as there
were over-mighty subjects and weak rulers.

Castle siting is tactical rather than strategic. There was no overall national plan and though an individual site might be skilfully chosen to command a line of communication (perhaps no longer used) or to protect a settlement (perhaps now shrunk in importance), other considerations operate such as proximity to hunting country (e.g. Odiham) or struggle for power (e.g. Orford).

Castles were scarce where there was a sparse population e.g. extensive woodland, fenland, moorland or bare downs. They were also infrequent where there were extensive abbey lands. Bishops had military office and obligations and there were episcopal castles in many places: Bishop's Stortford (London), Bishop's Castle (Hereford), Durham, Farnham (Winchester), Hartlebury (Worcester), Sherborne (Salisbury), Wells, Wolvesey (Winchester).

There are extensive abbey lands in the Cotswolds, South Lincolnshire, around St. Edmundsbury and Glastonbury, and consequently few castles.

(Bishop) Gundulf's Tower, Rochester

Scattered fiefs required a number of castles, whereas a compact fief needed only one. Thus a much-castled district was usually a region where proprietorship was much divided. Holdings were deliberately dispersed in William's original grants to avoid a concentration of strength which might rival that of the king, but this situation could be modified as a result of subsequent inheritance (mainly through marriage) or later award e.g. the Cliffords, based originally on Wye, acquired half of Westmorland through Vipon marriage; the Bigods of Norfolk obtained Chepstow through Marshall marriage and the Fitzalans of Clun acquired most of Sussex through marrying the heiress of Arundel. Edmund Crouchback, son of Henry III became Earl of Lancaster, received confiscated estates of the Montforts of Leicester and the Ferrers of Derbyshire, to which his descendants added by marriage the Earldoms of Lincoln, Salisbury, Hereford, and the Marches of Kidwelly and Brecknock. Consequently the holdings of John of Gaunt extended from Northumberland to Wiltshire, from Essex to South Wales and he owned about twenty of the most powerful castles in England.

DITCH

An often neglected aspect of fortification. Elaborate ones were designed by engineers and dug by 'fossores'. They were usually revetted with turf and sometimes stone or timber. They could be as much as 60 ft across and vary in shape from a sharp V to a more rounded U. They were usually further defended by palisades or a curtain and protected by outworks in the form of thorn-walls or other obstacles.

Whether natural or artificial, whether wet or dry, and however modest, the ditch was amongst the most vital defences of a castle. The first necessity of an assaulting force was to drain or bridge a wet ditch or to fill a dry one sufficiently substantially to allow the passage of siege-engines. Infilling was usually earth or stone, logs, brushwood or faggots. This would probably be attempted under cover of darkness and with the protection of 'cats' or penthouses (q.v.). The crossing often had to be 'paved' with logs to form a corduroy road along which belfries or other engines could travel. This road was often engineered to a gradient declining towards the walls or tower so that once a belfry was erected on it momentum would assist it towards its objective.

The vast majority of ditches were dry but wet ditches (moats) appeared in some places. The latter were of a U-shaped section, the former V-shaped. It must be remembered that so called dry ditches would normally have some water or mud and probably even more unpleasant material in their bottoms to provide an additional obstacle. In either case, the sides would be made as steep as possible and timber revetments on the inner face of a dry ditch would make them practically unclimbable without assistance. £5.16.8. was disbursed for 'mending ditches' at Aberystwyth c. 1288.

DOMESTIC BUILDINGS   see also Chapel, Kitchen etc.

Buildings outside the keep were of various materials: timber, half-timber ('post and pan'), or stone. Fireplaces and chimneys were usually stone. Contemporary documents call domestic buildings 'houses within a castle', accurately reflecting the lack of organic planning or integration with the prior military structures. These subordinate buildings could include courts, jails, clergy houses (Nottingham), even a treasury, as well as the frequently mentioned chapels, barns and stables.

Erecting Domestic Building in Bailey

About a third of Henry II's expenditure at Windsor was on domestic improvement: hall, chambers, larder, kitchen, almonry, chapel, furnishings and amenities (including pictures and garden). He showed similar concern at Winchester and Nottingham.

'It requires an effort of the imagination to recall that, in all periods of the Middle Ages and not only towards the end of its history, the castle was lived in more than it was fought in.' (Brown, 184).

DONJON   see Keep.

DOOR   see also Portcullis, Yett.

Castle doors were usually double-leaved and mostly opened outwards. There was often a small door or wicket in one of the leaves. They

Door, Bamburgh

were made of oak frames and usually fronted with oak planks often studded with nails. The frames were normally cross-braced to produce a large number of small squares or diamonds to avoid offering easily split end-grain to assaulting axes or other weapons. The wood could be re-inforced with iron straps.

Door and window arches were usually constructed around a temporary wooden centring but they could be made from self-centring units. The door itself hung on butt hinges which dropped on to pins embedded in the door-frame. Doors were barred or bolted but spring locks (known from Roman times) were also used. A two leaved door had a large 'flail' bar pivotted in the centre of the edge of one leaf to fasten both (like the smaller button catch still used in cupboards).

A simple, small door for a workshop cost 3¼ d in the C12.

DORSET

The explorer should begin with the shattered majesty of Corfe. After Sherborne there is Rufus and the scant remains of Marshwood. There are three Henrician coastal forts at Brownsea, Portland and Sandsfoot, of which the second is the most interesting. Sturminster Newton was possibly not a castle, Wareham has nothing to show above ground and Cranbourne and Woodsford are offered as examples of fortified manor-houses.

DOUBLE-SPLAYED   see also Splay.

An embrasure whose smallest aperture is at its mid-point.

DOVES   see also Pigeons

Doves or pigeons provided a welcome addition to the diet, particularly in winter or during a siege. Accommodation for such birds was frequently provided either at tops of towers or in special cotes at near ground level.

DOVECOTE

A dovecote or pigeon-house was a common, if not invariable, piece of castle furniture. There are examples on the summit of Conisbrough keep and in the bailey at Urquhart.

Dovecote

DRAWBRIDGE   see also Turning-Bridge.

A movable wooden bridge originally withdrawn horizontally to hinder access to defences. Later, the outer end was lifted by attached ropes or chains pulled through slots in the wall of the upper room in gatehouse. There are many variations by which the under-face of the bridge became an additional door, counterpoised with weights or the portcullis (q.v.) e.g. Alnwick.

A later development (C14) was to raise the bridge by lifting arms ('gaffs') which were continued to form the side-frame of a strong door pivotted above the entrance arch and acting as counterpoise for the bridge. The door came into position when the bridge was raised and was lodged close to the roof of the gatehouse passage when the bridge was down. A chamber for the windlass can be seen at Manorbier, the recess to contain the raised bridge at Carlisle, and slot to receive the lifting arms ('rainures') at Herstmonceux.

Some C14 drawbridges have walls on either side of the bridge pit e.g. Donnington, Launceston, Mettingham. The drawbridge pit at Rochester was 15 ft deep and the drawbridge at Warkworth is combined with a booby-trap to project unwary assailants into the pit.

The drawbridges for the two main gates at Caernarvon cost £8.6.8 in 1305.

Drawbridge with Drum Towers

DRUM TOWERS

Flanking towers of circular section.

DUMFRIESSHIRE

Caerlaverock is an outstanding example and other castles worth mentioning are: Annan, Hoddom, Lochmaben, Morton, Ruthwell (Comlongon), Tibbers and Torthorwald. There is a fine motte-and-bailey at Moffat and others at Dumfries.

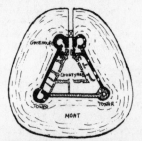

Caerlaverock, Dumfriesshire (plan)

DUNBARTONSHIRE

There is an impressive site in the county town and Cardross is worth mentioning.

DUNGEON   see Prison.

DURHAM

In a county disturbed by continual Scots raids, mediaeval military architecture was more developed than domestic or religious building. As Pevsner says, 'No student of mediaeval castles can afford to leave aside the County of Durham.' The cathedral city has a mighty castle and traces of walls (rather less than at Hartlepool). There were major castles at Barnard, Brancepeth, Lumley, Raby and Witton.

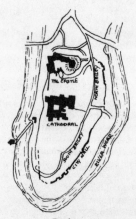

Durham

Of the small castles, Hylton is most impressive and there are interesting remains at Bishop Auckland, Bradley, Dalden Hollinside, Ludworth and an impressive fake at Lambton.

Daggers: (a) Misericord, (b) Anelace

EARLY CASTLES   see also Anarchy, Demolition.

As a reminder that these were wood and earth and long remained so, it is worth mentioning that the Bayeaux tapestry records that William ordered a castle to be '*dug*' at Hastings.

EARTHWORKS   see also Motte, Ditch.

The first castles basically relied for defence on a mound (motte), ditches and ramparts. The motte was a high truncated cone e.g. Thetford 80 ft high from bottom of ditch to its summit. The motte at York was erected in eight days.

Instead of a high cone the castle was sometimes built on a low mound or ring-work. It seems that the mound was preferred for a residential castle while a motte was more characteristic of a garrison fortress or siege-castle e.g. Topcliffe which was a siege base for the attack on Mowbray's castle at Thirsk. There are notable earthworks at e.g. Helmsley, Rising.

Dirleton, East Lothian

EAST LOTHIAN

Possesses at least two castles of the first rank: Dirleton and Tantallon (North Berwick). Others worth mentioning are Dunbar, Hailes, Yester.

Tantallon, East Lothian

EDWARD I (1272-1307)

'The reign of Edward I marks the climax of castle building as an exercise of royal

Hailes (from the South), East Lothian

53

authority. . . it was in the great fortresses
by which he guaranteed the conquest of
Wales that the mediaeval castle reached
the limits of its capacity as a military
device.' (King's Works in Wales, 228)

EDWARD III (1327-1377)

Edward I

His fear of French invasion led to great
military expenditure at Beaumaris,
Caernarvon, Calais, Carisbrooke, Conway,
Corfe, Portchester, Queenborough,
Rochester, Southampton, Tintagel,
Trematon, Winchester castles. Town walls at
Canterbury and elsewhere were
strengthened and many private houses
were granted licences to crenellate,
including: Amberley, Bodiam, Bolton,
Caister, Cooling, Chillingham, Leeds,
Maxstoke, Nunney, Old Wardour,
Penshurst, Scotney, Sheriff Hutton,
Shirburn, Wressle.

EDWARDIAN CASTLES

Two of the great C13
castles in Wales were built
by subjects, namely
Caerphilly (Gloucester
1267) and Denbigh (de
Lacey 1282). Edward's
own castles include
Kidwelly (1275-1325),
Flint (1277-86),
Rhuddlan (1277-82),
Conway (1283-9),
Caernarvon 1283-1330),
Harlech (1283-90),
Beaumaris (1295-1330).

Harlech, Merionethshire

Edwardian castles may be classified into three groups:

1. Keepless castles in which the flanked curtain wall forms the sole line of
   defence e.g. Conway.
2. Old castles which adopted a concentric line of defence by extending their
   site e.g. London Tower.
3. New-plan castles in which the defences are strictly and deliberately
   concentric e.g. Beaumaris.

'The Edwardian castles in Wales, which include among their number some of
the finest castles ever raised in this country, taken altogether form one
defensive system and one comprehensive undertaking which is by far the
greatest single achievement in the history of English castle-building.' (Brown,
127)

The astronomical cost of these great works has been well described as 'the premium Edward paid to insure his Welsh conquests against the fire of rebellion'. (J. G. Edwards)

The significance of Edwardian castles lies in their combination of three elements:
1. A replacement of keep by curtain with symmetrical flanking towers.
2. Outer curtain linking two successive defensive lines which can operate in concert.
3. A powerful keep-gatehouse with elaborate defences on the most vulnerable side.

EMBRASURE

The splayed opening in a wall for a window or to provide a firing point. Also used as equivalent for crenel (q.v.)

EMPLOYEES

Extended far beyond the castle garrison in some cases e.g. the royal castle of Pickering in C13 included among its employees a chaplain at about 2d a day, a watchman and a porter at about the same salary, together with a reeve, forester, park-keeper and four shepherds. The porter was sometimes paid in tolls and lesser servants in kind e.g. loaves and wine and perquisite of collecting kitchen scraps.

ENCEINTE

From the French 'engirdled'. The entire enclosure of a castle within its continuous walls or other defences.

ENFEOFMENT (Infeofment).

The act of giving symbolical possession of inheritable property. The terms often included 'when required' and the act was often the offering of a very minor tribute such as 'a rose at Whit Sunday', 'a horseshoe at Martinmas' etc.

ENFILADE

A fire of arrows or other missiles which sweeps a line of works or men from end to end; hence a part of the field which is so swept from the fortifications is said to be 'enfiladed'.

ENGINEER

There were no 'architects' in the Middle Ages. Cathedrals and other master-pieces were the work of master-masons, master-carpenters, master-glaziers etc. The designers of mediaeval castles, when they were not amateurs of architecture and professionals of war (i.e. the owners themselves – a contemporary described Geoffrey Plantagenet as 'highly skilled in engineering and carpentry.'), seem to have been called engineers (cf. our Civil Engineer).

During C12 the king had in his employ skilled professionals responsible for the design and maintenance of castles and other royal buildings. Two, Geoffrey and Ailnoth, had the office of keeper of Westminster Palace and a stipend of 7d per day. Richard, a friar-engineer much employed in the North, was paid 20s in 1171 in connection with building the keep at Bowes. He held

Engines

lands at Wolviston, possessed his own seal
and a relic of St Cuthbert. Henry II
employed Maurice who probably designed
the great keeps of Dover and Newcastle.
During the course of his employment at
Dover his salary was raised from 8d to 1s a
day and in 1181 he was given an allowance of
£3.0.2 for his robes. Ralph of Grosmont was
probably the engineer involved (1177-88)
with castles at Hereford, Grosmont,
Skenfrith and White Castle.

Engineers were rewarded either by
gifts of land or by regular salary with
'perks' such as robes or a horse, or 'tips'
for his pains which varied from two marks
to £2. Their duties varied from building
supervision to the making of
siege-engines. The king or feudal lord
might make known his requirements in
general and require the engineer to carry
them out in terms of space, building,
defences, and site, and to plan the overall
construction and supply. This
professional, therefore, combined in
himself military engineering, quantity
surveyor, logistics expert and many other
skills besides.

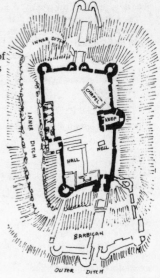

Helmsley with massive Earthworks

ENGINES

Large mechanical constructions, including
cranes, and the normal word for mediaeval
artillery. We think readily of 'siege-engines'
but it must be remembered that castles
themselves were often equipped with 'heavy
artillery'. At Harlech, for example, platforms
were provided for engines in advance of the
outer ward on high ground protected by
flanking walls and natural defences. These
were intended to attack ships. Criccieth had an
'engine-tower' at its N.E. corner.

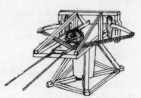

Engines: Ballista

Edward I had an official, Master Bertram,
styled 'machinator', whose main concern
seems to have been the construction of engines
at Caernarvon and London Tower.

The names for war engines include ballista,
catapult, mangon, mangonel, onager, petrary,
sling, springar, torment, trebuchet. Some of
these seem to be synonyms, while others are
used inconsistently due to the variety in
translation. None have survived and our

Engines: Trebuchet

56

knowledge of the details of their construction or performance is defective.

Projectile (q.v.) engines were used for bombardment – to 'soften up' defenders and their mere appearance could cause surrender. Otherwise they were used to destroy defence positions (especially hoardings) or to breach walls.

The belfry Edward I used for assaulting Bothwell was built in Glasgow and payments are recorded for the carpenters, plumbers etc. as well as for materials including lead, wheels, cables, wax. The parts were carried to the siege in 30 wagons, taking two days to cover the nine miles and involving a bridge over the Clyde and a log road from the bridge to the castle.

There were other engines in castles besides war machines. In construction, primitive pile-drivers were used and there were simple pulley-cranes operated by hand or treadmill. (There are still mediaeval crane-wheels in the cathedral towers of Canterbury, Peterborough, Salisbury). There were also winches and windlasses for operating drawbridges and portcullises and for lowering the buckets down the well. Sometimes these latter were operated by animal power.

ENTERTAINMENT   see also Zoo.

Castles were the scene of a good deal of entertainment which was not confined to its lord or garrison. Players and mimes often found in the liberty (q.v.) of a castle an opportunity for their art which might have been denied in the neighbouring township. The hall of a castle was frequently entertained by musicians and there was a gallery over the screens for minstrels with their 'chansons de geste' (epics) and 'chansons d'amour'. There were also jesters, acrobats and contortionists or tumblers. There are frequent representations of entertainers juggling weapons such as three daggers or balancing a sword, spear etc. on their forehead and chin (usually by their points). There are also illustrations of acrobats balancing on the (blunted?) points of swords.

Entertainment

Entertainment

Some of the entertainment we might regard as childish e.g. blind man's buff, storytelling etc. but much was concerned with the acquisition of knightly skills which could vary from conduct of arms to order of precedence and the recitation of heroic deeds. In the neighbourhood were opportunities for hunting and hawking (q.v.). The bailey might hold mews (q.v.), bear- or cock-pits (Warwick, Richmond), bowling green, butts (q.v.), lists or tiltyard (q.v.) and the immediate vicinity might offer a park or 'plaisaunce' (Kenilworth), formal gardens and ponds.

ENTRANCE   see also Gatehouse.

Originally, seems to have been a simple gate in the palisade or an archway with doors in a stone wall (e.g. Eynsford, Richmond. The latter subsequently had a keep built over the original entrance to form an awesome gatehouse). Later, the opening was protected by a small gatehouse tower with its entrance through the lower storey (e.g. Durham).

The entrance to the Great Tower or Keep was usually on the first floor and originally by a movable ladder or a 'broken' stair. When this was replaced by a permanent stone staircase it had an added forebuilding (q.v.) Exceptionally, entrance was gained on the second floor e.g. Dover, Newcastle, Norwich, and even more unusually there was an entrance to the basement at ground level e.g. Bamburgh, Colchester.

EPISCOPAL CASTLES   see also Distribution.

Because mediaeval bishops were also feudal lords and landowners they had the function and duties of that state. This included the lordship of castles. In some particular cases he had military responsibilities of a very high order e.g. the Prince Bishop of Durham was Lord of the County Palatine with responsibility for defending it against the Scots, as well as bishop of an extensive see. Hence his seal shows him in pontificals on one side and armed 'cap-a-pie' on the other.

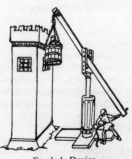

Episcopal Seal of Prince-Bishop

ESCALADE

Assault on walls or palisade by scaling ladders (q.v.) Escalade was a much employed method of forcible entry throughout the castle period, though it was rendered more difficult and hazardous by the introduction of high curtain walls. Nevertheless, Norham was so taken in 1327 and there is an account of another castle being defended by heavy beams hung from the battlements and when the enemy attempted a night escalade the ropes were cut and the logs fell, smashing the ladders or sweeping the assailants to the ground. Some of the problems of high curtains were met by the use of the great movable tower or belfry (q.v.) and there were probably other methods of gaining the ramparts by the use of cranes or lifts (see illustration) but they look extremely hazardous if not downright

Escalade Device

impractical. Still hazardous but practical was the use of a rope and grapnel.

ESCHEAT

To forfeit an estate.

ESSEX

Colchester once possessed the largest keep in Europe and Essex also has perhaps the greatest tower-keep in England (Hedingham). There are remains of greater or less interest at Chipping Ongar, Great Canfield, Great Easton, Rayleigh and Stansted Mountfitchet. Further examples include Hadleigh, Pleshey, Saffron Walden and Stebbing.

Colchester

FALCON

Small C16 cannon of 2½ ins bore, throwing ball of 1½ lbs weight.

Most loops at Noltland would accommodate these pieces.

Early Cannon

FALCONER

Highly skilled (and very patient) expert responsible for the care and training of hawks for sport of falconry (see T. H. White: *The Goshawk*, 1951). The nervous and volatile birds were calmed by falconers blowing water from their mouths in a gentle shower.

FEUDALISM see also Feudalism, Bastard; Livery and Maintenance.

A system whereby the holding of a fief (q.v.) was associated with vassalage, a condition only possible within a military social class, since both lord and vassal were

Falconers

alike gentlemen-warriors with reciprocal obligations, duties and rights. The latter included military support, local government (q.v.), taxation and maintenance of order.

The standard form of feudal tenure required homage (q.v.), fealty, knight-service (q.v.), 'aids', hospitality, suit to court and feudal 'incidents' (relief, wardship, marriage, escheat, forfeiture). Other forms included castle-guard (q.v.), serjeanty (q.v.) and prayer (limited to some rare church endowments).

Ecclesiastics originally held their fiefs under the same conditions as lay tenants but modifications exempted their investiture with 'spiritualities', added a limiting clause in their oath of fealty (saving the rights of the clerical order) and excused their personal appearance in arms (see Flail).

All land belonged to the king who bestowed parcels of it in separated lots as fiefs to various feudatories on condition that they supplied soldiers when required. This was called military tenure and provided for a specified number of fully armed soldiers for 40 days in a year ('a knight's fee'). The number was based on the income from the land: in C12 it was one fully armed and accoutred soldier (knight) for every £20 per annum income.

Black Prince pledges Fealty
(for Aquitaine)

On the death of a tenant, theoretically lands reverted to the lord (king) but in practice they were usually returned to the heir on payment of 'a relief' (a form of Death Duty). When the heir was a minor, the king had possession of the land during the minority; if the heir was a girl, the king could dispose of her in marriage provided the chosen husband was of appropriate social status. If a tenant-in-chief died without heir, the lands reverted to the Crown (escheated). A vassal's lands became forfeit for serious crime, especially treason, or for failure in feudal obligations.

Tenants-in-chief parcelled out portions of their land to sub-tenants (tenants in mesne) on similar terms of military obligation. These in turn might be 'sub-let' so that a manor might be held of a small castle which in turn was held of its owner's mesne-lord (sub-infeudation).

Military tenure was increasingly commuted for a money payment from the time of Henry II.

FEUDALISM, BASTARD

C14 and C15 development by which feudal dues, having been commuted from service or kind into cash, could be used to hire retainers (see Livery and Maintenance).

Great landowners could thus acquire very sizable retinues to support their quarrels, intimidate judges and juries, and attack the persons or possessions of their enemies. They could even seize the crown or fight each other for it. In Scotland the situation was a good deal worse, and prolonged for centuries more, than in England.

FIEF (Fee)   see also Escheat, Enfeofment.

A land-holding involving vassalage which was effected by homage (q.v.) A fief was inheritable providing that the heir was capable of vassalage i.e. an adult male. It was legally indivisible but could be sub-let (sub-infeudation). If vassal's heir was a girl or an under-age boy, the fee passed into wardship which terminated either when the boy came of age, was knighted and did homage, or when the girl married (with her lord's permission or instruction) a man capable of homage. Each fief was assessed at a specific number of knights and its holder, when required, took the field with this number of companions for a maximum of 40 days per annum. Suppose the king gave Sir A. de B. 25 manors as a fief for the service of ten knights, then Sir A. could keep all 25 'in demesne' or sub-infeudate for part of the service. In the former case he would receive the produce of the manors directly and, when called, present himself with nine knights (hired or from his household). Alternatively, he could e.g. keep 12 manors in demesne, grant a fief of eight manors to a relative, Sir C. de B., for four knights service and gain the homage of five landless adventurers (probably younger sons) for a manor apiece.

FIFE

Easily accesible castles include Aberdour, Ravenscraig, Rosyth, St Andrews, Scotstarvit. Other castles worth mentioning are Rossend (Burntisland) and Tulliallan. There was a royal hunting lodge at Falkland and there are scant remains at Crail.

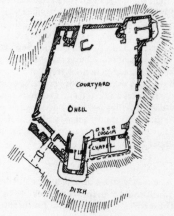

St Andrew's, Fife

FIELD

The area from which attack comes; the enemy's side of a fortification.

FIFTEENTH CENTURY

Castle building seems marked by greater attention to domestic comfort, even at some expense of defensive quality (e.g. the hall at Tutbury and the entire palace-castle at Pontefract.) The process had begun earlier but increasingly great houses are developing in which fortifications are a measure of precaution against unruly mobs rather than defences against professional armies. The everyday needs of occupants are the first consideration though the building may include a strong tower e.g. Haddon, Mortham, Wingfield, Yanwath. Brick is increasingly used especially in Lincolnshire (Kyme, Hussey, Tower-on-Moor between Tattersall and Horncastle. None of these can compare with Tattersall in beauty, size, or balance of defensive and domestic arrangements).

Tower House, Scotstarvit, Fife

FIGHTING PLATFORMS

The main defensive positions, in earlier castles at least, were a. the wall-walk or b. the keep which was provided with a roof-walk, triforium windows and covered fighting galleries (e.g. Newcastle 1171).

Fighting Platform

FINIAL

A slender pinnacle crowning gable, canopy or larger pinnacle. In military architecture it is applied to the vertical stone spikes which were fixed in the coping on merlons in Edwardian (and perhaps other) castles. Caernarvon seems to have had three set in each merlon. Their purpose is obscure but it may have been to hinder the lodgement of grapples which would have been impossible, or very temporary, at the shutter-protected and manned crenels. Other uses may have been to hinder the fixing of the hooks on the top of scaling ladders. They might also have helped to locate the upper beams of hoardings.

Finials

FIRE

A potent weapon of both attack and defence which could take form of Greek fire (q.v.), fire-arrows tipped with tow, fire-brands, burning pitch, boiling fat, fire wagons holding wood or hay made more combustible with animal fat. (An early account speaks of fire 'fed with bacon and grease'.) There seem to have been hand-thrown 'incendiary bombs' and there was incendiary ammunition for the great siege engines.

Much of the castle was susceptible to fire attack: palisades, doors, gates, brattices, hoarding, roofs and floors. So was much of the besiegers' material: towers, mantlets, pentises and engines.

The defences against fire were water, raw hides, metal plates or tiles, the replacement of wood by stone (especially by vaulting floor) or replacing inflammable materials generally.

Castle put to Torch

Little could be done to protect human flesh against fire weapon. 'With fire and sword' represents the essence of mediaeval assault as it also depicts the immemorial practice of war.

FIRE-ARMS

The earliest picture of a cannon appears in 1326 while the first mention of a hand-gun seems to be in 1338. Their development was slow and the long-bow would remain the predominant arm of individual soldiers into C16. The effect of fire-arms on castles can be indicated as follows:

(a) When developed it produced a powerful weapon requiring less man-power.
(b) It discharged the missile with greater force.
(c) Its more horizontal trajectory produced a direct impact on curtain walls together with increased accuracy.
(d) The very height of curtains and towers increased the size of the target and thus made them more vulnerable (c.f. the walls of Berwick with e.g. the walls of York).

Hand-Gunman

FIREPLACES

At first they were open hearths (q.v.) in the centre of the room and when they began to be placed against the external walls (towards the end of C11) they usually consisted of an added arched opening with semi-circular heads and backs. The flues rose within the thickness of the wall for a short distance and then passed to the outside, terminating in one or two loop-holes, often protected by a nearby buttress (e.g. Canterbury [1090], Colchester, London). The fire-back was usually built of selected stones, generally laid in a herring-bone pattern to resist the effects of heat.

This important amenity was decorated from early C12, jambs turned into small shafts and arches decorated with chevron mouldings (e.g. Hedingham c. 1130, Rochester 1126-39). The decoration would also include vivid painting and, later, heraldic motifs of which all trace has been lost. At this time the fireplace is beginning to project slightly from the wall but there is no real hood. There were great circular fireplaces in the kitchens (e.g. Canterbury, Portchester, Rising). In the later keep-fireplaces at Newcastle (c. 1175) the flues are still carried through the wall though the semi-circular back has been replaced by a straight back with splayed sides.

The great development took place at Conisbrough, in this as in other matters the

Fireplace

63

expression of advanced thinking. For the first time flues are carried to the battlements and a tall hood is built over a projecting fireplace whose head is a flat lintel built of voussoirs with joggled joints. Henceforth the fireplace normally had a straight back and boldly projecting hood supported either on corbels or small pillars with carved base and capital (very good example at Edlingham).

Fireplaces appeared in chambers when halls had only a brazier or central hearth (e.g. Chepstow). For examples of chimneys see Framlingham, Christchurch. There is a good kitchen fireplace and chimney at Rising. Rochester and Dover were well provided with fireplaces in the keep, though Portchester seems to have had none. Aydon (c. 1280) has three. Newcastle had fireplaces in the large mural chambers but the main apartments were probably warmed by braziers.

A hall fireplace at Conway (1285-6) cost 16s.

FLAIL

A weapon used extensively on the continent and not unknown in England. It consisted of a hand-shaft to which were attached many whips terminating in iron points. A popular form had a spiked iron ball on the end of a chain. This was somewhat ironically called a 'holy water sprinkler' because of its vague resemblance to an aspergil. It was said to be popular with the Lords Spiritual when they fought cynically in their baronial capacity, since it wounded by crushing and unlike the lance or sword did not 'spill blood' which by Canon Law clerics were forbidden to do.

Flail[1]

FLANKING

A curtain is said to be flanked when its line is broken at intervals by projections whose defenders can cover the face of the intervening wall. Projecting towers serve this purpose and improve observation of assaults on the curtain by mine, ram or scaling-ladder. The development of this defence was slow, beginning in the later C12 and becoming more frequent in the earlier C13.

FLINTSHIRE

Though only a small county, it is rich in important castles. There are motte-and-baileys at Mold, remains of a C13 at Caergwrle (Hope) and ruins of Edwardian castles at Flint, Hawarden and Rhuddlan and of a strong native fortress at Ewloe.

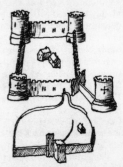

FLOORS

Ground floors might consist of beaten earth, flag-stones laid in the earth, or an integrated stone floor supported on the vaults of a basement. Upper floors usually consisted of heavy wooden planks supported by massive oaken joists whose ends were either located in

Flint

the wall during building or rested on corbels. Another way of supporting joists was to inset the wall at each floor level and rest them on the resultant ledge (e.g. Conisbrough). When the span was too wide even for the mighty baulks available in the Middle Ages, a central supporting pillar or arch was built up from the storey below. The floor surface was usually covered with rushes and sweet herbs, renewed monthly.

FLOOR ARRANGEMENT (Keeps).

Loftier keeps usually have a basement with three upper floors (e.g. Hedingham, Portchester, Rochester, Scarborough). The number of floors was not necessarily proportional to the height of the building e.g. Corfe (80 ft) and Guildford (63 ft) both have three floors.

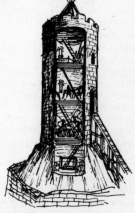

Floor Arrangement

At Dover (83 ft) and Newcastle (75 ft), the second floor was surrounded by a mural gallery, high above floor level, so that second and third floors were combined into one lofty room. Similarly at Rochester (113 ft) and Hedingham (100 ft) there are mural galleries above the second floor whose height corresponds to two external storeys. Examples of other arrangements: Norham (90 ft), four upper floors; Kenilworth (80 ft), lofty basement and upper floor; Bowes, two upper floors; Middleham and Rising, one upper floor but, as a result of sub-division, there were two floors in some parts.

FLYING PARAPETS

Little crenellated bridges connecting gatehouse towers, giving increased defence over entrance. Forerunner of machicolation (q.v.) Examples at Chepstow, Pembroke, Warwick.

FOOD   see also Provisions.

The staple diet of garrisons seems to have been bacon and herrings, cheese and beans, with bread and beer or wine.

Flying Parapet, Pembroke

The normal rations at Dover in the reign of King John were ½ lb of bread, ½ gallon of biscuit, five pints of wine. In addition, the soldier received, on 22 of his 40 days services, five herrings or a ration of cheese and oatmeal. On the other days, he was given half a mess of meat (a mess of pork was $1/24$ part of a hog). It is not usually appreciated that the amount of food required to maintain a garrison for a long siege would be extremely substantial and produce considerable problems of storage.

FOOTING

The lowest section of a wall including the foundation. Usually wider than the rest and sometimes with batter (q.v.).

FOREBUILDING

An extension to the keep, primarily to protect the great external stair but which also served to provide additional accommodation, sometimes including a prison and/or chapel. The forebuilding was a substantial annexe and was planned in various ways e.g. Scarborough (simplest form), Kenilworth (slight development), Rochester (more complicated), Dover and Newcastle (very elaborate). The forebuilding at Rising is the best preserved and there are other good examples at Berkeley, Norwich and Portchester.

Forebuilding, Newcastle

FOREST

Not necessarily woodland, rather hunting land or game preserve but to be distinguished from common or ordinary woodland. More than a recreation ground: a source of food (nuts, berries, mushrooms etc. as well as game), and of the principle building material and fuel. Forest was thus a natural resource of great value. Kings were always trying to increase it and barons to acquire it. Forest had its own law, its own courts and its own officials as well as a special circuit of justice – the forest ayre (every seven years). Forest inspectors ('regarders') circulated every three years. Other officials included justices, wardens, foresters (gamekeepers), agisters (rent and due collectors), woodwards.

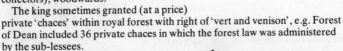

The king sometimes granted (at a price) private 'chaces' within royal forest with right of 'vert and venison', e.g. Forest of Dean included 36 private chaces in which the forest law was administered by the sub-lessees.

FORTIFIED CHURCHES ETC.

Ecclesiastical buildings were intrinsically comparatively strong and usually possessed a battlemented tower. Durham cathedral was described as 'half house of God, half castle gainst the Scot' and Tynemouth priory was as much fortress

Fortified Church, Edlingham

as monastery. Abbeys often had strong towers (e.g. Blanchland, Farne) and a crenellated gatehouse (as did university colleges). At Bridlington, Tewkesbury, Whalley (c. 1348) gatehouses are clearly for defence and not mere enclosure and that at Alnwick (C14) is a miniature keep with loops and machicolation. There are strong gatehouses at Battle, Bury St Edmunds, Tutley, Ely, Suffolk, St Albans. Ewenny priory, Glamorgan, is one of the most completely fortified religious houses and Holne, Northd., has remains of a strong defence including crenellated walls. Carlisle and Lanercost incorporate pele-towers. Paradoxically the gatehouse at Thornton (c. 1389) had a portcullis yet presents an oriel window and fragile niches to the field.

Blanchland Abbey Gatehouse

After the Danes had burned Peterborough in 1070, William built a castle on the abbey lands, supported by Tural, the abbot, who built a castle besides his abbey.

Cathedral closes were defended e.g. Lichfield, Norwich, Lincoln (Exchequer Gate and Pottergate) and the enceinte can be traced at Norwich and Wells (which also retains fine gatehouse of bishop's moated palace). Licence to crenellate was granted to the cathedrals at Lichfield (1299), Lincoln (1285), London (1285), Wells (1286), York (1285), and to religious houses at Norwich (1276), Peterborough (1309), Tynemouth (1295). Smaller churches had their defences: e.g. in Kent – Dartford, St. Radegund's, West Malling. With the exception of Wells, these ecclesiastical fortifications have not been entered in the Gazetteer.

Alnwick Abbey Gate

FORTIFIED TOWNS   see also Bastide, Town Walls.

There are early indications of settlement-enclosures in proximity to a castle – a kind of outer bailey. This association of castle and dependent township reaches an apogee in Conway and Caernarvon but there are other

Fortified Gatehouse, Bury St Edmunds

examples e.g. Caerphilly and Denbigh which also show the combination of baronial and national interest under Edward I (c.f. Chirk, Ruthin). A dependent township seems to have been planned at Dunstanburgh by Thomas, Earl of Lancaster in C14.

The fortification of free towns is generally a C14 development showing the shift of power from land to commerce. It is apparently paralleled by a contrasting decrease in the fortification of private residences.

FOUNDATION

The masonry or other structure below soil level to prevent settlement of a super-imposed heavy building when bedrock is too far beneath the surface of the ground.

Siege of Fortified Town

FOURTEENTH CENTURY CASTLES

Though the C14 saw the flowering of the concentric castle, this was neither common nor characteristic. The more usual C14 castle consists of a single bailey without a keep (Richmond, earliest forms of Carew, Ludlow, Manorbier) – castle of enceinte.

There were new castles with gatehouse keeps at Dunstanburgh and Llanstephan while Warkworth (acquired by the Percys in 1309) was made into a great tower-house (c.f. Raby). Middleham was much altered in the C14 and Knaresborough keep is entirely of this period. The great towers (Guy's and Caesar's) at Warwick are late C14 and French rather than English in inspiration. Other notable buildings of this period were: Bodiam (1385), Maxstoke (1346), Nunney (1373), Shirburn (1377), Stafford (1348). It also saw the building of the gatehouse at Lancaster, the great hall at Ludlow and the remodelling of domestic buildings at Portchester.

C14 Tower (Caesar's at Warwick)

Tower House Keep, Warkworth

FUNCTION

Besides being a defensible residence, a castle could play a limited aggressive role (hence large proportion of mounted soldiers in garrison). Even a small force could command countryside, protect or enforce local loyalty, devastate nearby hostile lands, attack marauders etc. e.g. Leicester garrison plundered Northampton (1174), Lincoln was assembly point for harrying forces (1215), sorties from Newark and Nottingham harried neighbourhoods (1216) and in the same reign relief forces for Lincoln assembled at Newark.

They provided administrative centre, safe storage (wool and money at Pickering) and Pickering's functions also included housing royal stud of 50 horses, court-house, residence for royal hunting parties, prison for offenders.

FUNDIBALUM

War engine for hurling heavy missiles – see Mangon, Trebuchet.

FURNISHINGS

A C13 hall would have on its dais a high table, perhaps elaborately carved. This was called a 'table dormant' (i.e. permanent as against the trestle tables which served the rest of the hall). Facing down the hall would be high-backed narrow chairs, perhaps with heraldic decoration, for the lord, his family and distinguished guests. Opposite them would be the minstrel gallery erected over the highly decorated screens. The body of the hall would be furnished with massive tables on trestles so that it could be cleared on suitable occasions. Three tables with their accompanying benches and occasional stools ran parallel to the length of the hall. All this furniture was usually oak.

The halls were painted and/or hung with tapestries and further embellished with trophies of chase or war. Perhaps there were stands of armour. The open roof had timbers or corbels carved or painted. The stone floor was covered with rushes or straw and scented with herbs. The great fireplaces were also painted, often with heraldic motifs. The dishes on the lord's table, at least, would be elaborate and costly, consisting not only of well-designed pottery but of pewter and silver (perhaps gilt). The bedrooms of honour were rich and elaborate with private oratories, massive carved bedsteads furnished with feather beds, quilts and silken counterpanes. (Edward II's bed at Caerphilly, 1326, was furnished with a canopy and curtains of red silk, a counterpane of red silk lined with green, two linen sheets, two down-filled pillows and overall a fur-lined covering of panelled silk.) Body-servants or pages might have a truckle bed and probably slept wrapped in their cloaks, while lesser folk would have to be content with bunks, straw

Furnishings: State Bed

State Bed Curtained

pallets or even the straw-covered floor of the hall itself.

There was not a great deal of other moveable furniture except perhaps for chests. cupboards and wardrobes (aumbries and gardrobes) were normally recesses with wooden doors in the thickness of the wall. Main rooms often had a slop-basin, sink or laver, also let into the wall.

The most sumptuously furnished part of a castle was usually the chapel which, like all other mediaeval places of worship, was richly ornamented and splendidly equipped. The kitchen had some built-in facilities, metal cooking- or boiling-vessels and pots.

There is a tradition that the great oaken tables in the hall at Snape had scooped-out depressions instead of trenchers with a chained knife and fork on either side. (The mention of a fork indicates that a mediaeval usage was persisting long after the Middle Ages.)

Royal Feast in Hall

GALLERIES

There are many galleries and passages in the thickness of tower walls. Newcastle has a number; one is a cul-de-sac but that is possibly an accident due to change in plan during building.

Open galleries run round the upper level of unusually high halls e.g. in the keeps of Dover, Hedingham, Norwich, Rochester and Newcastle (the latter may be due to a reduction in the planned number of floors). The Rochester gallery surrounds the entire tower and communicates with the vices in the S.W. and N.E. angles. It opens on the tower interior in 14 places, each corresponding to a loop on the outside wall. The gallery at Hedingham is also complete.

GARDEROBE

Properly, not a latrine or privy but a small room or large cupboard, usually adjoining the chamber or solar and providing safe-keeping for valuable clothes and other possessions of price: cloth, jewels, spices, plate and money.

Galleries in Keep

GARRISON

Defenders usually excluded lord (see Command) but might include lady (see Women). The castellan was usually commander

70

with knights as officers. 'Other ranks' included
men-at-arms (both horsed and on foot),
crossbow-men, archers, with support from
smiths, farriers, watchmen, porters,
carpenter-engineers (q.v.). More or less
non-combatants included chaplain (q.v.) and
miscellaneous servants (q.v.).

The number of fighting men in a garrison
depended on conditions, status of castle, means
of castellan and loyalty of those who owed
service. Early in the Middle Ages castles were
garrisoned by the feudal obligation of 'castle
guard' (q.v.) but there were many disadvantages
to this system and, by the second half of C12,
this duty had, in most cases, been commuted for
a money rent so that at this time the most
common method of garrisoning castles was
through mercenaries. Garrison numbers in
C12-13, when the importance of castles was at
its height, were quite small and disproportionate
to their military significance and power.
Rochester held out against John in 1215 with
some 100 knights and 'many men-at-arms',
in the same war Odiham held out for a fortnight

Man-at-Arms, (Garrison)

with only three knights and ten men-at-arms. (In C11 Dover was garrisoned
by ten knights with retinues.) At Burton in Lonsdale (1130) the garrison was a
knight, ten sergeants, a watchman and a porter at a total of £21 per annum.
Other known garrisons include: Orford (1174) 20 knights, Wark (1174) ten
knights and 40 men-at-arms, Norwich and Canterbury (1193) each had a total
garrison of 75 including knights and mounted and dismounted men-at-arms,
Framlingham (1216) 26 knights, 20 men-at-arms, seven crossbow-men,
chaplain and three others.

A little later Orford had a garrison of 20 men while the neighbouring
Walton had a peacetime strength of four knights and two servants. Larger
garrisons seemed to have been responsible for
the extension of the bailey, often by adding an
outer bailey on the opposite side of the motte
to produce 'hourglass' plan e.g. Arundel,
Windsor. About 1280 Chepstow had, besides
a constable, chaplain and his clerk, a garrison
of a porter, three watchmen, ten men-at-arms,
ten archers, and another 15 men-at-arms
based on the castle.

In the late C13 the garrisons of the great
royal castles in volatile Welsh Marches were as
follows: Caernarvon – constable, two sergeant
horsemen (who were responsible in his
absence), ten sergeant crossbow-men,

Knight, Man-at-Arms

71

a smith, a carpenter, artificer, 25 men-at-arms; Conway – constable, 15 crossbow-men, chaplain, smith, carpenter, mason, artificer and ten others (including janitor, watchmen etc.); Rhuddlan – included 12 crossbow-men and 13 archers serving for 24 days; Harlech – governor and 24 men; Criccieth – governor, chaplain, surgeon, carpenter, mason and 36 soldiers; Beaumaris – ten men-at-arms, 20 crossbow-men and 100 foot-soldiers.

At the beginning of C15 we find the following figures: Caernarvon – 20 men-at-arms and 80 bowmen; Conway – 15 men-at-arms and 60 bowmen; Harlech – ten men-at-arms and 30 bowmen; Beaumaris – 15 men-at-arms and 140 bowmen.

At the beginning of C16 the great border castle of Wark accommodated a constable and 40 men-at-arms in the keep, and the inner bailey had a two-storey barracks for 140 men and their horses.

GATE

The main entrance gate to a castle usually had two leaves, with a wicket in one, closed by locks and bars which slid into slots (bar-holes). The gates were made of oak planks with thick cross-braces behind external planking to prevent axes splitting timber. These defences were re-inforced by external metalwork, including studs, to blunt assailing axes and swords. Rare survivals e.g. Chepstow.

Gate

GATEHOUSE

As the entrance was the weakest part of the castle, its strengthening was a first priority and probably the first part to be rebuilt in stone (e.g. Lewes, Tickhill). Even when the perimeter of palisades was never replaced by a stone curtain the entrance was covered by a gatehouse (e.g. Chipping Ongar). Examples of early gatehouses: Alnwick, Arundel, Egremont, Rising (almost lost in later earth rampart), Sherborne.

Warkworth represents the latest military thinking of C12 and Renn describes it as the first true twin-towered gatehouse since Roman times. It had three storeys: a vaulted entrance hall, a first floor for the constable's lodging and a second floor housing the machinery for operating the porcullis (c.f. Pevensey).

Gatehouse, Alnwick

The word gatehouse extends to a complex system of fortification which can include bridges, gates, barriers and the defensive walls and towers which cover the entrance.

The conversion of the entrance to stone was primarily a fire precaution. But the gate had to be protected against other kinds of assault, usually by the proximity of a high tower, motte or keep. The closest proximity was produced by an enormous gate-tower (e.g. Exeter, Ludlow, Newark, Richmond – where the keep is actually over the gate). Gate-towers developed in the later C12 and seem to have housed the constable (in spite of the incursion of machinery in this accommodation) and imply a 'forward-looking policy' where defence was at the front and not at the rear. The first gatehouses were small square towers with their entrance through the middle of the bottom storey. In C13 with its fashion of projecting wall-towers, a pair of wall-towers was built to flank and protect the gate. The next development was to connect these two towers into one broader tower which could house guards and porters on the ground floor and provide a large useful chamber on the first floor. This model persisted as long as castles (e.g. C14 example at Caldicot) but a doubled wall-tower provided an alternative development (e.g. Helmsley). Sometimes these gate-towers bestrode the wall and provided an extended tunnel through which intruders would have to pass and run the gauntlet.

The position of the gatehouse in relation to the curtain varies: inner face flush with curtain (Exeter, Portchester, Richmond); partly outside but mostly inside (Ludlow, Newark, Tickhill); wholly internal (Lewes).

Some characteristic dimensions: Portchester 23 ft long by 28 ft deep, Lewes 30 ft by 30 ft, Tickhill 36 ft by 36 ft, Ludlow 34 ft by 31 ft; Newark occupied the largest area and probably served as a keep. The keep-gatehouse is characteristic of C13 e.g. Barnwell, Chepstow, Kidwelly, Leybourne. Perhaps Denbigh was the most elaborate. Some Edwardian castles have two gatehouses e.g. Beaumaris, Rhuddlan.

Gatehouses maintain their importance even in the later castles which were not much more than fortified manor-houses e.g. Donnington, Rockingham, Saltwood. They even survived as a stately entrance when all trace of fortification had vanished.

Notable gatehouses: Constable's Tower, Dover, Dunstanburgh, Llanstephan, Newcastle (Black Gate), St. Briavel's, Tonbridge. Lancaster has been described as 'the greatest of English gatehouses' but the King's Gate at Caernarvon is surely the apogee.

The fully developed gatehouse seems to have had a fixed pattern: it was usually of three storeys arranged as follows:

Gatehouse (Exterior)

1. Ground floor – a hall of entry flanked by cylindrical or octagonal towers which contained guard-rooms and were pierced with loops to command approach and internal passage. Usually the gateway was placed behind an arched recess which formed a porch. The portcullis normally descended in front of the gate which opened inwards and was secured by one

or more draw-bars.

2. First floor – often residence of castellan and might contain machinery of portcullis or at least its hearse.
3. Second floor – contained guard house, weapon-stores and engines.

Developments of defence included mutiplication of portcullises and doors, murder-holes, machicolations and barbican.

From later C13 it was usual to carry parapet on arch in advance of front face of gatehouse from one flanking tower to other and to leave space between parapet and main wall open to command field immediately in front of portcullis. Finest architectural designs : Caernarvon, Denbigh. Pembroke treats *inner* side of gatehouse in similar way

Gatehouse Entry Chamber
(from within)

to provide further harassment to such enemy as managed to penetrate through entrance passages.

The one necessary upper chamber was that in which the machinery controlling the portcullis was operated. In the floor of this room was the groove, through which, by means of a pulley in the ceiling the iron frame was drawn up or down, hanging here when not in use to close entrance below. Holes for the beam to which this pulley was fixed are visible at e.g. Conway, Rhuddlan. Portcullis chambers exist at e.g. Berry Pomeroy, London Tower, Bootham Bar, York.

GAUNTLET

Armoured protection for the hand, originally made of mail and integral to the hauberk (q.v.). Later made of leather with attached steel plates. With the full development of plate armour in late C14 it became a

Gauntlet

complex arrangement of articulated steel plates covering the back of the hand and each separate finger. Sometimes the knuckles were furnished with 'gadlings' (spikes or steel knobs) which made the gauntlet a useful offensive weapon. Because of its association with the hand, the gauntlet acquired a number of symbolic uses : to throw down the gauntlet was a challenge to single combat or trial by battle ; to take it up was to accept the challenge ; a thrown gauntlet (gage) could be a pledge to return to do battle in support of assertion or claim.

GLAMORGANSHIRE

Over 30 castles in this county are mentioned but most of them can be dismissed as having either extremely sparse remains or as being castles only in name. Yet there remains the stupendous Caerphilly, the interesting Coity, a good motte-and-bailey at Kenfig, a mystery at Fonmon,

Gatehouse, Caerphilly

a reconstruction at St Donat's, a wall at St Fagans and rather more at Cardiff, Neath, Newcastle Bridgend, Penard, Penrice, Ogmore and Oystermouth.

GLASS WINDOWS

Appeared in cathedrals early in Norman period. By C13 began to replace parchment, horn or wooden shutters in rich men's castles. Henry III introduced glass into most of his halls and chambers (and even into royal privies at Clipstone). Glass was so valuable that it was removed and replaced by wooden shutters in absence of owner.

A rare and generally late amenity. Normally the first rooms to be glazed would be those of the chapel. The royal chambers at Caernarvon had nine windows, imported from Chester, inserted in 1284 (probably just in time for the birth of Edward II). More glass windows, probably in the Eagle Tower, were inserted in 1285. Nevertheless C12 window-glass has been excavated in Oxfordshire in the castles of Ascot d'Oilly and Deddington. When glass windows became general it seems that usually only the upper half was glazed and the lower half was closed by shutters.

GLOUCESTERSHIRE

The castle in the county town has disappeared entirely but there are interesting remains at Berkeley, Beverston, St Briavels and Sudeley. Nothing is left of Kempsford but there are a few stones at Brimpsfield and rather more at Thornbury (rebuilt beginning C16).

GONFANON (Gonfalon)

Small ensign or standard carried beneath head of lance or spear.

Gonfanon

GORGE

(a) The neck of a bastion or other outwork, the entrance from the rear to the platform or body of a work.

(b) Often used of the rear of a tower. Open-gorged means that the tower was not closed towards the interior of the castle e.g. Corfe, Framlingham. When the gorge was left entirely open from the base it was provided with a moveable bridge at the level of the wall-walk. Open-backed towers are relatively weak and this design may be due to economies in labour, material and time in construction.

GRAFT

An earthwork, especially a ditch. The mediaeval word for a ditch or moat, hence graft – to work hard, dig.

GRAPPLING ENGINES

Used to sieze ram and thus neutralise it. A subsidiary purpose may have been to attack besiegers. Prince Henry of Scotland, observing too closely the siege of Ludlow in 1138, was caught by such a machine and was only prevented from being hauled helplessly up to the battlements by the prompt action of King Stephen who forced open the jaws of the machine by brute strength.

GREEK FIRE

Invented in Constantinople in C7. It had the characteristic of igniting spontaneously when wetted and was much used in sea battles. Its secret was so jealously guarded that its formula remains obscure to this day. What was sometimes called 'Greek fire' or more commonly 'wild fire' in the Middle Ages seems to have been a mixture of sulphur, pitch, charcoal and tallow to which saltpetre, turpentine and crude antimony may have been added. Its properties seem to have been adhesion and great difficulty in extinction. There is little ancient evidence of its use in Britain though this is sometimes assumed by modern authors. It may have been introduced by Richard I and seems to have been used at the siege of Dieppe (1195).

GRILLES   see also Yett.

It appears that the large windows of later great halls were protected by strong iron grilles cemented into the window-frames. These provided protection not only against the incursion of escaladers but also the ingress of large missiles. (Traces of their fixing survive at e.g. Kenilworth).

GROTESQUES AND GARGOYLES

These decorations, typical of churches, also existed in castles but there are few survivals due to the demolition of roofs and upper stages of walls and towers. But rare examples are worth looking for e.g. in situ, e.g. Raglan, Middleham (on ground).

Grille, protecting Window

GUARDROOMS

Usually provided by gate or within gatehouse, often on both sides of entrance. There was often also a guardroom at the entrance of the keep. Their manning was the responsibility of the porter or janitor (gate-keeper). Sometimes there was a prison associated with them (often underneath).

GUISARME

Combination of scythe and bill, fixed to end of long pole and used by infantry to unhorse horsemen and then despatch riders.

Guisarme

GUNS

The first use of cannon in England seems to
have been during Henry II's siege of Berwick
(1405). The Scottish kings also had a notable
siege-train of guns (including 'Mons Meg')
which were deployed against castles in the
North of England in C15. They were of
various sizes ranging from the large-bore
bombards to little pivot guns. The latter were
about four feet long and five to six ins wide,
mounted on an iron rod which could be driven
into ground and ending in a swivel which
allowed elevation to be varied.

The most common guns towards the end of
the castle period were probably the
serpentines which fired a four lb ball with an
effective range of about 1,000 yards.

Hand-Gun Man (c. 1470)

GUN-PORTS

The artillery or hand-gun equivalent of the
older arrow-loops. Some gun-ports were
simply modifications of arrow-loops (e.g.
Bodiam, Canterbury Westgate). The earliest
'custom-built' gun-ports appear at the bases of
the walls of Kirby Muxloe where they are set
low because of the technical problems of
depressing a gun-barrel. Here the sighting slot
is above, and separate from, the gun-port. At
Herstmonceux the sighting port has been
developed to provide a supplementary loop for
the (still more effective?) crossbow. Bow and
Arrow (Rufus) Tower overlooking Church
Ope Cove on Portland is equipped with late
mediaeval gun-ports. They also occur in the
late fortification at Cooling, Saltwood and
West Gate, Winchester.

Hand Gunner (C15)

GUNPOWDER

Much has been made of the appearance of
gunpowder as signalling the end of castles. Its
main function seems to have been 'slighting'
them *after* they had been captured by the
rebels in the C17 Civil War.

Drake's eyewitness account of the siege at
Pontefract at this time testifies to the
ineffectiveness of contemporary cannon and to
the danger which muskets presented to their
users. He also indicates that mediaeval engines

Cannonier (C15)

were still in effective use and the comparative casualties among the besieged and the besiegers also have their own message. The thorough 'slighting' which Pontefract received after its final capture is testimony to the danger which castles still presented.

HALF-TIMBER

Warwick Gatehouse (from inside)

Apart from primitive hovels, the commonest form of mediaeval structure. A timber frame (usually of oak beams pegged together), outlining window and door openings, was constructed and the gaps filled in with whatever was the most convenient and accessible material, usually wattle-and-daub (q.v.).

HALL

The principal and all-purpose room of a mediaval house. From mid C11 the hall tended to be raised over a storage basement, accessible only from the floor above. Where the hall was wide its floor was usually supported by a row of columns down the centre of the basement (Chepstow, Newark, Spofforth).

The first halls were usually of timber and probably placed against the walls of bailey to leave its centre free for stores and military activity. There were early stone halls at Richmond (probably the first in the country), Brough, Chepstow, Ludlow and Durham. Though the latter has been subdivided it still retains its entrance ('the most beautiful Norman doorway in all England').

Bishops' castles seem to have generally provided a hall for the accommodation of the bishop (as distinct from the castellan's quarters) e.g. Bishops Waltham, Sherborne, Taunton, Wolvesey.

Early stone halls did not have fireplaces but were warmed by a central hearth with a ventilation louver above. With the increasing

Hall, Hedingham

pressure of domestic requirements in C14 halls had improved lighting, more elaborate architecture and such refinements as panelling with 'wainscot' and the erection of more draught screens (e.g. Caerphilly, Conway, Kenilworth, Manorbier, Newark, Stokesay, Spofforth).

There are particularly fine survivals at Durham, Oakham, Westminster, Winchester.

All halls have common features: the entrance is usually in side wall next to the bailey and near one end with easy access to kitchens. When the kitchen and servery is incorporated this section is divided off, first by curtains and later by wooden screens containing one or more doors with a connecting passage. The passage thus enclosed later carried a gallery entered by a vice in a corner of the end wall. The side of the screens' passage opposite the hall had service hatches or doors from buttery, pantry and kitchens. At the opposite end from screens and minstrels' gallery was a dais for high table which was set across the hall at right-angles to the long table(s) in the body of the hall. Its floor was usually paved or of beaten earth, strewn with rushes and its roof was high-pitched, carried on timber trusses. Original central hearth was usually replaced later by a fireplace in one of the side walls. Windows (larger than usual) were pierced in the wall looking on to the bailey and, where security permitted, in both sides (Durham, Ludlow, Warwick). These windows were usually of two lights, divided by a mullion, with simple tracery at their head. The upper part was glazed quite early but the part below the transom was usually closed by shutters. Large windows were also protected by grilles. The central hearthstone was sometimes supported by a pier in the cellar beneath (Ludlow).

The hall was not only the chief living room in which the majority of retainers ate and also slept, but also the ceremonial and legal centre of the castle, hence tables in its body were on trestles so that the space could be cleared.

Hall, Stokesay

The later (C13 and after) tendency by which the lord began to withdraw more and more to his private chambers was regarded by thoughtful contemporary commentators as retrogressive, as an emphasis on class-distinction and a breakdown of communality (so thought the saintly bishop Grosseteste (C13) and the poet William Langland (C14)).

The first halls were in the keeps, later descending to the more convenient bailey, but the normal development seems to have been reversed at Chepstow where the early Norman hall was raised and crenellated in C13, whereas the keep at Okehampton has the hall and bower end to end, exactly as in contemporary unfortified houses. The magnificent open fireplaces and the impressive timber roofs of surviving halls may give point to the description of Kenilworth as 'the finest hall in the kingdom' in spite of its ruined state.

Hall, Oakham

Trial in Hall

HALL-KEEP

A keep whose length or breadth is greater than its height. Sometimes hall-keeps were later raised into towers. Fundamentally it is a fortified and elaborated version of a typical house, whereas the tower-keep is the normal arrangement erected on its side. The building of hall-keeps seems to have ceased when the replacement of the wooden defences of the enciente by stone made the erection of a hall in the bailey safe. In the case of tower-keeps there was a tendency (from mid C12) for the great hall to be built as a separate building and contemporary keeps either had no hall or merely a small private one for the lord. Examples of hall-keeps at Appleby, Bamburgh, Bowes (unusual plan), Canterbury, Carlisle, Colchester, Corte, Duffield (foundations), Lancaster, Middleham, Norham, Norwich, Pevensey, Portchester (later converted to tower), Rising, Sherborne (ruinous), Wolvesey.

HAMPSHIRE

Though Hampshire is not a castle county, it has examples of military architecture which the explorer can hardly afford to miss. First is Portchester, secondly the two episcopal castles of Bishops Waltham and Wolvesey, thirdly the walls of Southampton and Winchester. Beyond these, Carisbrooke represents all periods and Odiham has a unique octagonal keep. Our additional examples include, Basing, Christchurch, Merdon, and Warblington.

HAUBERK

A close-fitting long tunic of leather or woven material with long sleeves and a hood (coif) covered with metal rings (either attached separately or interlinked). It was divided at its lower half to protect the legs of its wearer when mounted. This is the almost universal mail shirt which was standard armour through most of the castle period until it was superceded, among the wealthy, in the C15 by plate armour which sometimes had a hauberk

Hauberk

and leather jerkin underneath to provide armour 'of triple proof'. It was always a costly item and valued as loot. (The margin of Bayeux Tapestry shows casualties being stripped of their hauberks.) It had at least one advantage over plate (which had to be bespoke) – it fitted almost anyone. Spares seem to have been kept in the armoury where many were captured after the siege of Bedford (1224).

Should not be confused with the habergeon which was a short light mail shirt sometimes worn as a protection for the throat and breast.

HAWKING   see also Falconer, Mews.

The aristocratic sport 'par excellence'. In its fully developed forms the birds themselves were associated with a social hierarchy so that among the upper classes themselves no-one could fly a bird above his station (e.g. eagles and pergrine falcons were reserved for emperors, kings and princes; goshawks for lower nobility and knights; merlins for ladies; sparrow-hawks for clergy; while kestrels were only fit for knaves).

Hawking

Hawks were divided into two groups: the long-winged, including the gerfalcon, peregrine, saker, lanner, merlin and the short-winged goshawk and sparrow-hawk (usually used for hunting among trees).

Only the female bird was properly called a falcon, the male was called a tiercel and regarded as inferior. The training of these proud, nervous and temperamental creatures required infinite patience and mental strength (see T. H. White: *The Goshawk*).

Hawking had its own language, mystique and mythology. The falconer was a valued member of a castle household and his charges received great care (there was almost a pharmacopoeia for their ailments). A favourite hawk was a treasured possession who might share a lord's bed-chamber and always accompany him on his wrist when he moved abroad.

HEARTH

A central hearth was the commonest form of fireplace (q.v.) until the major technical advance of the wall fireplace. It was placed before the high table and the dais but away from the traffic at the lower end of the hall. Few remain, though the pillar in the basement that supported its weight sometimes survives. The hearth was square, circular or octagonal in shape, bordered by stone or tile and sometimes with a central fire-back (reredos) of tile, brick or stone.

It was a source of danger when the hall was on a first floor made (perhaps together with the entire hall) of wood. A fire-cover ('couvre-feu' hence 'curfew') of tile or clay was placed over it at night when the company retired to minimise the hazards to a straw-covered floor. There was a church bell to signal the time of curfew and sometimes the castle supervised its obedience (e.g. Warwick).

HEDGEHOG (c.f. Herrison)

A 'chevaux de frise', or bristling barrier of pointed stakes or a thorn hedge planted at the far side of the ditch and providing the outermost defence. In the later Edwardian castles it was sometimes replaced by mantelet (q.v.).

HEIGHT

Examples of the height of keeps: Appleby 80 ft, Bamburgh 77 ft, Bolton 95 ft, Conisbrough 90 ft, Kenilworth 80 ft, Rising 50 ft, Scarborough 90 ft, Tattershall 112 ft.

For curtain walls, 30 ft seems to have been a standard height (e.g. Barnard) but there were inevitable variations (Framlingham 44 ft and Knaresborough 40 ft).

HELM (Helmet, Heaume) see Lady's Favour.

The Norman casque with fixed nasal persisted into C12. It was usually of cuir-boulli or of wood with added mail or scale armour and worn over hood of hauberk. It developed two ways:

(a) Into bascinet which became favoured battle-wear in C14.
(b) Into chapelle-de-fer, a cumbrous cylindrical, flat-topped helmet which was carried at saddle-bow until needed but became popular for tournaments and was further elaborated as 'tilting helm'.

Henry II (1154-1189)

Early in C15 the salade (sailey) was introduced and became common head-gear among all arms, worn in simpler version by archers and pikemen and in more developed forms by knights and men-at-arms. The later C15 saw the arrival of the armet with a separate gorget to join it to the cuirass.

Helms: 1. Norman Casque   2. Heaume (C14)   3. Salade and Bauier (late C15)

4. Bascinet (C1400)   5. Armet (early C16)

HENRY II (1154-1189)

On his accession after Anarchy, Henry found royal castles outnumbered by baronial in a ratio of nearly five to one. He set about correcting this imbalance by building or strengthening royal castles and confiscating or destroying baronial ones (see Demolition).

Malcolm of Scotland surrendered Appleby and Brough, the keep at Bowes was begun (c. 1171), Norham rebuilt (c. 1155) and there was work at Newcastle, Scarborough, Wark, and Warkworth with a new castle at Orford. Avranches tower was built at Dover, Windsor was strengthened and there was considerable expenditure at Bolsover, Nottingham and Peveril. Some of this work, costing over £21,000, seems designed to counterbalance local baronial power.

After rebellion of 1173/4. Henry 'took every castle of England into his (own) hands, and removing the castellans of earls and barons, put in his own custodians; he did not spare even his intimate counsellor, Richard de Lucy, Justiciar of England, but took from him his castle of Ongar'.

Henry II (Seal)

HENRY III (1216-1272)

Reign saw some advanced design (Dover, Kenilworth with 100 acres of water defences, London, York) but the main emphasis was on gatehouse defence (barbicans at Bristol, Dover, Lincoln, Marlborough, Scarborough, Shrewsbury, Windsor) or on strengthening enceinte by replacing palisades with masonry or adding flanking towers to existing walls. Particular attention was given to Bamburgh, Bristol, Chester, Corfe, Dover, Grosmont, Hereford, London, Montgomery, Newcastle, Nottingham, Scarborough, Winchester, Windsor. Henry III had a concern for hygiene, style and comfort (see Amenities, Domestication) being 'one of our most fastidious kings, living in an age which represents

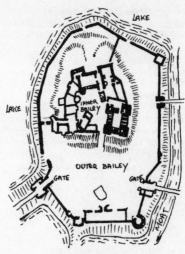

Kenilworth (plan)

the high-water mark of mediaeval civilisation'. A prodigious builder, spending over £113,000 on castles and £40-50,000 on Westminster Abbey.

HENRY VI (1422-1461)

Weak rule led to increase of bastard feudalism (q.v.) and baronial gangsterdom. In a rare charge of such robber-barons (q.v.), William de la Pole, Duke of Suffolk, was accused that 'many of your true lieges (have been) by his might and help of his adherents disinherited, impoverished and destroyed and thereby has purchased many great possessions by (livery and) maintenance (q.v.) and done great outrageous extortions and murders'. Another such criminal was Lord Saye and Sele who was eventually executed, along with his creature, the sheriff of Kent.

HERALDRY

Originated as an essentially practical method of identification in the confusion of hand-to-hand combat and when faces were increasingly obscured by head armour.

Warwick Badge

Heraldry

Initially the distinguishing blazons were personal and idiosyncratic and as old as shields and banners. In England the Bayeux Tapestry shows such devices which became hereditary in C12. About the same time crests became common with the advantage of being visible above the press.

Scrope Banner

Arms became codified in C13 as a result of the tournament heralds' expertise in identification of devices (hence 'heraldry'). 'Differences' were introduced to distinguish one member of a family from another and a technical language and rules were created. The 'coat of arms' (from its appearance on surcoats when shields became small and insignificant) became a badge of nobility, the mark of armigerous status, visually setting its wearer apart from the common herd. The lord's bearings were emblazoned on shield, jupon and horse-trappings and his non-armigerous following were provided with livery marked with his badge which was non-hereditary and designed by the lord, often for its personal significance (fetterlock, rose, sun in splendour). Mottoes appeared in C13.

In the High Middle Ages, brightly limned shields-of-arms, pennants, badges and banners distinguished leaders, followers, the castles they held and their places of temporary or permanent residence. Banners and badges were hung outside inns when occupied by a lord or his retinue and this is the origin of such inn signs as the Bear (Warwick), the Talbot, Elephant and Castle, Rose and Crown, Swan, White Hart etc. and Devonshire (or whatever) Arms.

Banners and pennants fluttered from towers and shields were hung on walls and from battlements to indicate not only ownership but responsibility for defence of a section.

Badges and shield-of-arms were often carved in the masonry (and, of course, were coloured or limned). The boar of Richard III occurs on an oriel at Barnard and heraldic shields appear at Warkworth (Lion Tower and keep) on fireplaces e.g. Tattershall, and frequently on gatehouses e.g. Alnwick, Arundel, Bothal, Cockermouth, Framlingham (itself having fetterlock shape), Herstmonceux, Kenilworth (Mervyn Tower).

A C14 Register of the Honour of Richmond shows the location of the individual contingents of castle-guard provided by the holders of land or office under the Earl of Richmond. The arms of the contributors are blazoned on or near the buildings in which they are stationed. It would seem natural for the arms to be displayed in reality on the actual sites both as an obvious form of non-verbal communication in an illiterate age and in situations where words might not be heard. Such displays would also help coherence, perhaps healthy rivalry and certainly 'esprit de corps'.

Fauconberg (Skelton)

Matters affecting the honour of a gentleman (by definition armigerous), including claims to pedigree and arms were dealt with by the court of chivalry (the Earl Marshal's Court, some of whose functions were later continued by the College of Heralds). A controversy

between Scrope and Grosvenor over the right to
'azure, a bend Or' required nearly 20 years to resolve
at the end of C14.

Scrope

HEREFORDSHIRE

From the point of view of military architecture, the
county is disappointing. It was once littered with castles
as is evidenced by surviving earthworks (e.g. Clodock,
Downton, Frome, Kentchurch Tump, Kingsland, Kington),
but nothing remains of the mighty castle of
Hereford, the great fortress of Ewyas Harold is reduced
to earthworks and the extensive Wigmore is disgracefully
neglected. But there is Goodrich and Pembridge and other interesting remains
from C12-C16 which include: Brampton Bryan, Bredwardine, Bronsil,
Clifford, Croft, Eardisley, Hampton, Kentchurch, Kilpeck, Llancillo,
Longtown, Lyonshall, Penyard, Snodhill, Treago, Weobley, Wilton.

HERRINGBONE

Form of building consisting of courses of rubble, flat stones or tiles bedded
diagonally in mortar, alternating with horizontal courses of thin stones (or
thick layers of mortar alone) so that the whole resembles the backbone of a
fish. Usually indicates C11 work (e.g. curtain, Richmond) and may be
evidence of hasty construction (cross-wall, Colchester; curtain: Bramber,
Corfe, Egremont, Hastings, Lincoln, Peveril, Tamworth). It provided a very
convenient bond for walling on a slope (e.g. wing-wall, Exeter) and was also
decorative (e.g. keeps at Benington, Guildford).

HERRISON   see also Hedgehog.

Palisade of pointed stakes on top of a bank to improve defence. Usually
replaced later by a stone wall.

   The herrison at Pickering remained until C14 and was maintained by
labour-service of bondmen and socmen, falling due every third year when
each tenant was responsible for one perch (about 5½ yds). The service was
commuted into a cash payment in time of Edward I and survived to C19!

HERTFORDSHIRE

The county possesses over a hundred moated houses (none of which are
architecturally important) and has little to offer the castle-explorer. There are
the poorly preserved remains of the important castle at Berkhamsted,
earthworks of the episcopal castle at Bishops Stortford and the more
impressive earthworks at Anstey. The small keep at Benington and gatehouse
with a little masonry at Hertford completes the tale.

HOARDING (Hours)   see also Put Holes.

A wooden gallery which, in time of war, erected outside crenellations to cover
dead ground at foot of the walls and towers. These erections were also called
'brattices'. The joists of the flooring passed through holes at the foot of the

85

parapet and were often common to both
the outer gallery and an inner gallery
('coursière') which roofed the rampart
walk. This roof was sometimes gabled
with the timbers resting on, and following
the slope of, the coping of the parapet.

Hoarding Holes, Richmond

Between the floor joists of the outer gallery were apertures through which
missiles could be projected onto assailants at the foot of the wall. There were
also slits in the face of the gallery for more horizontal firing.
Defenders were thus able to work under shelter
while covering both the field and wall-foot. These
projections were, however, vulnerable to
incendiary missiles and heavy artillery.

The records of Rhuddlan record that in the first
years of C14, 400 seven ft planks were purchased to
provide hourds for towers. In 1241, Henry III
ordered that a hoarding should be made around the
summit of the White Tower 'of good strong timber,
entirely and well covered with lead, through which
people can look even to the foot of the said Tower,

Hoarding round tower

and ascend and better defend it, if need be'.

The stone brackets (e.g. Norham) or the holes to support this structure (e.g.
Aydon, Clare, Richmond), are worth looking for.

HOMAGE

The declaration of fealty ('I am your man
(homme)') by which a vassal swore loyalty to his
lord as the preliminary to his investment with
lands or other income. The consequent
obligations were both passive and active: not to
harm his lord's lands, interests or person, and
positively to give him 'aid and counsel'. Aid
included a variety of military assistance: 'ost' –
40 days service in full armour and equipment,
'chevauchée' – escort duties or a raid of a few
hours or days duration; 'castle-guard' (q.v.) and
specified special duties e.g. supporting his lord's
head during an unpleasant channel-crossing.

These obligations tended gradually to be
replaced by money payment ('scutage') except
the ones which might be regarded as conveying
honor or privilege.

'Aid' also included 'reliefs', a sort of entry fee
e.g. 11s for a knight's fee (fief) which by C12
had risen to £5 for a knight's fee and £100 for a
barony.

Edward III doing Homage for
French lands to Philip Vl

Accepted monetary 'aids' (where a donation of something like 1s in the pound was usual) were ransoming the lord, contributing to the marriage of his eldest daughter and to the knighting of his eldest son.

HOMESTEAD MOATS

A form of defence of which traces are to be found in almost every English parish. It is the sole remnant of the moated house of the lesser gentry when the timber or half-timber house and palisade have vanished.

HONOUR

'That which gives a man distinction', hence a large feudal estate, usually centred on a castle ('the head of the honour'). A baron could hold many honours and they were usually widely separated at their first presentation in order to prevent the concentration of power in other than royal hands e.g. William de Warenne, Earl of Surrey, had honours in Lewes, Sussex and S. Yorkshire. There were exceptions to this principle in the Marches where the safety of the realm demanded strong military concentration.

Richmond

The honour of Pontefract substantially consisted of Airedale and Calderdale and had Pontefract castle as its 'head', with subsidiary castles at Almondbury, Barwick-in-Elmet, Kippax, Mirfield, Whitwood.

The honour of Richmond contained 424 manors between the Yore and Tees. Its first lord sub-infeuded with his two brothers from whom descended the Fitzralphs and Fitzhughs, the former with their chief castle at Middleham and the latter with castles at Cotherstone and Ravensworth.

Pevensey was the head of the 'honour of the Eagle', so called from its early lord, Gilbert de Laigle.

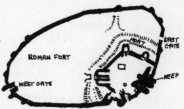

Pevensey, Head of Honour

HORSE

'Without a "cheval" nobody could be a "chevalier"' (Stephenson). The essential knight's mount, or 'destrier'

was a rare breed, strong and highly
trained, resembling a 'shire' and often
called a 'great horse'. All horses were
expensive and as early as C8, when
the European heavy cavalryman
probably originated, a horse cost 12s,
compared with a shield and lance 2s,
mail shirt 12s, sword and sheath 7s,
helmet 6s, leggings 6s, – a total of 45s,
or 12 times the worth of possessions
of an average peasant. In C10 an
ordinary horse was valued at 120d or
24 times that of a sheep, while a
destrier might cost £100 or more – the
equivalent of a small fief. Possessions
of a horse, therefore, symbolised
social class as well as military caste
and a poor knight's first aim was the
acquisition (usually by capture) of a
worthy mount.

Chamfron (Horse Head Armour)

Hospitality

HOSPITALITY

Generous provision of food and drink and lavish entertainment were an
expected and universally admired trait in aristocratic circles. This was to be
offered not only to the lord's superiors as obligation, but also to peers and to
the poor, particularly at church and agricultural festivals. It took place in the
hall and provided opportunities for communal celebration even of the lord's
personal occasions such as marriage or knighting.

HOUSE KEEP

A name for the development, particularly characteristic of the North of
England, of a type of castle or strong house which became common in
C14-15.

It consists of a high building, rectangular in plan, with four angle towers and
in the larger examples, containing a central courtyard e.g. Bolton (lc. 1379),
Sheriff Hutton (lc. 1382).

The structure provides a logical combination of castle and house where the
usual precautions for defence were taken and where more convenient external
opening had little effect on solidity. The domestic buildings are thoroughly
integrated and the curtain is their outer wall and not merely a defensive
covering.

Raby (1378) and Langley (early C14) show similar tendencies, but are less
perfect examples than Bolton, and might be compared with Lumley (lc. 1392)
and Chillingham (lc. 1344).

All these examples are undoubtedly castles, whereas Spofforth and Wressle
might be better described as 'princely manor-houses dignified by the name of
castle'.

A similar development can be seen in the Pele-tower (q.v.) or Scottish
tower-house (q.v.) but it is less logical and convenient.

HOUSE OF FENCE

The name given to fortified houses in Scotland which were erected in C15-17 (and after). They usually take the form of tower-houses (q.v.) designed for the use of handguns. See also L-plan, Z-plan.

House of Fence

HOUSEHOLD   see also Butler, Chaplain, Falconer, Knight, Marshal, Servants, Squire, Watchman.

Size depended on castellan's resources and needs but, besides his family, it always included:

(a)   Military personnel – the 'mesnie', retainers who might include household knights, outsiders doing 'castle-guard', squires, men-at-arms, porter and watchman.

(b)   Civilians headed by steward (seneschal) who was responsible for estate administration, routine legal and financial business and management of non-military household.

The smallest castles had at least three permanent officials: chaplain who added book-keeping and correspondence to his spiritual duties; watchman with eye for both external enemies and internal security including safeguarding goods and chattels, furniture and stores; porter (janitor) who kept the doors, particularly main entrance, and was responsible that no-one entered or left castle without permission. (Also known as 'door-ward' especially in North. The powerful Scots family, Durward, derived their influence from being the hereditary 'door-wards' of the royal palace.) Later and greater castles had two stewards: one for estate and one for domestic administration, butler in charge of cellar, chamberlain responsible for great chamber (and later for personal finances of castellan), keeper of wardrobe, marshal in charge of stabling and transport etc. Each department of a great castle had its head: marshal, butler, cook etc., all of whom had a subordinate staff which might include specialists varying from farriers to wafer-makers, from candle-makers to sauce-cooks, from poulterers to falconers and each of these might have apprentices or boy-helpers.

HUNTING

In the Middle Ages, hunting was more than a sport. It was almost a way of life for the rich and a means of life to the less well-endowed. In its highest form – the hunting of the deer, it was a privilege of the upper class and particularly of kings. The Conqueror, a rabid huntsman, introduced 'Forest Law' into England to preserve great tracts for his hunting provided with special agents to administer the law and to reserve the game.

King John Hunting Deer

Poaching was punished condignly and the slaying of royal deer carried the penalty of blinding.

Rights of 'warren' were for small game: not only rabbits and hares but foxes, badgers, squirrels, wild cats, martens and otters. It also included rights of hawking. Warren was granted more generally than hunting because it was considered to improve the latter.

The most dangerous quarry was the deadly wild boar which could 'slit a man up from knee to breast and slay him all stark dead with one stroke'. It should be remembered that mediaeval England contained quarry which is now extinct, including the wolf.

William the Conqueror's passion for hunting led to the devastation of villages and the dereliction of churches (in New Forest) and some considered the death of Rufus and his brother and cousin as Divine retribution. Henry II was described both as 'immoderately fond of the chase' and 'inordinately fond of hawking'.

One of the peripheral functions of a fortified dwelling in the right locality was to act as a hunting-lodge or tower (e.g. Barden Tower of the Cliffords, Knaresborough of the king). Castles also provided centres for the administration of forest and its laws and a gaol for offenders (e.g. Peveril, Pickering).

Hunting Lodge, Falkland

Hunting lodges were provided with security precautions. They were at least ditched around: the one in Kinver forest had a brattice over its gate and Woodstock was garrisoned in 1199 and 1212.

HUNTINGDON (and Peterborough)

A very small county and therefore cannot be expected to provide substantial remains of mediaeval building but Longthorpe gives a vivid and unique picture of civilised life in a large house. There remains a fragment of Woodcroft and rather more at Buckden and Elton. Examples of earthworks at Great Staughton, Hartford, Wood Walton. Hemingford Grey is a fortified manor, as is Northborough and there are other remains at Huntingdon, Kimbolton, Leighton Bromswold, Maxey and Peterborough.

Longthorpe Tower, Huntingdonshire

INCENDIARY WEAPONS see also Fire.

Large darts and other missiles surrounded with burning tow were fired from catapults and red-hot stones were sometimes shot from petraria. Use was also made of fire-wagons with hurdles and brush-wood liberally laced with animal fat. Blazing torches thrust through windows were also decisive in a number of known cases.

INCOMES, COMPARATIVE (C13)

Roger de Lacy, Constable of Chester, subsequently Earl of Lincoln and one of the richest men in the country, had a yearly revenue of about £800. At this time only seven barons had an income exceeding £400 a year and a knight or country gentleman could live in comfort on between £10 and £20 a year. A university student would be adequately supported by £3 or £4 a year. The constable of a castle might receive no more than £10 or £12 while his chaplain might be paid 1d a day i.e. about £1.15s a year.

Incendiary Weapons

INSCRIPTIONS

Apart from the symbolic communication of heraldry there may have been written inscriptions on castle walls, over gates and along battlements. The fashion certainly existed in the houses which replaced castles and it is recorded that in C19 there was still an inscription round the outside wall of Ravensworth as follows: 'Christus dominus Ihesus, via fons et origo, alpha et omega' but the date of its writing is unknown. A copper tablet attached to the outer gatehouse at Cooling reads:

'Knouwyth that beth and schul be That I am mad in help of the cuntre In knowyng of whyche thyng Thys is chartre and wytnessyng.'

Halbert,
Langue-De-Boeuf

There are Scottish examples: Muness, Shetland (1598) commemorates the builder, Laurence the Bruce, and prays offspring 'to help and not to hurt this work always'; Drumcoltran (C16) bids the reader (in Latin) to 'conceal what is secret, speak little, be truthful, avoid wine, remember death, be merciful' while sinister Noltland (c. 1570) bears the barely decipherable Biblical quotation: 'When I see the blood I will pass over you in the night'. (Exod. xii, 13).

Kisimul, Invernesshire
(plan)

INVERNESSHIRE

The list of notable castles should perhaps begin with Kisimul on the Island of Barra, followed by Urquhart, with a mention of Dounie (Beauly), Castle Tioram, Dunscaith, Dunvegan, Inverlochy and Roy.

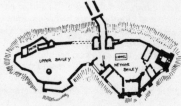

Urquhart Castle (plan)

JAMB

The straight side of an archway, doorway or window.

JOHN

Spent a good deal building and modernising castles – though little survives of his work. A number of moated manor-houses date from his reign e.g. Bridgwater, Kirkoswald. He left about 60 castles to his son, having spent over £1,000 p.a. (more than $1/10$ of revenues).

JOIST

Heavy horizontal timber to support floorboards, ceiling etc.

JOUST

A form of tournament or tourney in which the main event was a series of paired combats (as distinct from melée q.v.). The general principle was that of a knock-out (or knock-down), competition with matched pairs fighting with a variety of weapons. Generally mounted knights charged each other with the object of unhorsing their opponent with a lance. A direct hit often broke the lance and it was a considerable achievement for the one on whom the lance had broken to remain on his horse. A combat could start or continue on foot until one or other was disabled or cried, 'Hold, enough!'

The setting was one of splendour: bright pavilions, rich vesture, costly armour and great feasting accompanied with music.

KEELED   see also Spur.

Pointed at its foremost extremity. There are keeled towers (otherwise round) on the Norfolk Towers and the Fitzwilliam Gate at Dover (1220s) which perhaps represent a rare example of preference for intimidating appearance over the strongest defence. (If they face the point of expected artillery assault, perhaps not.)

KEEP   see also Hall-keep.

The strong-point and 'last resort' of earliest castles, normally separate from first line of defence and often with direct communication to the field. A modern word, the earlier popular word was 'donjon' while the contemporary word seems to have been 'tower'. The contemporary word for shell-keep (q.v.) was 'motte'. The mediaeval use of 'tower' has survived in the case of London and given its name to the whole castle. 'Motte' and 'donjon' have been metamorphosised and change their meaning

Keep, Richmond

with 'moat' and 'dungeon'. Moat is used for the fosse or ditch surrounding the enclosure and dungeon for any prison since the keep, and particularly its basement, was occasionally so used.

The keep originates as a defensible residence consisting of a common hall and a private chamber. At least by C12, latrines had been added to these essential rooms though the kitchen and store were still separate (the latter sometimes provided in a basement). If a hall and chamber are placed alongside each other over a common basement we have the nucleus of a hall-keep whose two large rooms might also enclose a kitchen and chapel with latrines at either side of the cross-wall dividing the ground plan into unequal hall and chamber areas. Keeps are characterised by massive external walls, an external staircase and a well-defended door. The defence is completed by a roof protected by higher walls ending in a crenellated parapet covering the wall-walk.

Keep, Conisbrough

If the chamber is placed over the hall (with a basement beneath), then we have the nucleus of a tower-keep e.g. Broughton, Goodrich, Hedingham, Newcastle, Portchester, Rochester, Scarborough. Internal access to the floors was usually by a staircase in the thickness of the wall and often situated in a corner.

Keeps were originally square or rectangular in plan but their corners were susceptible to mining, picking and battering and the corner staircase was a structural weakness; hence the development of towers without right-angles e.g. Orford (1165). The weakness of even a great rectangular keep like Rochester was demonstrated by its successful mining by John and it is significant that when the corner was rebuilt it was replaced by a circular tower.

The first circular keep was Conisbrough (c. 1170) followed by Pembroke (c. 1190) and Skenfrith. Curious shapes were devised in experimental development e.g. Mitford (pentagonal), Knaresborough (octagonal to field, square within), Helmsley (round to field, square within), Warkworth (a C15 tower-house of complex cruciform shape occupying the original motte).

The tradition of the great tower persisted even when the military value of the old keep had been superceded by other developments and later wall-towers often have one noticeably larger than the others e.g. Barnard, Caldicot, Chepstow, while Flint seems to represent an experimental return to the notion of a great tower (1277). With the development of perimeter defences, the donjon degenerated in military importance from a 'last resort' to 'private chambers' thence to storehouses and prisons and thus to 'dungeons'. It may be

Keep, Portchester

93

significant that there are no keeps in Leicestershire. When stone keeps were raised on an artificial mound (see motte) their foundations sometimes penetrated to the virgin soil (e.g. Skenfrith). When this precaution was not taken there was danger of slippage and consequent damage (e.g. York).

KEEP ENTRANCE

The obviously vulnerable point in an otherwise very strong position. Access was usually at first floor level and occasionally at second. It was approached by an external stair (sometimes movable or easily destructible) or by a stone stair with a removable bridge. The forebuilding (q.v.) developed as an entrance protection which also provided extra accommodation. It also tended to produce a communication bottleneck.

KEEP, INTERNAL COMMUNICATIONS

Because of the superimposed accommodation of tower-keeps, communication can never have been convenient. It was sometimes made less so for defensive reasons: a narrow spiral stair, breaks in the stairs to different floors, the necessity of crossing floors to continue etc. These precautions produced practical difficulties in domestic living which occupied far more of a castle's existence than the rare state of war. Attempts to solve these problems without unduly weakening the defence can be traced, as well as attempts to avoid the keep in wartime being a trap as well as 'a last resort'.

KEEP, HALL AND TOWER FORMS   see also Keep.

Nomenclature is not very satisfactory as any keep used for residence is, in a sense, a hall-keep and presumably any high building is a tower. We have tended to use 'hall-keep' of any great tower whose length and/or breadth exceeds its height and 'tower-keep' where the height exceeds the other dimensions. Norham is intermediate, being 90 ft high and 86 ft broad.

KEEP, POSITION

The keep may be built on an old motte, on a motte that was designed to carry it from the beginning, or be built independently of the motte so that there is a keep-and-bailey type of castle equivalent to the motte-and-bailey. The keep was sometimes placed on the curtain between wards (Bamburgh, Scarborough) or at the corner of an inner ward (Kenilworth, Norham, Portchester) or detached in a central position (Dover, Newcastle, Rochester). There are rare examples of early gatehouse keeps (Ludlow, Richmond).

Norwich, Hall-Keep with Forebuilding

KENT

Because of its wealth and proximity to the continent (see Inscriptions), Kent is very rich in military architecture. There are remains of town defences at Canterbury and Rochester but, above all, there are castles of every period and size. Our examples are not exhaustive but include: Allington, Canterbury, Chilham, Cooling, Deal, Dover, Eynsford, Folkstone, Garlinge, Godard's, Hever, Ightam Mote, Leeds, Leybourne, Lullingstone, Lympne, Penshurst, Queenborough, Rochester, Saltwood, Sandgate, Scotney, St John's Jerusalem, Sutton Valence, Thurnham, Tonbridge, Tonge, Upnor, Walmer, West Malling.

Rochester, Kent (from seal)

KINCARDINESHIRE

Crathes is a good tower-house, Dunnottar an interesting castle and in the neighbourhood of Inverbervie lie the Tower of Benholm and Allardyce castle.

KINROSSHIRE

Castle on the island in Loch Leven.

Loch Leven, Kinrosshire

KIRKCUDBRIGHTSHIRE

There are remains in the county town, while near Palnackie (Orchardton Tower) is a rare example of a circular tower-house. There are also interesting castles at Cardoness, Carsluith, Drumcoltran and Threave and some motte-and-baileys e.g. Urr.

KITCHENS   see also Ovens.

Castle kitchens seem to have been originally wooden buildings occupying a corner of the bailey. Henry III's kitchen at Oxford was blown down by a gale in 1232 and archaeology at Weobley has identified a wooden kitchen, thatched with reed and linked to hall by pentice. There are kitchen fireplaces contrived in the angle-turret of the keep (e.g. Canterbury, Norwich) as a result of removing the kitchen to the hall floor. Kitchens seem to have become a regular part of the hall-complex in C13, accompanied by pantry, buttery and screens at the opposite end from the dais and solar. Within the kitchen were enormous fireplaces and ovens and possibly a scullery where the scullions would wash dishes over sinks, often contrived in the wall and emptying into the ditch (e.g. Durham).

Cardoness, Kirkcudbrightshire

McLellands, Kirkcudbrightshire

95

King John ordered new kitchens in his castles at Marlborough and Ludgershall to have ovens large enough for each to roast two or three oxen at a time. These were apparently inadequate for Henry III who ordered further new kitchens at Ludgershall as well as a new hall with its own pantry and buttery (1244).

There are fine kitchens at Ashby, Cockermouth, Farnham, Durham and Raby (both octagonal). The latter (c. 1380) is complete, of two storeys with a stone vault and louvred lantern. Ashby (c. 1360) is partly destroyed but there are considerable remains of a spacious vaulted building. At Cockermouth a whole tower is given up to kitchen service. The kitchens at Skipton (c. 1315) are well preserved and include roasting hearth, baking hearth and servery.

The kitchen wing at Caernarvon is some 20 yds away from the hall across a courtyard (which seems to presume a connecting wooden corridor).

Owing to the castle's confinement within the curtain, when the kitchen became a feature its position was not as fixed in castles as it was in ordinary dwellings. It does more or less occupy its normal place at Berkeley where it is a polygonal building divided from the screen by the buttery. It is in a similar position at Warkworth, though it may originally have been separate, while the original kitchen at Cardiff was probably next to the hall. At Kenilworth it is near the East curtain with access to the hall stairs and the cellar passage. At Ludlow it is also in a separate building and so at Conway, Caernarvon and Harlech where it lies against the curtain near the hall.

Kitchens were complex buildings and their planning shows signs of 'time and motion study'. They usually had their own water supply, were convenient for the dining room and contained ovens, open fires for roasting and smoking meat, spits and grills, storage cupboards and often a stone sink. Water may have been drawn from a well but sometimes the kitchen supply was piped from a cistern on a higher floor of the castle. In great households there were sometimes separate kitchens for lord and lady and in 'livery and maintenance' castles there was a separate one for the garrison.

KNIGHTHOOD   see also Horse, Squire.

Knights were made rather than born and the rank was achieved only after long and arduous training which began in infancy (see Squire). Any knight could elevate a suitable candidate to this status but the honour was usually conferred by the boy's father, another relative, or a great lord and warrior.

A complex ritual for the making of a knight had developed by C11 at least and had reached its full form by end of C12. Among its elements were: a nightlong vigil in the castle chapel, a ritual bath at dawn, mass and breakfast with friends and family, clothing in new white vesture. The dubbing or accolade which followed these preparations usually took place in public and in the open air accompanied with fanfares and other music. It began with armouring, a process which concluded with the presentation of a blessed sword which had accompanied the vigil. The central act of dubbing was the 'colée' or buffet given with a swinging blow of the open hand, a powerful knock-down blow intended to make the knight remember the occasion, the admonition and the accompanying oath. He swore to be a true knight and to fulfil the obligations of his profession (see Chivalry). Of the many formulas which might accompany the accolade the most eloquent was 'Sois preux' – 'be gallant' i.e. valorous, honourable and faithful to pledged word. After this there was sometimes a return to the church and finally there was his presentation with the valuable horse which was a necessary adjunct to his station. Once mounted he was formally handed his lance and

Colée, William knights Harold (C11)

shield and performed a kind of 'lap of honour' which might include a mock attack on the quintain or other display of military skill.

Apart from this formal ceremony knights could be created on the field of battle (a special distinction).

The status of knighthood made its holder a member of the upper classes: through the honourable profession of arms, the economic status indicated by the possession of horse and armour, and the tenure of an official degree given with religious sanction. But there was social mobility: the successful middle class could buy themselves into the estate of knighthood and a poor soldier might attain knightly rank through valorous martial service or notable exploits. Nevertheless, its members formed a closed class or caste and the obligations of chivalry seem largely to have been limited to their fellow members or class equals.

KNIGHTLY CAREER

The career prospects of a knight were: inheritance of estates, marriage to a wealthy heiress, royal service or service to a noble as a high official in his household. Knights who were not eldest sons were mostly penniless and their possible careers tended to be limited to serving in the retinue of a great lord or being a mercenary soldier with prospects of loot and/or ransom. It was the hope of this last possibility or the rarer chance of a profitable match which was their

Knight being vested (C13)

highest hope in spite of the attempts of the
Church to develop the notion of chivalry and
'noblesse oblige'. If the knight was a skilful
fighter his best chance, in the later Middle
Ages with the decline of local and
international wars, probably lay as a
'professional' in tournaments where there
was a fair living to be made in ransoms and
prizes. (The victor usually claimed the value
of the defeated knight's armour.)

Knightly Skills

KNIGHT SERVICE

The obligation of a tenant to provide one
knight for every £20 of annual income from his
estates. This obligation dated from the time of
Edward I (1272-1307). A knight's wages were
8d per day and he was expected to serve for 40
days so that knight service could be commuted
for two marks i.e. 26s 8d = 40 × 8d. This was
a normal practice by the reign of Henry II.
Sometimes the knight service due from the
tenant to his overlord was earmarked for
garrison work in one of the latter's castles. It
was then called 'castle-guard' (q.v.).

The royal valuation of knight's fees due
from an estate was nicely calculated to
produce few 'spares' and thus prevent the
raising of a private army.

'Knight service' was onerous for it involved
finding not only highly trained men, but
several very superior horses for each, costly
equipment (including 'spares'), numerous
servants and enough food to supply the entire
contingent (including servants and horses) for
40 days.

Knightly Banners

A tenant had also to provide his lord with
'aids' (money payments on the knighting of his
eldest son, marriage of eldest daughter or
contribution to his ransom) and hospitality –
free entertainment whenever lord visited (with
small army of retainers and servants). This
latter obligation could be so burdensome that
its requirements became strictly defined.

He also had to attend on lord at his own
expense and in person on ceremonial
occasions, at lord's council, or at legal
proceedings ('suit to court'). In return,
together with other vassals, he could

Knight (C14–15)

determine customary law and have right to
judgement by his peers.

LADY'S FAVOUR

Chivalry made much play with the token given
to a knight by his chosen 'donna' (often a
sleeve). Leland has an enlightening story
about a helm given as a token:

Knight Armed with Grace
(Allegory of God's Grace arming Knight)

'About this tyme (1319) there was a greate
feste made yn Lincolnshyr, to which cam many
gentelmen and ladies; and amonge them one
lady brought a heaulme for a man of were,
with a very riche creste of gold, to William
Marmion, knight, with a lettre of
commaundement of her lady, that he should
go into the daungerest place in England, and
there to let the heaulme to be seene and
knowen as famose. So he went to Norham;
whither withyn four days of cumming, cam Philip
Moubray, gardian of Berwike, having yn his

Knight Armed by Ladies

bande 140 men of armes, the very flour of men of the Scottish marches.
Thomas Grey, capitayne of Norham, seying this, brought heis garison afore
the barriers of the castel, behynde whom cam William, richely arrayed, as al
glittering in gold, and wering the heaulme his lady's present. Then says
Thomas Gray to Marmion, 'Syr Knight, ye be cum hither to fame your helmet.
Mount up on yor horse, and ryde lyke a valiant man to your foes even here at
hand, and I forsake God if I rescue not thy deade or alyve, or I myself wyl dye
for it.' Whereupon he toke his cursors, and rode among the throng of
ennemyes, the which layed sore stripes on hym, and pullid hym at the last oute
of his sadel to the grounde. Then Thomas Gray with al the hole garison lette
prik yn emong the Scottes, and so wondid them, and their horses, that they
were over throwen, and Marmyon sore beaten was horsid agayn, and with
Gray pursewid the Scottes yn chace. There were taken fifty horses of price,
and the women of Norham brought them to the foote men to follow the
chace.'

The inspiration was still potent in some
quarters two centuries later, for a strong
element in drawing the chivalrous 40-year-old
James IV to invade England (and to the
disaster of Flodden) was a letter from the
Queen of France, calling James her knight and
enclosing her turquoise ring as a token. She
urged him to go 'but three feet on English
ground' for her sake. He went rather more,
with her ring on his finger, and died
courageously in the forefront of the battle,
together with more than 10,000 of his men.

Lady offers Heart.

99

LANARKSHIRE

Besides the famous castle of Bothwell, the
following may repay a visit: Avondale
(Strathavon), Black Castle (Motherwell),
Carnwath, Craignethan.

LANCASHIRE

North Lancashire was poor and thinly
populated in the Middle Ages and therefore
there are few castles in this region. They
include Clitheroe, Lancaster and Piel. There
are plenty of pele-towers e.g. Ashton, Borwick,

Bothwell, Lanarkshire
(Reconstruction)

Broughton, Dalton, Gawthorpe, Gleaston,
Greenhalgh, Gresgarth, Hoghton, Hornby,
Turton, Wraysholme.

   South Lancashire is even poorer in major mediaeval buildings: castles are
totally absent (if one excepts the C19 Wray) and there is only one pele-tower
– Radcliffe.

   The remains of the fine defensible gatehouse at Cartmel are worth
mentioning.

LANGUAGE

The interested may care to collect phrases by which castle life has enriched the
English language. Here are some examples: A bolt from the blue, To pick a
quarrel, Hoist with his own petard, With fire and sword, Below the salt, Break
a lance, The last resort, Kick against the pricks, Draw a bow at venture, Shot
his bolt, Two strings to his bow.

   Literature has also been enriched, from the Anglo-Saxon riddles about
ballistas and battering-rams, to novels such as 'Ivanhoe' and 'We Speak No
Treason.'

LATE CASTLES

After the C14, so-called castles (in England
at least) were rather impressive and romantic
fortified houses than serious castles. They
were the result of chivalric fashion and
French influence and some of the motivation
seems similar to that which inspired the
outburst of Victorian Gothic. These late,
nostalgic castles were generally modelled on
a simplified (and cheaper) version of
Beaumaris e.g. Herstmonceux, Kirby
Muxloe, Maxstoke, Nunney, Raglan.

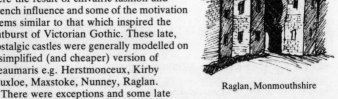

Raglan, Monmouthshire

   There were exceptions and some late
castles (e.g. Bodiam, Cooling, Mettingham)
had a serious military purpose which was at least supplementary in their
building. Even in others, the gatehouse at least had some strength (e.g.
Donnington).

LATRINE   see Privy, Sanitary Arrangements.

LAUNDRY

Laundry was done in wooden troughs containing solution of wood-ash and caustic soda for bleaching. There was doubtless a laundry hut but remains are unidentifiable. There seems to have been a daily wash of clothes, sheets, tablecloths and towels. In some cases the laundress washed the hair of the lord.

LAVABO (Laver)

A stone basin, half-built into the wall and half projecting (not dissimilar to but normally less ornamented than a church piscina). It was a wash-basin and sink whose main use was for the washing of hands before and after meals (forks were unknown in the castle period). The similar facility in Scotland is called a 'slop-basin'. Some were served by a refillable tank placed above them with bronze or copper taps. These cisterns were castellated and elaborately decorated and often had spouts in the form of leopard heads.

Lavabo-Slop Sink,
Corbridge

Examples on the second and third floors of Conisbrough keep and on the second (hall) floor of Dacre where the lavabo closely resembles a piscina. Other examples at Beverston, Goodrich, Harewood, Woodsford.

LEAD

Used in considerable quantities – the unit was a carrat (2,184 lbs) – for roofing, plumbing, sealing metal inserts into stone, providing counterweights for trebuchets, covering allures (rare) but not for anti-personnel purposes.

When resources were adequate, it was used to cover minor as well as major roofs. It was naturally used in such exigent plumbing as existed: water-pipes, water-spouts, making water-proof joints, drain-pipes and cisterns (occasionally). Fall-pipes did not exist (except at London Tower), their function was carried out by stone spouts and gargoyles which threw roof-water clear of walls. There is no evidence of its use, boiling or otherwise, against besiegers.

John de Maréchal lost an eye through being splashed by lead when the tower in which he had taken refuge was fired (c. 1140). (It was this same John who, when Stephen threatened to kill his hostage son unless he surrendered a rebellious castle, replied that he was not troubled by the threat since he had 'the hammer and the anvil with which to forge still better sons'.)

LEGAL TERMS

Scottish, see Scottish Legal Terms.
English, see Attainder, Escheat, Enfeoffment,
             Fief, Feudal, Pit and Gallows,
             Liberty.

LEICESTERSHIRE

The two finest remaining castles in
Leicestershire were built by the same man, Lord
Hastings, at Ashby and Kirby Muxloe. Beyond
these, there is not a great deal to mention:
Belvoir is an essay in Gothic romanticism,
Leicester has some interesting fragments and,
for completion, we might add Castle Donington,
Earl Shilton, Groby and Hinckley.

Ashby-De-La-Zouche Castle,
Leicestershire

LIBERTY

A place outside normal (royal) jurisdiction.
Even when castles lost their jurisdiction over the
town beneath their walls they often retained an
attenuated area bounded by their outermost
defences. Thus a refuge was created for fugitives
from town justice such as bad debtors and
undesirable characters. Hence the
expression 'to take a liberty'.

The liberty of Norwich castle began at its
outermost ditch and survived until 1345 in spite of
continuing complaints from the town. The
'bounds' of London Tower are still 'beaten'.

Castle liberties had a positive side in
occasionally providing freedom for dramatic
performances which were intolerable for
small-minded burgesses.

Liberty

LICENCE

To crenellate Allington (1282).

'Edward, by the grace of God, king of England,
Lord of Ireland and Duke of Aquitaine,
greeting to all to whom these present letters
come.
You are to know that we have granted on our
own behalf and that of our heirs that our
beloved and loyal Stephen of Penchester and
Margaret his wife may fortify and crenellate
their house at Allington in the County of Kent with a wall of stone and lime,
and that they and their heirs may hold it, thus fortified and crenellated, in
perpetuity without let or hindrance from ourselves, our heirs, or any of our
ministers.
In witness whereof we have caused these our letters to be made public
(patent). Witnessed by myself at Westminster on the twenty-third day of
May in the ninth year of our reign.'

To this licence, in the form of Letters Patent, was appended the Great Seal of
Edward I (in green wax suspended on silk cords). Note the mention of
Stephen's wife.

LICENSING   see also Adulterine.

It was one of the principles of Norman
government that no castle might be built
without royal consent and even if one were
held in fee, it could be requisitioned by the
Crown in case of need. (In early C12 one
nobleman warned another that to add unduly
to one's fortifications was to invite royal
expropriation.)

Great Seal of Edward I

Feudal custom apparently limited the extent
and strength of private fortification and by end
C12 it was the 'crenellation' or battlementing
of its walls which distinguished a castle from a
manor (which might well have gate and
ditches) and rendered it liable to forfeiture if
unauthorised.

Formal permission was granted by a 'licence to crenellate' (lc.) and these
are found in the Chancery Rolls from the reign of King John. Such licences
might express the legitimisation of an existing structure and therefore their
date is not conclusive evidence of a castle's original date. Exceptionally,
licences might be granted by another than the king e.g. in the County Palatine
of Durham such licences were issued by the bishop (and in French instead of
the normal Latin).

The first licence was possibly Bishopton (1143) though there were earlier
ones giving permission to strengthen an existing castle as distinct from
creating one by crenellating a house. The last was granted in 1533 to Sir
William Fitzwilliam for Cowdray, Sussex, though it represents something of
an anachronism, if not legal fossilisation.

LIFE OF A CASTLE

In spite of the air of long continuance and near permanence which surrounds
the masonry remains of surviving castles, the life of a castle could, in fact, be
extremely short, especially in the Welsh Marches. The same was true of
England during the Anarchy when some castles were abandoned before they
were completed. Selby was captured within a week of its building and
thenceforth vanishes from history. Reading was built in 1150 and destroyed in
1153.

LIGHT, ARTIFICIAL

Supplied by flambeaux (resin-soaked torches held in wall brackets), candles,
tallow dips (made from animal fat) or oil lamps (sometimes in form of cresset
e.g. Urquhart).

The dark entrance to the great keep of Newcastle, Northd., is provided on
either side of the stair with a small lamp niche with a dished sill to retain its oil.
In domestic quarters of some castles the corbel for supporting a candle or oil
lamp survives and privies often have a shelf or recess to hold a light. The
watchman's quarters on the summit of Scottish tower-houses sometimes have
a recess for his lantern.

LINCOLNSHIRE

Singularly poor in castle remains. Apart from earthworks, all survivals up to C14 are covered by mentioning (Old) Bolingbroke, Grimsthorpe, Lincoln, Somerton, South Kyme. Apart from these, Tattershall is one of the most important late castles in England and Thornton deserves a mention. There are traces of about a score of motte-and-baileys e.g. Bourne, Bytham, Fleet, Folkinham, Goxhill, Owston Ferry, Stamford, Swineshead, Welbourn and of town defences at Stamford.

LINES OF DEFENCE

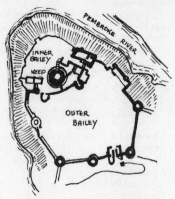

Early castles developed on the principle of successive lines of defence, defenders retreated as each was captured until they reached their 'last resort'. Though such lines caused considerable trouble to the adversary, they also hampered the defenders by not being mutually supportive (e.g. Barnard, Norham). Occasionally the keep was located so as to support curtain and external field (e.g. Rochester) or, in the rare case of Richmond, it commanded the one side from which serious attack was possible and thus stood in the very forefront of the defence. But such examples seem to have been innovations of individual

Pembroke Castle (Lines of Defence)

engineers and not part of a general development. This was inspired by Crusading experience and hard acquaintance with advanced fortifications possessing complete flanking protection and lines of defence which rose closely behind their predecessors so that all could combine against assailants.

LISTS

Originally, this was the space immediately in front of defences and was kept smooth and free from cover. It provided a convenient area for arms drill, especially for the mounted knights. When this area was enclosed by a further concentric wall (list wall), it provided a ready-made arena for jousting (q.v.) with seating or standing-room for spectators on the wall-walks on either side. Hence the word became used for the tournament field wherever it was located.

Lists

LITURGICAL LIFE

The life of a castle's inhabitants, as of any mediaeval group, was linked to and revolved round the church's festivals. Michaelmas marked the beginning of its fiscal year. Sieges and assaults often seem to have been undertaken on festivals (to bring luck?) and there was devotion to the martial saints (St. George, St. Michael) in the castle chapels though the dedication (q.v.) of these latter was by no means confined to saints with military associations.

The castle provided a social centre for the great Feasts. There seems always to have been a general Christmas dinner in its hall (though the tenants often made a substantial contribution to the food). Apparently, too, the licence of the Feast of Fools brought some apprehension and we know of the posting of extra watchmen on the castle walls as a precaution against riotous behaviour getting out of hand. On major festivals there were gifts from tenants to lords and vice-versa and munificent gifts from lords to each other. There were carols and mummery, music and dancing, and a variety of seasonable dramatic performances.

There were also celebrations, of pagan origin but a tolerated part of agricultural life, associated with Fire and Fertility, with Spring and the New Year. There were jollifications which represented an amalgam of pagan and Christian elements, carols and eggs at Easter, exchange of New Year gifts, the ceremonies of St John's Eve, Beltane's fire, Lammas and Harvest Home and the Wakes which celebrated the local saint.

Some part of nearly all these events took place in the castle hall or in the castle grounds.

LIVERY AND MAINTENANCE   see also Man-Rent.

A C15 development whereby small tenants contracted to wear a lord's livery and badge and to fight for him in return for his protection in their need. It often degenerated into something little different from paying and feeding mercenary soldiers.

The contract took the form of an indenture e.g. in 1449 the Earl of Salisbury entered into such an indenture with one of his vassals, Walter Strickland, by which, in return for a yearly salary and a share of the spoils, Walter bound himself to provide a ready force which would go anywhere, at home or abroad, at Salisbury's command. This force comprised a total of 290 mounted and unmounted soldiers. Earlier we hear of Roger de Clifford retaining Sir Robert Mowbray for £10 per annum.

It is possible that Sir Edward Dallyngridge, builder of Bodiam, was indentured to Sir Robert Knollys who gained a fearsome reputation as the leader of a 'free company' in the French wars of Edward III.

This development led to anarchy, private armies and the decay of chivalry and true feudalism. (It is sometimes called Bastard Feudalism.) It was an important element in the Wars of the Roses. Lord Hastings', property executed by the Duke of Gloucester in 1483, had indentured two lords, nine knights, 48 squires – all sworn to aid him against anyone.

Livery Badges (York)

105

LIVERY AND MAINTENANCE, CASTLES OF

These are characterised by the provision of defence against treachery within as much as against attack from outside. There is a return to a quasi-keep in which the lord is safe from a disaffected garrison, there are arrangements for his apartments to be cut off from the rest of the castle and for their defences to face inwards as well as to the field. He usually has control of the main gate and its defences and there is separate provision for housing and feeding his retinue, two halls, separate kitchens, bailey, barracks etc.

The garrison is no longer part of the 'family' as, in a sense, tenants and servants were with ties of loyalty and tradition. Mercenaries had no loyalty apart from the purse, their services ceased if pay ceased and could be switched for a better offer. They were frequently 'men without ruth or conscience, distrusted even by their employers, whose trade was war and whose gain was plunder'.

There are many examples of this type of castle e.g. Bodiam, Llanstephan (lc. 1385) and Thornbury, one of the last, with accommodation for a whole regiment of retainers, strictly secluded from the lord's accommodation which ensured personal control of gatehouse.

LOCAL GOVERNMENT

Focused on and directed from the castle. The baronial castle, as head of the lord's honour, was often the gathering point and communication centre for widely scattered estates and franchises. Royal castles might also stand at the heads of estates or districts but more commonly they were in the custody of sheriffs and thus became centres of county administration.

It was in the castle hall that usually the local courts met, whether courts of shire, hundred or honour. Thus it was to the castle that a man went to pay his taxes, to seek justice, to answer a summons or to present his services. Through its gates passed not only knights and soldiers but, far more frequently and in much larger numbers, litigants and supplicants, tenants and bailiffs, tax-collectors and messengers.

In 1186 the royal castle at Nottingham was provided with a 'chamber of the clerks' to which, as a government office, royal writs came and from which they were issued, from which juries were impanelled, and where rolls, vouchers of dues, payments and summaries of cases pending were made up (sometimes in triplicate).

LOOK-OUT   see also Crow's Nest, Watchman.

As in all warfare, siege-warfare required intelligence of enemy strength, movement and disposition. Castles required knowledge of mines and saps, of siege works, of the activities of rams and bores, of movement and significant activity. This was provided by high towers, by overhanging bartizans and galleries, and by spies. (Often heralds and other messengers were blindfolded on approach so that they could not carry back

Look-Out, Caernarvon

information. Sometimes they were retained for the same reason.)

Similarly, it was useful for besiegers to know what was happening behind the high curtain, what was the state of morale, food supplies etc. The gathering of this information was one of the purposes of the belfry (q.v.) e.g. at the siege of Bedford (1224), Henry included observers (exploratores) among the occupants of his two belfries.

LOOP

A vertical narrow slit, usually splayed, to provide light or an offensive aperture through a wall. Many so-called arrow-loops are merely narrow windows and would be impractical as bow loops as they are the wrong shape and provide no convenient accommodation or stance for a hypothetical bowman.

Loop

LOOPS, BOW

Their purpose is to allow defenders to fire from cover and, in the case of crossbows, to protect the bowman when reloading. They are sometimes provided in the merlons of a parapet. Interior loops usually consist of a long vertical slit which widens laterally from the outside to an internal recess for the accommodation of the archer which was usually provided with one or two seats.

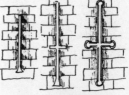

The loop for a long-bow requires a tall embrasure for plunging fire and a deep recess for drawing. A crossbow needs a broader recess, but less tall and deep, since it is fired horizontally. The splayed jambs of a bowloop permitted lateral as well as frontal fire and the sill was often deflected steeply downwards to improve command of dead ground beneath walls.

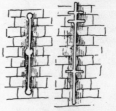

True bow-slits rarely appear before 1190 e.g. Avranches Tower, Dover; flanking towers at Framlingham, fighting tops in keeps of

Bow Loops

Kenilworth and Pembroke. The earliest form was a simple vertical slot, less than 2 ins wide at the outside. The length of the slot could vary from the norm of about 3 ft to as much as 12 ft (e.g. Corfe, c. 1280).

Developments included the introduction of a splayed foot to the slit (e.g. Skenfrith c. 1190) to improve command of the ground immediately below the loop and the addition of a horizontal slit, also widely splayed, which improved traverse (especially of the crossbow) e.g. Trematon (c. 1190).

During C13 both horizontal and vertical arms were terminated by circular holes called 'oillets' (e.g. Kenilworth c. 1240) and further developments included the addition of more than one cross-arm (e.g. Barnwell c. 1266) and the remarkable loops in Grey Mare's Tail Tower, Warkworth (c. 1260), 17 ft

7 ins long with triple arms and an unusually large splayed foot. The keep at Tickhill appears to have possessed an enormous loop, with oillets and a splayed foot, for the operation of a large fixed crossbow.

Mediaeval fire-power reaches its climax at the South front of Caernarvon which has, beneath the parapet with looped merlons, two superimposed fighting galleries in the thickness of the wall, thus allowing concentrated fire from three positions on an enemy attacking from the South.

In Edward III's reign, the outer ward alone at Dover was said to contain 555 loopholes not counting the gatehouses and 19 towers. At this time the ideal practice seems to have been to allow three men for every two loopholes, which led a contemporary to calculate that it would require over 1,000 archers to fully man every loop in the castle.

LOOPS, ELONGATED

Bow-slits whose lower half is prolonged below the level of the allure or fighting platform (e.g. Caernarvon, Warkworth). This development allows a greater angle of declination and seriously limits the area of 'dead ground' at the base of the wall.

Loops Elongated, Warkworth

L-PLAN

Development of tower-house whereby a wing was added at right-angles to the original rectangular house. It sometimes provided a location for a convenient newel-stair and always increased accommodation. The number of floors in a wing, given over to rooms, was often as many as five or six as against four in the main building. These additional rooms were usually for private and family accommodation whereas the larger and loftier rooms of the original house were more public and social. A further and important advantage of this development was that it provided flanking fire along the front of the house and, in particular, protected the door which could then be brought down to the ground floor and placed in the re-entrant angle.

L-plan, Greenknowe

Scores of examples of this type of tower-house in Scotland e.g. Drumcoltran, Greenknowe, Monikie, Scalloway, Turriff.

108

LOUVER (Louvre)

A lantern-like structure raised on the roof above the central hearth of a hall, designed to extract smoke. Its sides were covered in sloping slats to keep out the rain and provide an up-draught. It is said that, in some cases, these slats could be opened and closed by a cord like Venetian blinds. From C14, some louvers seem to have been capable of revolving so as to take advantage of wind direction.

It is claimed that some halls were equipped with pottery ventilators in the form of knights, kings or clerics and so designed that smoke was emitted from their eyes or from the tops of their heads.

MACHICOLATION   see also Flying Parapet, Murder-hole.

Since Hoarding (q.v.) was susceptible to fire, it was replaced during C14 by stone corbels which carried a masonry crenellation and provided openings in the floor for shooting, loosing stones, timber, boiling water etc. upon assailant approaching the foot of a wall or tower. The device seems to have originated in the Crusader castles of the Near East at the beginning of C13 and when it reached England was first confined to the main gate (e.g. Cooling, Kidwelly) but it had spread to the summits of towers and curtain walls by C14 (e.g. Bodiam, Nunney, Raglan, Warwick).

Machicolation

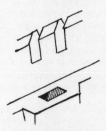

A form of machicolation most often found within a gatehouse takes the form of long rectangular slits in the vault of the passage and in the arch in front of the portcullis (sometimes called murder-holes q.v.). In some cases they may have been used to hold a heavy wooden frame or to allow the insertion of strong beams to reinforce the iron herse of the portcullis. The stymology of 'machicolation' – 'mâcher' : break or crush, 'coulis' : groove, may be helpful.

Machicolation (Diagram)

The slits which terminate above and in front of a gate seem originally to have been designed for the emission of water to quench fire assaults on wooden doors (e.g. Caerphilly, Leybourne).

MACHINE   see Engine.

MAINTENANCE

Not only modifications and updating in defence but included testing and upkeep of weapons (all liable to rust), engines of various sorts, clearing of gutters and roofs, plastering and painting of external walls, clearing of drains, emptying of cesspits, deepening or adding wells, renewing ditches and palisades, re-roofing, replacing timber constructions with stone, improving domestic facilities, re-decoration. Repairs could extend from 'mending a window and gutter in a wardrobe' to making good the damage of a siege. Castle ditches needed constant attention and c. 1288 'mending the ditches' at Aberstwyth cost £5.16.8.

MALVOISIN

'Bad neighbour' – a common nick-name for a great belfry or powerful siege engine.

MAN-AT-ARMS

A heavily armed infantryman (sometimes mounted) who provided the backbone of the castle garrison. He was usually accompanied by, and in charge of, three or four less well-equipped soldiers so that a force of 250 men-at-arms usually implies something like 1,200 soldiers in all. In C15, at least, men-at-arms were knights or squires e.g. John de Clifford accompanied Henry V to France with '50 men-at-arms, well accoutred' of which three were to be knights and the rest esquires, together with 150 archers.

Men-At-Arms (c. 1300)

MANGON

A siege engine which it is impossible to distinguish from mangonel (presumably a diminutive), introduced to the Normans by the Byzantines and was probably the only heavy engine in use for a century after the Conquest. It was an artillery piece consisting of a heavy frame which supported a long arm with a cup or sling at its free end. The other extremity passed through a skein (of ropes, sinew, women's hair) stretched between upright posts. The skein was twisted by capstans (called 'capitals') and then the free end was pulled down against their torsion by a winch or windlass. When it was horizontal it was locked

Mangonel

in position by a trigger-mechanism and the spoon or sling was loaded with the appropriate projectile (usually a stone or incendiary material). At the appropriate time the trigger was released and the arm flew up, impelled by torsion and its own springiness (some arms seem to have been constructed in narrowing sections to increase this 'whip' effect), until it hit the horizontal padded stop between the upright arms of the frame. This caused the whole machine to kick up its rear (hence the Romans called them 'onagars' (mules) and the Normans 'nags'). Inertia, sometimes assisted by sling, hurled the projectile towards its target in a lowish, and probably not very accurate, trajectory.

No mangon has survived and detailed information is scarce, but we do know that some of them had iron frames or junction-plates which were stored separately. Modern experiments have achieved a range of 200 yds with a stone projectile of 50 lbs weight but there is evidence that this performance is considerably inferior to that achieved by the mediaeval artillerymen and their engines.

MANNING   see also Castle Guard, Garrison.

In a large fortress, particular posts were always manned by the castle-guard contributed by a specific individual. This lessened confusion, increased familiarity and consequent efficiency, and developed 'esprit de corps'.

At Richmond in C14, the Constable and his men were posted in the keep, the barbican was the responsibility of FitzElias and his retinue, the gatehouse was in the charge of FitzRobert and his men; to the Chamberlain was committed the guard of the Gold Hole Tower, the roof and battlements of the great hall were the responsibility of FitzAlan, the neighbouring section of curtain was the charge of FitzHenry, the next of FitzHerbert, the next of de Burgh. Ralph FitzRobert occupied a position near St. Nicholas' chapel, while Torphin FitzRobert was conveniently located between the kitchen and the brew-house.

MANOR   see also Parish.

Some castles were in towns and had rights of toll or market or both, but most were rooted in the agricultural economy and organisation of manor and village.

The manor was an estate held by a lord and farmed by tenants who owed him rent and service and whose relations with him (and each other) were governed by the manorial court.

The word came to England with the Conqueror and the estate so described might coincide with a village and its lands, include more than one village or one village might contain part of several manors. The principal dwelling house of the lord was called the manor-house (in Scotland, the 'capital messuage').

MANOR-HOUSES, FORTIFIED   see also above.

Manors were always given some defence for privacy and protection against marauders, both human and animal (boundary ditch, moat, palisade), but the granting of licences to crenellate (q.v.) became common in the late C13 and C14 and many private houses achieved the status of castles., e.g. Ashby (1474), Hever (1340), Kirby Muxloe (1481), Leconfield (1308), Markenfield (1310), Maxstoke (1346), Nunney (1373), Old Wardour (1393), Raglan (1430), Spofforth (1308), Stokesay (1291), Tattershall (1434), Thornbury (1511), Wingfield (1441).

Fortified Manor (Hever)

MANRENT, BONDS OF

Scottish equivalent of English indentures (see Livery and Maintenance) by which a great lord rented services of armed men to support him in his quarrels in return for pay and protection. The Scottish form of the Bastard Feudalism which developed in Europe in C14-15.

Fortified Manor (Little Wenham)

MANTLET (Mantelet)

The row of protective fixed hurdles to protect besiegers, especially bowmen (c.f. Pavise). The name was also given to the large wooden shield carried by assault troops when storming a castle.

A mantlet wall is a low stone erection, crenellated and turreted, forming an outer ring round part of the whole or the curtain which overlooks and supports it. It replaced the 'hedgehog' (q.v.) as a defence beyond the main ditch and the clear space of the 'lists' (q.v.) and hence is sometimes called a list-wall.

Probably the best examples are in Wales: Harlech where the mantlet-wall has its own small barbican gatehouse and Beaumaris where the mantlet wall is well endowed with flanking towers.

Mantlet

MARSHAL

The officer in charge of a great household's horses kept for status, transport, hunting, warfare. His staff included farriers, grooms, carters and perhaps clerks. He was responsible for providing and maintaining suitable mounts for the lord and his family as well as for the garrison (a knight usually had three), for transporting household goods and organising the cavalcade when his superiors moved elsewhere (socially or on business), for deliveries to and from fairs, markets, and

Mantlet Wall, Beaumaris

merchants, for the supply of bran, hay and oats required by his many charges and for their care and exercise. He also saw to the acquisition and maintenance of carts and wagons, their containers, chests and barrels, the panniers for pack-horses, all harness and tack, greasing, repair and renewal of leatherwork, metalwork or woodwork related to his area of responsibility.

MASONRY   see also Architectural Terms.

Since masonry was often rubble merely faced with ashlar (q.v.), it could be pierced with comparative facility by miners and sappers once its facing stones were dislodged. This was easiest at sharp corners and was the purpose of the bore (q.v.).

Against this threat, plinths, batters and spurs were erected at the foot of walls and towers to produce a greater thickness of masonry, and projecting towers were re-designed with round or polygonal faces to obviate their vulnerable sharp corners. Some observers have commented on the comparatively small size of most ashlar. This is probably due to problems of transport and the weight that could be carried by two men or a packhorse.

It is useful to examine the quality of masonry and relate it to area, period and type of stone. It can vary from the evidence of a hasty and unskilled rush job to consummate skill with the finest of material. Material was normally that which lay conveniently to hand, though early castles have stone from Caen. Roman stones are re-used and so is Roman brick (see Brick).

MASON'S MARKS

Mediaeval masons undoubtedly marked their work in secular buildings as they are well known to have done in large sacred buildings. But mason's marks rarely remain, perhaps due to the considerable deterioration of the surface where they would be placed. There are examples at Bothal, Prudhoe, Tower of London, Warkworth.

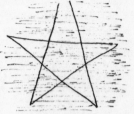

Mason's Mark, London

MASTERS

Practical education and training in the Middle Ages was largely an apprentice system controlled by the Guilds. At the head of training for each trade, mystery or craft were regent masters who judged the work offered for examination and decided whether it was a 'master-piece' i.e. qualifying its creator for the degree of Master.

The building of castles involved master-carpenters, master-plumbers, master-slaters or -tilers, master-plasterers and master-smiths as well as master-masons. Each of these master craftsmen would be supreme and responsible in his own sphere but would work in conjunction with other masters under the direction of the master of the works, normally the agent of the king or noble for whom the castle was being built.

Master Mason

MATERIALS   see also Ashlar, Rubble.

The first castles were constructed of earthen banks and timber for the palisades and buildings they enclosed. The most vulnerable timber was later replaced by non-combustible material, usually stone but it could be flint (e.g. Eynsford) or brick. A simple, but strong and large, motte-and-bailey could be made of easily available local materials and cheap unskilled labour but the construction of a stone castle was an entirely different matter, requiring complex organisation (q.v.) and expensive specialists.

If there was previous building on or near the chosen site, its materials were used. The large thin red bricks of the Romans can be seen in many Norman

113

Materials

and Saxon buildings and a number of Northern castles incorporate stone from Roman camps or the Wall.

Normans brought stone from Caen (used e.g. at Arundel, Orford, Portchester) but English stone was increasingly used under Angevins (quarries included Corfe, Egremont, Folkestone, Pevensey, Reigate). Among varieties of local stone are clunch (hard chalk), freestone (fine-grained sandstone or limestone), greensand (green limestone), oolite (granular limestone), tufa (cellular igneous rock) and flint. The quarries were owned by king or great monastery and either hired for a specific time or contracted for fixed amount. The stone was extracted from bed by wedges and then sawn or split to convenient size (usually about a foot cube) and face side dressed. Often transported by water for cheapness (quarries at Barnack, Maidstone and Quarr are near navigable rivers).

Herstmonceux

Both Saxons and Normans occasionally made bricks, which are used a little more in C13 and increasingly from C15 (e.g. Beverley town gate, Caister, Faulkbourne, Herstmonceux, Lullingstone, Sandwich town gate, Tattershall).

Mediaeval mortar is usually a mixture of lime, sand and water. Cockleshells are added to the compound used in the lower courses of the White Tower, ox-blood was mixed in at Bolton, and elsewhere crushed chalk is the main ingredient. Lime and sand were dug at the nearest available place and transported to the site which usually had its own kilns e.g. Denbigh, Weobley.

The fact that early castles were entirely, and later ones substantially, of wood should not give the impression of insubstantiality or rustic shed (see Ardres). Excavations at Weobley have shown that early C13 buildings were weather-boarded vertically and horizontally and surviving mediaeval roofs should leave no doubt of skill and sophistication of mediaeval carpenters (q.v.) Apart from structural use, masses of timber were used in construction process: rafts and piles for foundations, scaffolding, bonding masonry, temporary shuttering for rubble walls, arches and vaults. Structures included not only complete buildings but palisades, hoardings, ladders, bridges and doors. Once the castle was built, timber continued to be consumed in vast quantities for fuel, carpentry, engines, repair and maintenance. Pickering extracted from its forest ten oaks in 1250, four in 1251, 40 in 1256, 110 in 1315 and 300 in 1323. Part of the timber requirements for Edward III's embellishments at Windsor were over 3,000 oaks in 1354 and over 2,000 in 1362. Whole woods or forests were bought or contracted with as in case of quarries. Trees were felled and trimmed and usually used immediately without time for seasoning.

The chief metals used were lead and iron though some furniture and fittings were made of brass or latten (a brass compound) and there might have been plate of pewter or silver and occasionally gold. Lead came from Cumbria, Derbyshire and the Mendips and was chiefly used for plumbing and roofing though it was occasionally used for bonding stone particularly where water action was feared. Iron came from a variety of places, including Yorkshire, Staffordshire, Gloucestershire, Northumberland. Its uses, both domestic and military, were numberless. Both metals were usually delivered in bars and ingots and worked on site.

Conway

Materials occurring in the accounts of Flint (which took nine years to build and cost £7,000) include 87,000 bags of lime at 4d a bag, lead for roofing, iron for hinges and locks, and parchment for writing the accounts. In a single year (1286) the building of Conway castle and town walls absorbed the following materials: nearly 20 tons of charcoal, 524 tons of coal, 140 carrats of lead, 90 loads of iron, three barrels of steel, 500 lbs of tin, 125,000 nails, an unspecified number of ropes (costing £12.2.10), 13,500 wooden shingles, nearly 12,000 planks, 2,000 scaffolding poles and nearly 1,200 'clayes' which may have been some kind of scaffold union, not to mention miscellaneous items and the thousands of tons of stone and hundreds of tons of lime. (A carrat was a measure of lead weighing about 2,184 lbs.)

Some concept of vast quantities of materials used in castle-building may be gained from estimated 30,000 tons of stone in Borthwick tower and knowledge that vast remains of Warkworth lost 272 wagon-loads of lead, timber and other materials in 1672.

MELÉE

Form of tournament consisting of a mock battle, often between knights of different regions or loyalties. Its advent was proclaimed by heralds throughout the neighbourhood and it could attract international stars. At the appointed place and time, the two teams of knights lined up, horsed and armed, at opposite ends of a meadow or 'green'. They charged each other at a signal from the heralds. The field was

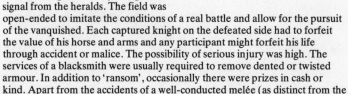

open-ended to imitate the conditions of a real battle and allow for the pursuit of the vanquished. Each captured knight on the defeated side had to forfeit the value of his horse and arms and any participant might forfeit his life through accident or malice. The possibility of serious injury was high. The services of a blacksmith were usually required to remove dented or twisted armour. In addition to 'ransom', occasionally there were prizes in cash or kind. Apart from the accidents of a well-conducted melée (as distinct from the

115

malicious wounding of an ill-conducted one), its aftermath could easily degenerate into an angry brawl among the supporters which might involve the principals and in these circumstances there could be the intention and act of inflicting serious injury on members of the opposing faction.

The civilised Henry III consistently opposed the holding of tournaments because of the danger to individuals and the state through convocation of treasonable assemblies with opportunities for plotting. The Church joined in condemning these exercises as occasions for all seven of the deadly sins: Pride, Covetousness, Lust, Anger, Gluttony, Envy and Sloth – and not without reason! Nevertheless, they remained popular not least among the avid spectators and those who made a good deal of money out of the preparations and accompaniments of these events, varying from great merchants to the equivalent of peanut vendors. Edward I introduced 'Round Tables' (q.v.) in the later C13 as an attempt to canalise and civilise tournaments, giving them a code and replacing the melée with single-combat encounters using blunted weapons.

Henry III

MERCENARIES see also Livery and Maintenance.

Professional soldiers who replaced the amateur feudal levies who could only remain in the field for limited periods and at specified times. They were full-time, instead of limited to a 40 day service, and they were paid daily wages instead of performing a feudal obligation. There were advantages and disadvantages in mercenaries and the three Edwards managed to overcome most of the latter and built a royal army, consisting mostly of Englishmen who were loyal, patriotic and proud of their ability. The archers were selected from the competitors at local archery contests at which they competed for the honour of being chosen to an elite corps composed of the best bowmen in Europe.

MERIONETHSHIRE

The county never seems to have had many castles. At Tomen-y-mur there are earthworks, rather more at Castell-y-Bere and then there is magnificent Harlech.

MERLON

The full height of the battlement between two embrasures. In war-time the embrasures or crenels were closed by wooden shutters

Harlech, Merionethshire

(q.v.) which swung from axles fastened to the tops of merlons either by iron collars or a hole and slot in the masonry. These shutters rarely remain in England but signs of their fastening or support may occasionally be found in the sides of merlons.

Merlons are usually from 5 ft to 6 ft wide and 6 ft high but taller ones, up to 9 ft 6 ins are known. Some are pierced with arrow or bolt-loops (e.g. Caernarvon, Warwick, York walls) and this practice begins about the end of C12. The C13-14 saw a tendency to narrow their width as the result of increasing the number of crenels.

Careful observation will reveal some merlons finished with a

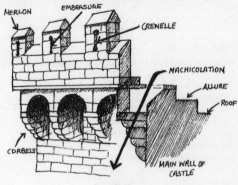

Crenellation

roll on the coping. This was to prevent arrows or bolts which had struck the inclined plane of the coping from glancing over the parapet into the castle enclosure. A refinement at Caernarvon continues the drip-mold down the sides of the embrasure to prevent arrows glancing across the merlons.

MESSENGERS

Full-time messengers were necessary servants to a great lord with scattered estates and much business. They carried receipts and commodities as well as letters and ranked in the castle hierarchy between the grooms and the men-at-arms. Their job was responsible and could be dangerous, especially if they were delivering an unwelcome message to an irascible recipient. (In 1250, Walter de Clifford forced a royal messanger to eat the king's Writ, wax seal and all.)

MEWS   see Hawking.

The accommodation for the hawks or falcons and an important inner-bailey building under the charge of the falconer. Mews were quite large buildings, sometimes taking the form of a miniature castle, containing enough space to allow short flights and high enough for the falconer to enter the door upright with a hawk on his wrist. They were probably of wood and

Mews

117

have left no identifiable remains. The perches within them were adapted to the size of the different birds used in falconry and the floor was covered in sand or gravel, changed regularly.

Outside the mews were blocks, made of wood or stone, usually consisting of a long cone whose point was driven firmly into the ground. They provided acclimatising perches on which the birds were 'weathered' i.e. grew accustomed to the conditions outside the mews.

MIDDLESEX

The only castle in the county is the Tower of London.

MIDLOTHIAN

Edinburgh possesses its famous and much altered castle as well as the more interesting Craigmillar. Borthwick and Crichton are important Scottish examples, whilst Brunstane (Penicuick) and Roslin deserve a mention. Dalhousie is listed, as is Luffness.

Edinburgh, Midlothian

Craigmillar, Midlothian

MILITARISM

Mediaeval society was as much military as churchly. There was a knightly education of hall and field which not only paralleled the clerkly education of school and college but even gave it some of its terminology: degree, bachelor. The mediaeval state was founded and maintained by military might and could be won or lost as a result of military engagements. One might even say that the Middle Ages in England are begun and ended with a battle (Hastings, 1066, Bosworth, 1485) and in both one king died and another usurped the throne.

Kings were warrior-kings who led their people from the front and the aristocracy that they gathered about them in service was largely a military aristocracy. The seals of great dignitaries usually portray them armed cap-a-pie and charging home with

Children Playing at Knights

sword and lance. The brasses and monuments which they left as their memorials in church are predominantly mailed and armed. A castle was the proper and significant abode for such leaders of society.

In all classes, games, sports and recreations had a noticeably large martial element. There were competitions with shield and buckler, quarter-staff, fencing, archery, tilting and quinting, jousting and wrestling. The literature of the period romanticised chivalry and the knightly quest, fabliaux and drolleries depict and sometimes mock knightly codes and behavious. Songs of battle and the loves of knights were the substance of the lay of the minstrel and the poetry of the troubadour.

Churches are bedecked with heraldry in stone and glass, entire chapels are occupied by the recumbent effigies of mailed knights and their ladies and more than one misericord depicts the interests or even the foibles of the knightly class.

Modern English (see Language) bears many a fossil of the knightly age though not all will recognise 'panache' as the proud plumes of a knightly helm.

Satire on Militarism

MILITARY DEVELOPMENT

The motte-and-bailey introduced by the Normans provided the plan for the subsequent stone castle whose first development was keep-and-bailey. The traditional function of the great tower as 'the last resort' dictated the arrangement of outer gate, outer ward, inner gate, inner ward, keep.

Meanwhile, the improvement of flanking defences led to the concentration of defence on the curtain hung between its own great towers so that the keep became of secondary importance and the 'castle of enceinte' appeared. Eventually the keep could be dispensed with altogether, as the defences and strength of a castle became concentrated and combined into a double or triple line which could offer simultaneous resistance and mutual support.

Perhaps the first sign of all the future development was the reduction of salient angles which both increased the castle's offensive capacity and reduced its vulnerability to boring or mining.

MILITARY ORDERS

An attempt to combine the virtues and work of a knight with the devotion and commitment of a monk. There were many such orders arising out of the Crusades, but the chief ones affecting this country were the Knights Templar and the Knights Hospitaller.

The Templars were an international and essentially military order concerned with the defence of pilgrims and the Holy Places against the infidel. Their houses in England (called Preceptories), apart from the London Temple, were mainly recruiting centres or farms for the

Hospitaller

119

support of the order though hospitality to pilgrims was practised at all of them. A former site is often indicated by the element Temple in a place name. At one time or another the Templars had about 60 houses in England and Wales but the order was suppressed in 1312 on dubious grounds of heresy and their property was either pillaged or transferred to the Knights Hospitaller. The Hospitallers (or Order of St John of Jerusalem) were very similar to the Templars but did not suffer papal suppression. The order was abolished in England, along with other religious orders, by Henry VIII and its houses (about 70) were plundered and secularised. It survived on the continent and continued to distinguish itself in works of hospitality and military enterprise, perhaps one of the greatest of the latter being its heroic defence of Malta in 1565.

Templar

There are remains of a commandery of the Hospitallers at Torpichen in Scotland and at Chibburn St John's Jerusalem in England. The old Grammar School at Skipton incorporates the remains of a chapel of the Knights Hospitaller.

MILLS

Castles normally received their flour from the manor mill but there would have to be provision for times of siege when communications were cut. All castles would probably possess hand-mills for this emergency but some had large machines worked by animal or water power (e.g horse-mill at Middleham, water-mills at Beaumaris and Leeds).

Water-Mill

MINE

A subterranean passage excavated under the walls of a besieged fortress either to gain entrance directly or by causing a breach in the undermined tower or wall. The word is particularly used of the large chamber supported by wooden props which was dug

Mending Water-Mill

under the building to be demolished. The approach tunnel is sometimes called a sap. Mining was a response to the invention of the great stone towers (keeps) which could not be burned, carried by assault or battered down by primitive siege engines.

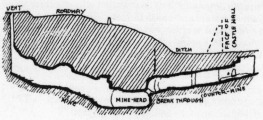

Local peasantry could doubtless be impressed to drive a tunnel towards and under the corner of a tower (its weakest point) but on at least some occasions, skilled professional

Mine, St Andrews

miners were employed (e.g. at Henry's siege of Bedford in 1224, the constable of St Briavel's sent miners from Hereford and the Forest of Dean). When the tunnel was under its objective, it was enlarged into a square chamber whose roof was supported by props and planks. As soon as the chamber was judged to be the right size, the space between the props was filled with brushwood laced with animal fat and the miners retired apart from the fire-lighter. The destruction of the roof supports led to its collapse and usually to the collapse of the masonry above, creating a breach which was attacked by assault troops ready and waiting for the mine to be sprung.

The mine was the most dreaded threat to a fort and much castle development was due to counter-measures: abolition of large salient angles, plinths and prows, galleries and machicolation, careful choice of a rocky site or a low site which could be provided with a moat (the most effective defence of all). Angles were attacked because they were less supported by pressure from the sides (a good deal of a wall's strength is inertial) and the collapse of an angle would tend to bring down sections of the two adjoining walls, thus

Miners at Work

creating a greater gap. Also at an angle the falling debris was less likely to fill up the breach.

There is a mine gallery under the keep at Bungay and St Andrew's has the remains both of a mine and a successful counter-mine (1546). Mines were sometimes detected by placing bowls of water above their suspected path. Ripples would indicate activity.

Perhaps the most famous mine was that which brought about the surrender of the great tower at Rochester which was holding out against King John (1215). John pressed on the work with all his energy and authority: Canterbury had to work day and night to produce as many picks as possible and when the mine neared completion (nearly six weeks later), the Justiciar was ordered to, 'send with all speed by day and night forty of the fattest pigs least good for eating to bring fire beneath the tower'. Their sacrifice was not in vain: lard produced a fierce blaze which swiftly collapsed the mine and brought down a sufficient portion of the keep corner for an assault party to gain the basement, though the defenders resisted stoutly for a time behind the protection of the cross wall. When the keep was repaired the corner was replaced by a round turret which still remains (though cracked) as a testimony to the power of a mine.

MINSTRELS

Part of the staff of a great castle and provided with a rostrum for performance above the great screen at the bottom of the hall, attained by a vice. Minstrelsy was part of the entertainment offered at a castle and usually consisted of chansons de geste, songs of derring-do, the heroic exploits of great lords and vassals or, later in the period, chansons d'amour, the love-longings and sufferings of knights for ladies. The performers were not always professionals: when Edward II stayed at Whorlton, the daughters of his host entertained him by singing 'Simon de Montfort' and other songs. They were rewarded for their pains with the princely sum of 4s.

Minstrels

MISSILE WEAPONS   see also Artillery etc.

Individual missile weapons included the long-bow and the crossbow (q.v.) and the small sling with a range of about 275 yds. Manuscript illustrations often show slingers among the attackers or defenders of a castle.

Missile

MOAT   see also Water Defences.

The water-filled ditch (usually of U-section) which provided the only sure defence against the mining that was the ever-present fear of those who sheltered behind stone walls. Moats were much developed in C13, not only around castles but all houses, so that the expression 'moated manor-house' savours of redundancy. Moats were fed by diverted springs or streams. Unlike the V-shaped dry ditch, a moat is not accompanied by a bank, the excavated earth was used to make dams which served either to divert water to the moat or keep it in its desired channel.

MONMOUTHSHIRE

This Marcher county was inevitably an object of raids and strife, particularly because of its pastoral richness. Consequently, it is well-endowed with castles and has examples

Great Tower with Postern to Moat, Raglan, Monmouthshire

ranging from mottes to the complex development of Chepstow. Other noteworthy sites include Abergavenny, Caldicot, Grosmont, Monmouth, Newport, Penhow, Raglan, Skenfrith, Usk and White Castle, Mottes survive, at Dingestow and Dixton.

MONTGOMERYSHIRE

Not rich in castles, even that of the county town which in 1610 was 'a faire and well-repaired castle' is now fragmentary and of the other half dozen in the county, only Dolforwyn and Powis are worth mentioning.

MORAY

Duffus is perhaps the most interesting castle but Brodie, Coxton and Elgin (Lossiemouth) rate a mention and there is an interesting motte at Forres.

Coxton

Coxton Tower, (Section)

MOTEHOUSE

The castle nearly always contained a court-house for the administration of local (manorial) justice, though sometimes the court was sited in a traditional out-door spot, often beneath an ancient tree. In a royal castle, the king's justice was administered, or could be administered in the hall. The various names of the New Hall at Pickering (King's Hall, Mote Hall) are an indication of its function.

MOTTE   see also Mound.

Mound or mount, the essential feature of the earliest Norman castles. The word in Norman-French, derived from the turf of which most mottes were composed. The Latin word was 'dunio' or 'domgo', a corruption of 'dominio'. In French this became 'donjon' and in English 'dungeon'. A motte at Canterbury is still called 'Dane John'. The motte was an effective and practical symbol of the lord's 'dominion', of his 'domesne'.

Motte

There are mottes in every county of England and to take Kent as an example, they exist at Newenden, Stockbury, Thurnham (two), and Tonbridge (well-preserved). The highest motte in England is at Thetford. Mottes could be made by the simple and obvious method of throwing the excavated earth inwards as the round surrounding ditch was dug. But the matter is not as simple as that: many mounds are not round or anywhere near, some are in fact square. Basically, there are two kinds of motte: the truncated cone of comparatively small surface area at its levelled summit and the much more extensive but less eminent erection, sometimes called a ring-work. Some writers use the word 'motte' for the former and 'mound' for the latter, a convenient distinction though the words are etymologically cognate. The raising of a truncated cone was quite a complex matter: the upcast was regularly levelled and reinforced with layers of stone or beaten earth. The nucleus of a motte may be a natural hill or eminence, modified by scarping, compressing or shifting earth. At Carisbrooke the motte is built of alternate layers of large and small chalk-rubble skilfully laid. At Rayleigh the motte slopes are revetted with stone and elsewhere there is evidence of timber revetments. The motte at Durham ascends in a series of high revetted steps.

Early Motte-and-Bailey
(Reconstruction)

Topcliffe Castle

The height of mottes can vary from 10 ft to 100 ft and their base diameter from 100 ft to 300 ft. Examples of natural mottes at Belvoir, Pontefract; of the artificial raising of a natural eminence at Tickhill, Tutbury; of entirely artificial mottes at York (two). When the motte had reached its full height it generally seems to have been finished by covering its slopes with an outer layer of clay to prevent uneven settlement and slippage on the face of the slope.

Generally mottes were crowned with a wooden tower which was basically an elevated fighting position and look-out point. It consisted of a platform raised on stilts so as not to impede the free movement of the garrison on the top of the motte and 'bore more than a superficial resemblance to the Roman watch-tower from which in fact it may have been derived'. When a motte was designed from the beginning to carry a stone tower, the foundations of the latter were laid in the virgin soil and were built up along with the motte until they emerged at the crest. Similarly, sometimes a well shaft was dug in the centre of the projected motte and as the latter grew the lining of the well was continued upwards.

Plan of Motte

Building a stone tower on a motte which was not originally designed for the purpose could have disastrous or near-disastrous results as the earth sank beneath the enormous weight. Clifford's Tower (C14) built on a motte (1080) has suffered from this, as has the C14 keep at Duffus built on the earlier Norman motte.

Clifford's Tower, York

MOTTE-AND-BAILEY

The very early but very effective type of Norman castle, constructed in hundreds all over the country. Basically it consisted of a mound with a ditch and a further area defended by another ditch and palisade. There were many variations on this theme. Renn distinguished five features of mottes which can be combined, six basic bailey plans, and four relations of the motte to the bailey. To these permutations we may add mottes with one, two or three baileys; baileys with one or two mottes and mottes without baileys and baileys without mottes. The chief advantages of this primitive castle were the availability of the materials, the cheapness of the (forced) labour and the extreme speed of construction (a matter of days rather than weeks).

A typical motte-and-bailey was laid out by striking a rough semi-circle from the base of the motte and curving this line so that its ends met the motte ditch at approximately right-angles. The perimeter of the motte was defended by a palisade and the palisades erected on the earth rampart, made from the ditch spoil, crossed the motte ditch and joined the summit palisade after climbing the sides of the motte. Later the timber tower and the wooden palisades were replaced by stone building (e.g. Oxford, Windsor). Additional examples of motte-and-bailey castles are included in the county lists.

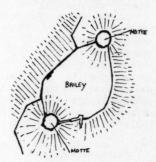

Plan of Lewes Castle

Gywas Harold Castle

The largest Motte-and-Bailey, Old Sarum

125

MOUND   see also Motte.

The typical feature of the early Norman
castle:
They make a mound of
earth as high as they can,
and encircle it with a ditch
as broad and deep as
possible. They surround
the upper edge of this
mount. . . with a stockade
of squared logs firmly
fixed together. . . Within

Plan of Mound

this stockade they build
their house, a central
citadel which commands
the whole place. The entrance may only be reached across a bridge which,
springing from outer edge of the ditch, gradually rises supported on pairs of
pillars or even triple pillars trussed together and suitably spaced, crossing the
ditch with a gradual slope until it reaches the upper level of the mound at the
level of the threshold of the gate.'

(Early C12 Flemish writer, cited Braun.)

Typical mounds at Cockermouth, Framlingham, Restormel, Old Sarum,
Rising.

Mounds scarped or carved out of a hill at Bletchingley, Bramber,
Conisbrough, Corfe, Whitchurch.

MULTANGULAR TOWERS   see also Keep, Tower.

Edward I's great engineer, Master James of St George, had
a great fondness for multangular towers (an idea probably
derived from Constantinople – though there was, and is, a
Roman one incorporated in town-walls at York). He built
two castles featuring them in the neighbourhood of Lyons
as well as his English constructions at Caernarvon and
Denbigh.

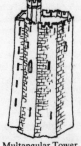

MURAL CHAMBER

Rooms in the vast thickness of keep walls. They are not a
universal feature of keeps (e.g. Corfe, and Portchester has
only two small ones which function as privies). On the
other hand, Conisbrough has a normal supply, Dover has
as many as 27, and those at Newcastle are large enough to
contain good-sized chambers with large fireplaces.
Occasionally chambers may be found in the thickness of
curtain walls e.g. Kenilworth, Richmond, Tantallon.

Multangular Tower
(Caernarvon)

MURAL PAINTING

A favourite castle decoration was to paint a large wall white and to divide the area into rectangles outlined in red in imitation of large masonry blocks, each embellished with a flower in its centre. (Remains of this fashion can be discerned in Durham cathedral.) In 1240 the Queen's chamber in the Tower was so ornamented and the chosen flowers were roses. Murals proper were not unknown: the hall at Winchester had a map of the world, a chamber at Clarendon had a frieze of kings' and queens' heads, while a room above this had paintings of St Margaret and the Four Evangelists as well as additional 'Heads of men and women in good and exquisite colour'. There are fine, and possibly unique, remains of mural paintings at Longthorpe Tower.

MURAL PASSAGES

Besides the normal staircases, corridors and latrines, large square keeps sometimes have mural passages designed as fighting galleries. These also occur in the curtain of Edwardian castles (e.g. Beaumaris, Caernarvon).

MURDER HOLES (Meutrières)   see also Machicolation.

A name usually given to holes in the vaulting of an entrance passage e.g. gatehouses at Bothal, Harlech, London (Byward), Newcastle (Black Gate), Pembroke, Tonbridge, Warwick. They may have occurred naturally in consequence of fixing the centring of vaults during building but their defensive possibilities were soon seen and exploited. They may have served either or both of the following purposes:

(a) To drop timber framework through in order to strengthen or replace a weakened gate.

(b) To provide an aperture for harassing an enemy by means of assault or missile weapons. The defenders would hardly have used valuable molten lead but powdered quick-lime was likely, with even more lethal effects. There were also the possibilities of boiling water, fat or super-heated sand.

'Murder Holes'

This term is also more generally used of any opening (including machicolations) through which lethal action could be taken e.g. the gun-ports at Wark were described as 'murder holes' (c.f. Shot-holes). It would seem more accurate to describe all vertical holes through which an enemy could be attacked as machicolations.

NAILS

Hand-made, of course (usually at ironworks of Newcastle-under-Lyme). They cost between 7d and 6s per thousand (including carriage) according to their size etc.

125,000 were bought in 1286 for the works at Conway.

9,000 board nails for Harlech (1286) cost 13s 6d i.e. 1s 6d a thousand.

40,000 nails for laths cost 7d a thousand while 20,000 nails for barrows cost 6s a thousand.

NAIRNSHIRE

Near Nairn itself lie the remarkably complete ruins of Rait, while Cawdor and Kilravock must be mentioned.

NEWEL   see also Spiral Stair, Vice.

The central column or post around which a spiral stair revolves. In the commonest construction of a stone spiral stair each step took the form of an eccentric keyhole. The circular terminations fitted on top of each other to form the newel, while the opposite and much broader end was built into the wall (see diagram).

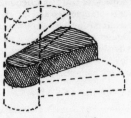

Newel (Diagram)

NEW TOWNS   see also Bastide.

Edward I was one of the great town planners: besides his plantation-towns attached to fortifications in Wales (Conway, Caernarvon, Flint), he built Kingston-on-Hull (no remains) and Winchelsea in England which were probably modelled on the 'villes neuves' of his Duchy of Aquitaine.

NORFOLK

The county is interesting for its early general use of brick. This material occurs at Caister, Middleton and Oxburgh. There are also substantial remains of great Norman fortresses at Norwich and Rising. The earthworks at Castle Acre have been designated 'the finest in England' and there are remains of motte-and-baileys at Buckenham, Horsford, Mileham, Thetford, Wormegay and elsewhere.

   There were major castles at Baconsthorpe and Gresham but their remains are hardly worth mentioning any more than those at Claxton, Dilham and Weeting (though the latter has been included as an example together with the sacrilegious use of N. Elmham).

Caister, Norfolk

NORMAN CASTLES

Though the Normans introduced the castle and were indefatigable castle-builders (about 32 between 1066 and 1071, about 100 by 1086 with countless mottes) yet there were weaknesses in their basic design of motte-and-bailey or tower-and-bailey: dead angles, communication problems, separated defence-lines, dead ground, susceptibility to mining, vulnerability to improved engines, passivity. The future of castles lay with activity, with mutually supportive defensive positions, with greater enclosures to accommodate larger garrisons for sortie, enfilading towers, machicolations, stone for wood, continous galleries and wall-walks and stronger defences against mining.

NORMAN CONQUEST

Introduced castles into England – any earlier ones were the erections of Normanised predecessors of William I.

'They wrought castles widely throughout the nation, and oppressed the poor people; and ever after that it greatly grew in evil. May the end be good when God will.'

(Anglo-Saxon Chronicle)

Previous lack of castles was given as a reason for the Norman's success:

'For the fortresses which the Gaul call 'castella' had been very few in the English provinces; and on this account the English, although warlike and courageous, had nevertheless shown themselves too weak to withstand their enemies.'

Norman Soldiers

(Odericus Vitalis)

It has been estimated that the castles built immediately subsequent to the Conquest numbered 99. They also extended into Scotland and motte-and-baileys survive at e.g. Annan, Duffus, Inverurie, Lochmaben, Moffat.

NORTHAMPTONSHIRE

Castles are rare: Barnwell is the most interesting, as an example of the monumental C13 type. There is a good gatehouse at Rockingham and sparse remains of the great castles of Fotheringay and Northampton. Woodcroft preserves a C13 fragment and there are fortified manors at Astwell, Northborough and Southwick. Longthorpe, though not strictly a castle, has been included because the exceptional survival of its wall-paintings are exemplary of decoration in a great house or castle. There are vestigial earthworks at Earls Barton, Higham Ferrers.

NORTHUMBERLAND

'The castle county of England.' The whole history of military architecture in these islands may be studied in Northumberland and illustrated with splendid examples, including some which are peculiar to this county. A recent book (Graham) lists 336 castles and pele-towers. Northumberland was, of course, a Marcher county and had been on the boundaries of civilisation since the Romans established their

Pele-Tower, Halton

129

delimiting wall. Furthermore, Scotland, unlike Wales, was never conquered or even partially integrated and warfare continued up to and beyond the time when Scottish kings became rulers of England. Selection has been difficult but the following list contains a selection of pele-towers and the most interesting castles are underlined: Alnwick, Aydon, Bamburgh, Belsay, Berwick, Bothal, Bywell, Callaly, Cambo, Cartington, Chibburn, Chillingham, Chipchase, Cocklaw, Cockle Park, Corbridge, Coupland,

Tower House Keep, Warkworth

Craster, Cresswell, Dilston, Dunstanburgh, Dunston, Edlingham, Elsdon, Embleton, Etall, Featherstone, Ford, Gatehouse, Halton, Harbottle, Haughton, Hexham, Langley, Mitford, Morpeth, Nafferton, Newcastle, Norham, Ogle, Otterburn, Ponteland, Prudhoe, Staward, Thirlwall, Tynemouth, Wark, Warkworth, Whitton.

NOTTINGHAMSHIRE

Not rich in military architecture with the remains of only about half a dozen castles. Of the great royal castles of Nottingham practically nothing survived Cavendish's palace. There is much more left of the former episcopal castle at Newark, a little masonry at Greasley and traces of earthworks at Cuckney. (At Hawton the site of a moated manor has been converted into the largest Civil War earthwork in the county.)

NUMBERS OF CASTLES   see also Scotland.

In the middle of C12 there may have been as many as 500. About 1200 A.D. there were probably about 400 and the number continued to fall, though those that remained were strengthened. The practice of building in stone increased expense and limited new building. Rebellion or disloyalty was punished by demolition which probably more than offset the few new castles built during C13 and C14. The number of castles further declined in C15 and C16 and the survivors were mostly devastated during the Civil War of C17. Today there are probably some 200 well worth the enthusiast's attention.

It has been estimated that there have existed some 1,500 castles of one kind or another in England and Wales (though not all at the same time). About 1,300 of these were founded in C11 and C12. In Wales there seem to have been rather more than 200 of which most were likewise of an early date. The settlement of the country's political affairs brought about the abandonment of most castles and increased the 'domestication' of the small proportion which survived. The spurt of building at the end of C13 was connected with the final subjection of Wales and after beginning Beaumaris in 1295 no other major castles, either royal or private, were initiated.

In 1322 there were 63 royal castles in England, an adequate number to police the country. There were some coastal fortifications built during this century but the private castles were the result of fashion and the cult of chivalry initiated by Edward I who introduced the tournament and imitated

Arthur's court at Kenilworth. (The Order of the Garter was introduced by Edward III.) Braun thinks such castles as Bodiam, Maxstoke, Nunney and Raglan were the result of romanticism rather than of real need (though some owners may have been glad of their defences during the Wars of the Roses). The walls of these castles would have offered but feeble resistance to the trebuchet (Herstmonceux has thin brick walls and large mullioned windows). They were elaborately fortified manor-houses of a nostalgic kind, perhaps affected by the influence of French chateaux on soldiers returning from the Hundred Years' War.

For examples of castle numbers in individual counties: Yorkshire is known to have had over 70 and Northumberland more than 300.

Arthur arrives at Caerleon

OFFENSIVE WEAPONS

Though a castle was essentially a defensive work it was not without means of retaliation which included personal arms (q.v.) and artillery. The latter was mainly used against the engines of assailants.

At Kenilworth (1266), the artillery of the garrison destroyed two great belfries (q.v.) erected by the besiegers commanded by Henry III and the Lord Edward. According to a contemporary chronicler the battery and counter-battery fire at this siege was so intense that the hurtling stones frequently collided and shattered in mid-air.

Artillery was rarely mounted on towers (unless they were solid bastions or strongly vaulted) because of the danger of recoil weakening the masonry.

Early guns could not be depressed and so, when any provision at all for their mounting was made, the gun-ports were located at the base of walls (e.g. Kirby Muxloe).

OFFICIALS See Household.

OILLET see also Spying.

An eye-hole. Small circular opening occurring singly and independently or as part of loop (q.v.). Examples in wall-tower at Warkworth.

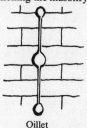

Oillet

ONAGER see also Artillery, Mangon.

A ballistic engine of Roman origin, deriving its energy from torsion. Late models could apparently project a stone of 60 lbs up to 750 feet. It could be used as an incendiary weapon, an impact weapon to destroy buildings and machines, or as a fragmentation weapon against personnel.

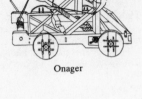

Onager

ORATORY

A small prayor-room for individual or family use. Castles are often provided with a private oratory as well as a more public chapel for general use. The fore-building at Dover contains both oratory and chapel and Henry II provided and embellished a separate chapel/oratory for his daughter-in-law at Winchester.

Sometimes used to mean merely a small chapel e.g. keep chapel at Guildford, constricted into L-shape, so that eastward-facing priest is out of sight of little congregation in north-south 'nave'.

ORDER

The military side of a great castle was governed by regulations or 'statutes' issued by the constable. Those for Dover seem to have been drawn up by the great Hubert de Burgh in the reign of John : sergeants are to see that the (night-watchmen) warders 'right royally keep their watch without going to sleep, since they have the constable's leave to sleep as much as they like in the day time' ; any warder found asleep on duty was to be marked by snipping off a piece of uniform or taking his duty staff as evidence (the penalty for this serious offence was remarkably light : docking a day's wage – 2d), aggression was to be confined strictly to the enemy, if a sergeant struck another man with his hand, he was fined 5s and 10s if he used his fist ; a sergeant and a warder were especially nominated for the duty of watching the lights in the castle chapel.

ORGANISATION see also Household.

The building of a great castle was a most complex affair involving detailed organisation, accurate co-ordination and difficult logistic problems. The process which resulted in a new royal castle can be studied in some detail.

Orders came through the king's writ, addressed to the shire-reeve (sheriff) as the king's agent, with supplementary writs to other sheriffs for help in regard to labour, transport and materials. In the case of a royal castle, because of priority and urgency, there would be commandeering and conscription.

The site-manager was either the constable-designate or another official representative of the king. For the king's works in Wales, the builders (masons, carpenters and navvies) were recruited from

Organisation of Castle Work

every shire. Yorkshire, e.g. supplied 20 masons, 40 carpenters, 150 diggers. Besides these basic workmen, the Edwardian castles had the services of dikers from the Fens and other specialists from France (Vaud, Valais, Viennois, Savoy).

Some of the complexities of supply may be indicated from the following: money was panniered and pack-horsed from London, Nottingham, Winchester and Ireland; there were ship-loads of stone, lime etc. from Bristol and Tenby to Aberystwyth, and from Anglesey to Harlech; lead was brough from Snowdonia and the Isle of Man; iron and steel from Newcastle-under-Lyme; coal from Flintshire and ropes from Lincolnshire.

If one considers the state of roads, the technology of ships and carts, the difficulty of communication, the state of accountancy and mathematics, the need to provide relays of draught animals and military escort, the magnitude of the achievement is astonishing.

Though most of the information available relates to royal castles, it seems a reasonable assumption that lesser lords worked on exactly the same principles with a difference only of degree.

ORIEL

Strictly speaking a 'look-out'. It originated from domestic desires for privacy and a 'Bellevue' or 'Belvedere' which may be related to the growing mediaeval love of nature. The facility developed in C13 as a 'nook' of timber projecting from the wall of the chamber, a non-military gallery, usually with a window and often with a fireplace. In C14 it became the delightful and aesthetically pleasing upper bay-window to which the word is generally applied (e.g. Newark). Earliest example in chapel at Prudhoe (c. 1300).

Oriel, Prudhoe Chapel

An oriel was built at Stirling by Edward I in 1304 to provide his queen and her ladies with a comfortable observation post during the siege!

In its fully developed form it served to lighten the high table on the dais in great hall (c.f. University colleges) but had a military use in the additions to Flint and Rhuddlan on the tops of towers nearest the towns, c.f. Crow's Nest (q.v.) at Warwick.

ORKNEY

Has a number of interesting castles; Cairston, Cubby Roo's, Kirkwall, Noltland.

OUBLIETTE

Noltland, Orkney

Prison (q.v.) wherein prisoners were lowered by rope through a trap-door and vanished from sight to be forgotten. Usually used of

prisons below normal level, sometimes even
beneath another prison cell. It was
characterised by a lack of facilities for egress
and shortage of light. It is often found in
Scottish castles ('pit') and there is a
bottle-necked prison under the N.W. tower of
Newark which might reasonably be styled an
oubliette. (Also e.g. Alnwick, Cockermouth,
St Andrew's).

OUTREMER

'Christendom beyond the sea' – the name
given to the Christian footholds established in
Syria and Palestine as a result of the Crusades.
The castles of this area, most especially the
splendid Krak des Chevaliers, reflected and
developed Byzantine and Arab military
architecture and the ideas behind them were
brought back to England by returning
Crusaders to affect castle design in this
country.

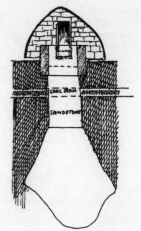

Oubliette, St Andrews

One wonders if 'Acre' as an English place-name is not a nostalgic
reminiscence of the capture of the great Syrian stronghold.

OUTWORK

A fortification advanced beyond the 'enceinte' to defend a vulnerable point
such as a gate or a bridge or to defend supply-route e.g. from dock. Most
commonly occurs to defend entrance – a kind of extended barbican. There are
notable outworks at e.g. Beaumaris, Bodiam, Caerphilly, Harlech, Helmsley,
Pontefract (Swillington Tower).

OVENS   see also Kitchens.

Remains of ovens identify kitchens, bakeries etc. Circular stone ovens survive
e.g. New Hall, Pickering. Some domestic ovens were of vast size e.g. Bolton
(14 ft 6 ins diameter), Ludlow (12 ft 6 ins diameter).

Ovens also had a military function. They were used for heating sand and
missiles to be projected from engines. This was probably the purpose of the
ovens on the summit of Conisbrough keep and the late oven inserted in the
base of a curtain-tower at Ludlow.

OWNERSHIP

Except for royal castles, their custody was related to lordship over
surrounding and supporting lands of which the castle was the 'head'. These
lands had been parcelled out as tenancies by William I among his Norman
followers in return for feudal service and duty. Subsequent proprietorship of
the castles descended to the heirs of the original grantees unless the estates
were recalled to the Crown for treason or rebellion. When this happened
castles and their estates could be redistributed as award for loyalty or in the
hope of maintaining support, or they could be retained in Crown custody, or

they could be returned to the baron from whom they had been escheated after a greater or lesser length of time.

Natural or violent death often changed the possession of castles with considerable rapidity and this process was assisted by forfeiture and dispossession.

OXFORDSHIRE

Never had many castles. There are some remains of the one in the county town but rather less survives of those at Ascott, Banbury and Deddington. There is more at Bampton, while Shirburn is substantially complete and still inhabited. Broughton is more a fortified manor-house and may be associated with Grey's Court and Hanwell. At Beckley, Middleton Stoney, Mixbury and Swerford there are earthworks only.

PALACE

Originally, means no more than a 'hall-house', irrespective of size of hall. Later appropriated to houses with great halls and later still to pretentious houses.

PALISADE

Wooden wall or fence of heavy timbers (something like old railway sleepers), set vertically and touching. One end was fixed deeply in ground and the members were locked together with horizontal beams and braced and propped at the back. The top was either pointed or looped and crenellated. These fences were so effective that they were often not replaced by stone walls for more than a century after a castle was first built.

PARADOS

The inner or rear wall of a wall-walk or allure. It is sometimes found in livery-and-maintenance castles where danger may be expected from within the castle-enclosure.

PARAPET

The battlemented wall protecting a rampart or roof-walk towards the field. It is divided into merlons and crenels (embrasures) (q.v.). At first the embrasures were placed at long intervals but there was an increasing tendency to increase their number by multiplying crenels and decreasing the lengths of the intervening merlons (which were sometimes looped) to give more fire-points for the same distance. Even at their most concentrated, however, the merlon

Parapet

remains broader than the embrasure because a reloading crossbow-man needs more cover than one firing and because of the comparative small size of garrisons. Examples at Caernarvon, Conway.

PARISH

After providing for material security, Norman lords took care of their own (and dependents') spiritual welfare. Castles were equipped with chapels at an early stage in their completion (sometimes there was a chapel even before the castle was built). The chaplain early seems to have developed his pastoral care to include the castle's dependents. Bailey chapels often seem to have become parish churches and some still exercise this function. The curious boundaries of existing parishes are often due to their following the 'marches' of a Norman manor. Originally, the parish was the manor considered ecclesiastically and the lord often provided the church for his tenants (hence continuing right or presentation or advowson) within the castle or in its immediate vicinity. Consequently the castle church sometimes survives as the parish church when the castle has disappeared.

PARISH CHURCH

Usually lies within village-enclosure often associated with castle and forming a kind of outer bailey. Sometimes an outer bailey was added to the castle defences to enclose the church, for the protection of both (since on more than one occasion the church tower was used as a counterfort in a siege).

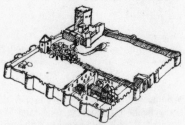

Porchester Castle
(with Parish Church within Enceinte)

In these cases the church seems to have served both the civil parish and the military garrison. A good example of this former dual purpose is the church of St Leonard, Farleigh Hungerford, which still contains a mural painting of a gigantic knight.

PARK

An area, enclosed with palings or ditches, associated with a castle or large house to provide a private hunting or recreational area, as distinct from the forest.

PASSIVE RESISTANCE

Castles have often been stigmatised (particularly in their earlier period) as offering only passive defence and showing the grave error of purely defensive thinking. This is unfair and shows a misunderstanding of their function. Most castles were the houses of great lords which needed to be defended against either local rising or invasion. The fact that it was necessarily static necessarily limited its military function. Nevertheless even the earliest castles were far from inactive. Their garrisons often met the enemy in the field and even sieges were characterised by offensive sorties which were often successful. Sally-ports (q.v.) are of frequent occurrence and the provision of a sally-port sufficiently massive to be almost indistinguishable from the main gate is a feature of late C13 and early C14 castles. It must be remembered that knights were always horsed and that infantry were often mounted (particularly when they formed part of a castle garrison).

PAVILION

The high peaked tents providing individual accommodation for the knightly class (and perhaps their servants). They appear in mediaeval pictures of sieges and tournaments, usually decorated with pennants and shields of arms. From this developed the later meaning of accommodation for players (and spectators) at outdoor sports.

PAVIS(E)   see also Mantelet.

Large wooden shield protecting individual, particularly used in sieges or during the tenancy of a fixed position. It is also used of the individual protection carried by miners or assault parties (some knights had a subordinate called a 'pavisour' to carry the protection). They were often provided with props to maintain them in a near vertical position and occasionally were mounted on a wheeled frame so that they could be moved easily.

   Pavises were often highly decorated and bore the armorial bearings of the knight they protected, or his overload.

Erecting Pavilion

PEEBLESHIRE

Near the county town is Neidpath Castle. Traquair is also worth a visit.

Scottish Soldier Behind Pavise

PELE-TOWER

Strong tower, rather less grand than the great tower-keep, erected as place of refuge and watch on the Scottish border. They were built from C12 to C17 (and after) and, without other evidence are often difficult to date on architectural grounds. Bowes comes from C12, while Chipchase and Belsay ('most handsome building of its kind in the North of England'), are C14. Another C14 example is Gilling which recalls the C12 keeps. The towers at Shortflatt, Shield Hall, Tarset may be C13. Most English pele-towers are C15-16 while most Scottish ones C16-17. 'Pele' is cognate with 'pale' and means 'enclosure' and the tower usually had an attached walled yard or 'barmkin' (q.v.).

Belsay Castle (Pele)

137

Typically, they are rectangular in plan with a tunnel-vaulted ground floor (as a protection against fire). The entrance was on this floor which served as stable or store. The door was wooden but protected by a heavy framework of iron on its outer face (see Yett). From the corner of the entrance floor a vice gave access to two (or more) upper floors which provided living quarters and defensive positions. The first floor was usually occupied by the hall or main living room with the sleeping chamber on the floor above. Both floors were usually provided with privies and their summits battlemented and often machicolated.

Pele-towers are particularly frequent in Northumberland where some of them provided accommodation for vicar or rector (see Vicar's Pele) but they also occur in Southern Scotland and were once popular in Derbyshire (both Peveril and Haddon seem to have developed from simple pele-towers). Peles sometimes had a chapel in the barmkin as castles had one in the bailey – one dedicated to 'Our Lady of the Pele-yard' is mentioned at Prudhoe in C14.

PEMBROKESHIRE

The great honour of Pembroke supported an Earl Palatine and there are plenty of reminders of the county's former military importance: Pembroke itself, Manorbier the home of Giraldus Cambrensis, the episcopal palace of Llawhaden. In addition there are substantial remains at Carew, Cilgerran, Haverfordwest, and rather less at Narberth. Newport, Picton, Roche, Tenby, Upton and Wiston.

PENNANT

Long tapering heraldic flag. In 1283 Adam the Tailor was paid 44s for four pieces of silk to make pennants and royal standard for Rhuddlan.

PENNON

A small flag, usually swallow-tailed at the fly, borne on a knight's lance just behind the blade.

PENTHOUSE (Pent, Pentise).

The basic meaning seems to be a sloping roof, either single or double (like an inverted V). A building with such a roof (e.g. those in bailey with roof sloping up to curtain) was called a pentise or penthouse.

The word is also applied to the covered passage, built of stout timber and covered with raw hides, which protected soldiers or workmen constructing a sap or mine within range of the enemy, or those building a causeway across a ditch, or hacking with picks, axes or martels at the footing or lower face of a wall.

The name is also given to the covered passages over the paths between isolated domestic buildings within the bailey. Such passages were often simple structures with open sides but, in later castles, they could be entirely enclosed with windows, panelling and even fireplaces.

PERTHSHIRE

Its notable castles include Claypotts, Doune, Elcho, Huntingtower and Kinclaven. Others well worth mentioning include Alyth, Blair Athol, Comrie

(Coshieville), Grandtully, Killin (Finlarig),
and Moulin.

Castle Fraser

PETRARIA   see also Mangon, Trebuchet.

A general name for the great
stone-throwing engines against
whose battering the prodigious
thickness of curtains and the
deflective spur were
developed.

   Ideally, the stone projectiles
were cut to a weight and shape
related to the engine and the
objective. Some stones were
intended to fragment with the
effect of shrapnel, others to
batter towers and walls. At his
siege of Bedford (1224),
Henry III ordered the sheriffs
of Bedfordshire and
Northamptonshire to send
without delay 'all the quarriers
and stone-cutters of your
jurisdiction, with levers,
sledges,

Elcho, Perthshire

mallets, wedges and other of
their necessary tools to work stones for mangonels and petraria'. He had six
mangonels and a trebuchet in action at the time.

PHEON

A heavy iron javelin fired from the great crossbow, springald or
springal. In a conventionalised form it figures as a charge on
numerous armorial bearings e.g. Smith, Colt, Baron De L'Isle
and Dudley.

Head of Pheon

PIGEONS   see also Dovecote.

Doubtless formed a useful supplement to the garrison's
provisions, fresh meat which did not require feeding. A vaulted
chamber survives at the summit of Conisbrough keep which was a
pigeon-cote, pierced by numerous holes about 6 ins square. There is a similar
provision at Threave.

PIPE ROLLS

The annual accounts which the sheriffs rendered to the king from C12. They
provide a rich source of information about expenditure on royal castles. They
get their name because the large rolled parchments have the appearance of a
pipe.

PISCINA

The 'sacred sink' of a church or chapel, used in ceremonies of Mass. In castle-chapels, as elsewhere, often richly and elaborately carved e.g. Bodiam, Conisbrough, Weobley.

PIT AND GALLOWS

Judiciary rights vested in some castles by which their court could commit an accused to prison or death. These barony courts were held either in the Great Hall or in the square before the castle gate. A C16 picture of Corfe shows stocks and pillory in front of the gate and the outline of the castle gibbet on a nearby knoll. (see Killin, Perths.).

PITCH OF ROOF   see also Creasing.

Earlier keeps had steeply inclined roofs, sometimes of double pitch (like letter M). Their vulnerability had to be masked by carrying the wall height to the level of the gable(s). This led to a great deal of wasted space and, when the use of lead became common, the pitch was lessened or even replaced by a flat roof to give extra accommodation for the same height. The interior of keeps often show signs of this modification.

A Felon Awaits the Scaffold

PLACE-NAMES

May give the explorer a clue. 'Tower' is pretty obvious, as is 'castle' whether as a separate word (Castle Bromwich, Castle Ings, Elmley Castle) or as an element in a word (Castleton, Newcastle). Burgh, Brough or Borough is both less obvious and even less reliable.

Wales offers 'castell' and 'Caer' may be a clue, as may 'Tomen'.

Scotland has Mains, Bordland (Borland), Ingliston, and variants of Fleming (Flemington, Flinders, Flanders) may sometimes point to an existing or vanished stronghold.

PLAN

Earliest mottes are generally a circle with additions often

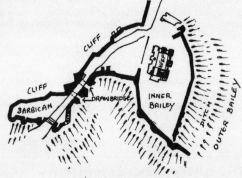

Plan of Scarborough

140

formed of segments of a circle.

The development of lofty stone walls and towers led generally to the abandonment of a curved plan, though there are some late examples (Sedgwick, 1257, Scaleby, 1307).

The logical and economic form was the late rectangular plan with a projecting tower at each corner e.g. Kidwelly (c. 1244), within earlier castle; Barnwell (1264), Goodrích (C13-14), Somerton (1281).

The C14 saw the appearance of the regular and standardised form of concentrated rectangular plan: curtain walls which served as walls of domestic apartments, forming a rectangle with towers at angles, gatehouse in centre of one long side, four ranges backing on to curtain with comparatively small central courtyard (or none at all). Bodiam (1385) is best southern example, Bolton best northern (1379). Off-shoots of this idea are found e.g. Cooling, Hever.

PLASTER

External walls were usually plastered and whitewashed. Orders of Henry III survive for whitewashing Corfe, Rochester and White Tower. Chaucer's 'Long castell, with walles white' (Dethe of Blaunche the Duchess) may be a reminiscence of Pontefract. Internal walls were plastered, sometimes with fine gypsum from Montmartre which gave name to 'plaster of Paris' e.g. dais end of Nottingham hall (1251). More common after discovery of gypsum at Purbeck but kept name.

PLINTH

Keeps were often raised on a battered (q.v.) plinth, e.g. Scarborough, to give additional protection against miners etc. The heights of these platforms can vary considerably e.g. Bamburgh 5 ft 6 ins Conisbrough 20 ft, Kenilworth 12 ft.

POMERIUM

Passage between rear of town walls and nearest houses to provide access to wall-walk and towers. (From Latin 'pone muros' – 'at the back of the walls'.) Southampton still has lane called 'Back of the Walls', Caernarvon has a complete pomerium except on west, there are survivals at Newcastle (particularly on N.W.) and the lanes exist at e.g. Bristol, Northampton.

Conisbrough with Battered Plinth

PORTCULLIS (Herse).

A gate which drops vertically through slots. It is normally of oak open-work, terminating in spikes, plated and shod with iron. Its massive weight is quickly released by knocking away a wedge or ratchet in the chamber above which also contained the windlass or winding-drum to

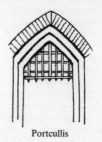

Portcullis

141

raise it by pulleys and ropes and chains. This task was often made easier by the use of counterbalancing weights.

The drop-gate seems to have been invented by the Romans as early as 208 B.C. The idea was preserved by the Byzantines and (re)-introduced into these islands in early C12 (e.g. Arundel, Colchester, Rochester, Tickhill) and became general in C13 and after. The grooves which guided and held the portcullis are still to be seen in the door-jambs of many gateways and doors (Bolton had a portcullis to every external door), but portcullises themselves are a very rare survival and noteworthy. The portcullis was sometimes worked in conjunction with the drawbridge as a counter-poise so that when the drawbridge was down, the portcullis was up and vice-versa. Windlass-rooms remain at e.g. Berry Pomeroy, London Tower, York bars. Many gatehouses show evidence of possessing more than one portcullis e.g. each gateway at Beaumaris was designed to have three portcullises and the keep-gatehouse at St Briavel's has three main portcullises with additional small ones to defend the doorways from the entrance passage to the porter's lodges.

Portcullis winding Gear
(London Tower)

In the Scottish attack on Linlithgow, the portcullis was rendered inoperative by a stratagem. A hay-cart, driven by disguised soldiers and with others concealed in its load, was deliberately halted under the portcullis. When they attacked the guard and the alarm was given, the loaded cart prevented full descent and supporting soldiers entered under it.

The portcullis is a familiar heraldic charge. It was the badge of the powerful Beauforts and adopted by the Tudors.

PORTER   see Household.

POSTERN   see also Sally-port, Watergate.

Postern and sally-port are often used as though they were interchangeable, but perhaps they should be usefully distinguished.

A postern is a small door or secondary gate for use when the main-gate is inconvenient or when its operation is unnecessary. They provide ingress for men and materials of the lighter kind and are often placed in close proximity to the kitchen e.g. Warkworth. They were also used for surreptitious entry and exits and their openings are often masked on the outside. They occur near keeps and almost always away from the main entrance where the attention of the besiegers would tend to be concentrated. They

Castellan escapes via
high Postern in Tower

also occur in the base of a tower or exit through the curtain (e.g. the posterns at Pontefract and Ludlow, the latter with a dog-leg). There is a good postern at Harlech, approached by a small doorway in the wall of the inner ward, which pierces the outer curtain flanked by a bastion and then doubles along the face of the rock to end at the water-gate. The postern at Scarborough leads to the harbour.

Some posterns seem very much an 'emergency exit' as they open high on curtain walls or in the flank of a keep and presuppose a rope-ladder. (The Bayeux tapestry portrays such an escape.)

A postern in the Black Gate, Newcastle, seems to have been gained from the drawbridge pit (c.f. Helmsley) and there is one at Carew from the basement of a wall-tower to the scarp of the ditch while the postern at Pickering had its own drawbridge.

PREFABRICATION

We know that oak roofs were sometimes made in one place, taken apart for transport and re-assembled in their designed position. The same seems to have been true of military engines and defences.

In 1221 we hear of a bretteche being moved from Nafferton to Newcastle, Northd. and in 1216 of towers being translated from Knepp, Sussex, to Dover. The king's siege train of artillery doubtless carried the great engines in sections designed for quick assembly.

PRICES

Examples from 1286:

Charcoal (for forges) – 1½d per quarter.
Sea-coal from 4d to 6d a ton according to season.
Lead – 26s a carrat, i.e. a cartload weighing c. 1200 lbs.
iron – 2d a piece, 8s 10d a cartload, including carriage.

Charcoal Burners

Steel – £3.6.6 a barrel, including carriage from Newcastle-under-Lyme to Chester.
Tin – 500 lbs for £3.11.4 (about 8½d a lb).
Timber – shingles (for roofs). 3s 6d a 1,000 boards from 1s 4d to 3s a 100 (according to size presumably).
Sand – about 3s 6d a ton-mile for transport.

PRISONS   see also Oubliette.

A good deal of variety, from lightless and damp holes to comfortable 'house arrest'. Mediaeval records are full of references to the castle goal and from time to time resound with complaints, true or false, concerning unjust imprisonment and other misdemeanours of the constable responsible.

The constable could incur a crippling fine if a prisoner committed to him escaped and an angry constable of Banbury, having recaptured one, executed him on the spot. Escape from 'durance vile' cannot have been easy but distinguished prisoners often seem to have been kept under a quite loose, and not uncomfortable, form of restraint in which their prison walls were co-extensive with the walls of the enceinte and they had their own servants and food (though they had to pay for both e.g. in the reign of Richard II, a yeoman and some servants confined in the Tower 'with their master' had a weekly food allowance of 3s 4d.) In John's reign some loosely restrained prisoners at Corfe rioted and took over the keep.

Gaoler incarcerating
Prisoners in the Tower

Prisoners could vary from minor criminals awaiting trial to high-ranking prisoners for political offences or in protective custody. Eleanor of Aquitaine was held for many years in Salisbury keep, though she was able to maintain accurate political intelligence and communication. Another Eleanor, sister of the Arthur whom John allegedly murdered, languished 40 years in Bristol before her death in 1241. John was also accused of starving to death in Windsor the entire family of his former comrade, William de Braose. Berkeley witnessed the atrocious murder of Edward II in 1327 while London Tower received many who never passed out of its gates, including the Duke of Clarence and the children of Edward V among others less distinguished. The mighty stronghold of Pontefract saw the imprisonment and death of Thomas of Lancaster (1322), Richard II (1400), Earl Rivers and four other noblemen (1483). Scrope, Archbishop of York, was imprisoned and condemned to death there and other distinguished captives included James I of Scotland (1405-1424) and Charles, Duke of Orleans (1417-30).

Prisoner attempting Escape

The association of prison and tower led to the change in the meaning of dungeon, though few towers (except Scottish ones) were initially equipped with a prison. Exceptionally, London Tower had an unpleasant chamber called 'Little Ease' two floors beneath the chapel and Lydford keep (1195) was built specially as 'a strong building for prisoners' who were kept in the basement which was half-buried in the earlier motte and lit only by three loops. Special chambers for holding prisoners seem usually to postdate C12 when they are found in gatehouses and the basements of mural towers. There is a large prison tower annexed to the King's Gate, Caernarvon, while at Goodrich it is next to the keep.

Most prisoners were probably only short term, awaiting trial or paying the penalty. Imprisonment was not a usual punishment for criminal offences in the Middle Ages. The Coleman Tower, Pickering, was probably to hold those accused of offences against the forest laws until the justice's arrival. Though many chambers described as prisons were in fact storehouses or even latrines, later castles usually had a strong-room for this purpose e.g. Bolton, in the basement of tower, still with staple for fetters; Knaresborough, cellar under kitchen – itself in basement of keep; Pontefract, beneath bailey; Rising – basement of forebuilding, 'a gruesome pit'; Skenfrith – basement of S.E. tower, more an oubliette (q.v.); Warkworth – basement of keep, equipped with fireplace, cupboards, privy; Warwick – basement of tower with observation gallery for warder; Windsor – basement of (aptly named?) Devil's Tower.

The gatehouse was probably the commonest location of the castle prison (e.g. Arundel, Cockermouth). The prisons in the gatehouse at Alnwick have oubliettes below them and there was a similar arrangement at Cockermouth.

PRISONERS' CARVINGS

Prisons contain many inscriptions (mostly from C17 e.g. London Tower, Pontefract, Warwick). The most interesting are C14-15 carvings in Carlisle which have many typical mediaeval subjects including heraldry, dragons, mermaids, stags, fox preaching to geese, Justice, Wheel of Fortune, Our Lady, and the Crucifixion.

Prisoners' Carvings, Carlisle

PRIVACY   see also Hall.

There was not a lot in earlier castles where eating and a good deal of sleeping was communal. One can trace the gradual withdrawal of the lord and his family into increasingly private apartments but even Henry III, during his occupancy of the Council Chamber at Rochester, complained that his privacy was disturbed by the garrison passing through on their way to chapel.

PRIVY (Chamber)   see also Sanitation.

Mediaeval name for latrine, along with 'necessarium', 'jakes', 'draught', 'gong'. There is even evidence of early euphemism if 'petits mesons' in a constable's letter of 1306 refers to this convenience. The latrine-pit emptiers are called 'mudator latrinarum'

Persisting Mediaeval Tradition

or 'gong-farmers'. Unlike the monastic 'reredorter', castle privies were generally crude and often consisted simply of a stone seat over a voiding shaft which discharged into a pit or ditch. A wooden seat survives at Bungay and it is likely that the stone seats were generally covered. Some outlets were flushed by a stream (e.g. Christchurch, Langley) and more sophisticated systems were provided in later castles (e.g. Beaumaris, Caernarvon, Denbigh, Rhuddlan). Most privies at Bolton were equipped with lights and wash-basins.

Chateau Gaillard was entered via latrine shaft and subsequently the exits were blocked by stone division or iron grilles and sometimes concealed by masonry screens or grotesque masks (e.g. Beaumaris, Conway, Harlech).

Keeps had their privies in mural chambers (often approached through dog-legged passages) and the seat was often corbelled out from the wall (e.g. Chipchase, Corbridge, Guildford, Peveril, Portchester), or carried on a squinch-arch e.g. Conisbrough. Keep chambers often had a privy 'en suite' (e.g. Newcastle) as had prisons (e.g. Bolton). In major apartments they were supplemented by the 'chamber pot' and later by 'close stool'. Hay seems generally to have been used for 'bumf'. Most latrines had facilites for natural and artificial light and seem to have been used for private reading as recommended in the popular 'Life of St Gregory'.

Larger castles grouped the garrison privies into a latrine tower (e.g. Dunstanburgh, Framlingham, Ludlow, Manorbier, Middleham, Richmond). Entire N.W. turret of Kenilworth is given over to latrines with pit in basement. Coity has outstanding provision of this kind with a hierarchial arrangement. They were also located in walls (curtain at Conisbrough, town walls at Conway where 12 cost £15 in 1282). One gets the impression that they were often sited so as to provide additional hazard for assailants.

PROFESSIONALS

Among the highly skilled persons employed in the building and maintenance of castles were engineers (q.v.), masons and carpenters who were essential for offensive and defensive siege structures in addition to their normal duties.

Master-carpenter Nicholas worked for King John for 9d a day, his robes and a gift of land. Similarly, Master-mason John was paid 20s a year, a mark for robes every alternate year and occasional 'gifts' or tips of one mark (13s 4d). Master-craftsmen were assisted by their 'mates' or 'associates' (the Latin word is socii, the one used for 'fellows' of a college).

Records refer to 'ingeniatores' (engineers), 'cementarii' (stone-masons), 'petrarii' (stone-cutters), 'quaeretores' (quarrymen), 'carpentarii' (carpenters), 'minatores' (miners), 'fossatores' (ditchers). These professionals did not consider their area of competence in a narrow spirit, as carpenters could erect a hall roof or carve a stall in the college chapel, so ditchers worked on mines, siege-engines, moats, vaults and foundations.

There were also 'hurdatores' who constructed hoarding (q.v.) and 'piccatores' – demolition men who assaulted occupied castles or sometimes 'slighted' surrendered ones with their picks.

PROJECTILES   see also Arrows, Bolt, Quarrel.

Both mangonel and trebuchet were 'petraria', machines designed to hurl specially shaped and weighted stones, but in the exigencies of a hard-pressed siege they could make use of anything that came to hand. In particular, they frequently discharged containers (usually pottery) of inflammable liquid ('Greek Fire' q.v.). There are also illustrations of them loaded with dead horses ('germ warfare') or even human heads ('terror').   The ballista (and its successor, the springal) was an enormous fixed crossbow whose ammunition

Human Heads as Ammunition (Nicea 1097)

was iron shafts, wooden stakes or large javelins (pheons). Often these had incendiary material attached.

Stones had both impact and shrapnel effect. Bolts were accurate missiles for individual targets.

At last siege of Bedford (1224) a lord among the besiegers was seriously wounded by a bolt which penetrated the front of his armour and over 200 of their artillerymen became casualties as a result of the besieged's concentrated fire on the siege-engines.

PROVISIONS   see also Stores.

Perhaps the most vital factor in a castle's resistance to siege was an adequate supply of provisions without which even the strongest and most stoutly manned castle must fall in time. The most necessary provision was water (see Wells) which could usually be secured permanently. Food, without the resources of canning and refrigeration, was a more difficult affair. Sometimes a garrison was reduced to a diet of water and horse-meat (Rochester 1216) while Kenilworth's surrender in 1266 was largely the result of starvation.

Provisions

Records give some insight into the implications of stocking royal castles in preparation for hostilities: corn is bought in bulk and hand-mills are supplied to grind it within the castle (though some castles had mills powered by animals or water). The meat is usually pork or bacon, bought 'on the hoof' together with vast quantities of salt to preserve it when slaughtered. In 1215, 80 cows (costing £16) and 130 sheep (£6.10.0) were brought into the bailey of Lancaster. Bedford had livestock in the outer bailey when the castle fell in 1224. There is much mention of cheese, beans and oats (presumably for horses, at least in part), malt and barley for beer, and vast quantities of wine. When the besiegers of Bedford stormed into its outer bailey in 1224 they captured many stores including horses and harness, hauberks, suits of mail, crossbows, livestock and corn. In face of threat from his son, Henry II ordered Salisbury to be stocked with, inter alia, 125 measures of corn (£21), 120 'bacons' (£10.16.8), 400 cheeses (£8), 20 measures of beans (60s), 20 measures of salt (30s), 60 measures of malt (£9.0.10). Caerphilly (c. 1320) contained:

78½ quarters of corn (three years old)
34 quarters of corn (two years old)
10½ quarters wheat malt
71½ quarters new beans
41 quarters old beans
7 bushels of mixed beans and barley
2 tons of pilcorn
9½ quarters of oatmeal
7 bushels of oatmalt
64 new carcasses of salted meat
14 old carcasses of salted meat

147

81 oxhides
40 mutton carcases
20 new hams, 52 old hams, 1,856 stockfish
Large quantities of wine, honey and vinegar.

Provisions could also be critical for the besiegers, particularly if the enemy had adopted 'a scorched earth' policy. An English army besieging Dirleton (1298) was reduced to eating field beans and would have been forced to abandon the siege but for the timely arrival of a provision ship in the Firth of Forth.

PUT-LOG HOLES

Holes or recesses high in the face of masonry are for the support of put-logs i.e. the horizontal members of the scaffolding used in building or repair. They should not be confused with similar holes facing the field below the wall-walk which held the brackets to support the hoarding (q.v.) or with holes to carry the end of joists etc.

Put-log holes often lie on a quite sharp diagonal line whereas the other varieties are horizontal.

QUARREL   see also Bolt.

Bolts and quarrels were the missiles fired from crossbow. As with arrows, different ammunition was used for different purposes. The word 'quarrel' is probably derived from French 'carreau' meaning 'diamond' or 'with square facets'. This missile is developed from the bolt and designed to reduce the chance of its glancing off heavy armour. It had a heavy four-sided metal head, usually with a small sharp point on each corner, and was capable of delivering a tremendous smashing blow on almost any surface. If, occasionally, it did not achieve complete penetration, it still could unhorse a mounted knight or smash a foot-soldier to the ground and the wounds it caused were of a particularly fearsome nature.

The expression 'to pick a quarrel' derives from the crossbow-man's careful choice of a particularly effective missile to discharge against a specific and chosen enemy.

Another kind of war-head was called a 'pile' which possessed a cylindrical head or one drawn to a bullet-shaped point.

QUERN

Small hand-mill for grinding corn.

QUINTAIN

Apparatus to provide military exercise or sport. It usually consisted of an upright stout post or plank which made a target and might be provided with a dummy head or shield at which darts or javelins were hurled or which provided a mark for tilting at with a lance. A more complex form had a long horizontal arm whose centre was pivoted on a post and which carried the target (usually a shield) at one end and a counter-balancing sand-bag at the other. A hit

Pike-Heads

Tilting at Quintain

caused this weight to swing round and unhorse a careless rider who had failed to take avoiding action or who rode an inadequately trained horse.

RADNORSHIRE

In spite of its strife-torn history and legend (Vortigern is associated with Glasbury-on-Wye and the last Welsh prince was slain in its mountains), the county has few notable remains.

Radnor was a fortified town 'with a large and strong castle' in 1610, all that remains of the town walls is street-alignment and, of the castle, earthworks. Little survives of the Mortimer stronghold at Dinbaud, there are traces of about eight motte-and-baileys e.g. Bleddfa, Crug Eryr, Cymaron, Painscastle.

RAM

Heavy beam swung from a massive timber framework or a smaller version carried by an assault party. The great engines had a heavy iron-shod head (sometimes depicted as that of a ram – which might have been used in early versions) that could deal weighty blows against heavy doors and/or against masonry until they broke up. Its operators were either protected by cats (q.v.) or the ram was suspended from the ridge of a stout timber house on wheels with its roofs (and sometimes its sides) covered with iron plates or raw hides as a protection against missiles, particularly incendiary ones.

Ram

In order to approach objectives protected by ditches etc., the path of rams had to be cleared, levelled or filled by men working in cats. The heavy ram, as distinct from the great log picked up to assault a gate, was slung from the ridge-pole or poles of its penthouse by a series of chains and was swung rhythmically by a team of trained soldiers once they came within range. The penthouse was propelled towards its object by men using poles and when they had gained the operational position, the wheels were taken off and the frame pegged down.

The ram was no doubt effective against wooden defences but with the coming of masonry they were only useful against corners or thin walls. They were also slow and vulnerable to counter-action which could be directed against the operators or the machine itself whose head might be grasped by forks or large pincers or its effect nullified by lowering thick matting to absorb impact. From the late C12 they tended to be replaced in formal siege-operations by trebuchets and other powerful battering engines.

RAMPART

In earthworks and timber fortifications, it consisted of a broad earth baulk with a stockade along its outer edge to provide a protected fighting platform for defenders. Loosely used for any fortification in which defenders are defended by a parapet; thus the tops of curtain, or towers where the men stood behind battlements are called ramparts.

As the earthbank was replaced or heightened by a wall, so the palisades in front of the fighting platform were replaced by a narrow stone wall and the allure sometimes had an even lighter wall (parados) at its rear. From a very early date in stone fortification (probably continuing a practice used in the earlier stockades) it was customary to indent the wall facing the enemy with openings called 'crenels' which gave protection to the archer and provided a limited field of fire towards the field. Sometimes the full height of the parapet wall (merlon) was pierced by loops.

RAMPART WALK   see Allure.

RANSOM

Seems to have been the main material object of mediaeval warfare as far as officers were concerned. A 'king's ransom' was no idle phrase (Richard I's was 100,000 lbs of gold) and that of a noble could produce the wherewithal for his captor to build a castle. Less distinguished prisoners seem to have been assessed at the value of their armour (as in a tournament). The third earl of Douglas, taken at Poitiers (1361) clad in a splendid suit of armour, was saved from a crippling assessment of ransom because a fellow prisoner convinced their captor that he was but a worthless servant masquerading in his master's mail. From his ransom and plunder in the French wars, Sir John Falstolf not only built Caister castle but left in his will (1459): £2,643 in ready cash, 98 ozs of gold plate and 14,813 ozs of silver. In his life-time he had been accustomed to banquet 100 guests served from silver and silver-gilt plate and wined from over 200 gallons of fine red wine which he habitually kept in his cellars.

RECREATION   see
Amenities, Entertainment.

RENFREWSHIRE

Not rich in castles but Crookston and Newark (Port Glasgow) deserve a mention.

RETINUE   see also
Robber Barons.

The personal following of a tenant based on his land-holding and its sub-letting into manors. C14 retinues include: Richard, Lord Talbot – 14 knights, 60 squires, 82 archers; John de Vere, Earl of Oxford – 23 knights, 44 squires, 63 archers. The Clifford lords of the honour of Skipton put into the field 60 men-at-arms and 40 archers (c. 1380) and 50 men-at-arms and 150 archers (1415).

Newark (from South), Renfrewshire

A Humble Retainer

150

These personal followers wore the lord's livery (q.v. and heraldry) and constituted an escort for display of status, a bodyguard, a means of intimidation and sometimes a private army.

REVENUES

Incomes to castles could come from many directions, including re-routing from the Exchequer or Wardrobe in the case of Royal establishments. There were also rents from manors, work-service (including agricultural work), receipts from pasturing in its forests and the sale of timber. Many of its needs were self-provided: hay from meadows, game from forests, pigeons and fish, beef and mutton. There were cash profits from farming too, especially from the sale of wool from the castle sheep (Pickering had 1,600 sheep in 1322). There were also fines from the castle courts. Pickering's revenues in 1314 came to £385,19.3½ and its expenditure to £367.1.9 (almost all on New Hall). There were occasional 'windfalls' due to a fortunate marriage or inheritance and there was always the profession of arms: loot and ransom in war, tournaments in peace. Not a few castles were built from the spoils of the French wars e.g. Caister, Herstmonceux, Nunney.

REVETMENT

An outwork, embankment or bastion faced with layer of masonry for additional strength. Walls of revetment are walls used to face a sloping surface (of earth or rock) for strength, to prevent slippage and to produce more nearly vertical surface (e.g. keep at Pontefract whose underlying motte is enclosed on three sides by such walls).

RICHARD I (1157-99)

Brought from Crusades new concepts and techniques: exemplified at Chateau Gaillard, renovation of London Tower at cost of £3,000, introduction of round towers e.g. Bell Tower at London, keep at Pembroke.

RING-WORK

A roughly circular earthwork of bank and ditch.

ROBBER BARONS   see also Anarchy.

Richard I (from seal)

There was a spurt of baronial castle-building when the direct royal succession was broken by loss of Henry I's only son in the White Ship. Disaster and power was gained by such ruffians as Geoffrey de Mandeville who in 1146 had 'not only the Tower of London in his hand, but also castles of impregnable strength built around the city; and all that part of the city which recognised the king [Stephen] he had so securely subjected to his control that, throughout the kingdom, he acted in the king's place'.

Roofs

Similar situations occurred at other times. A Florentine visitor reported in later C13:

'We passed through many woods considered here as dangerous places, as they are infested with robbers; which indeed is the case with most of the roads in England. This is a circumstance connived at by the neighbouring barons, from the consideration of a share in the booty and these robbers giving personal service to their protectors on all required occasions with the full strength of their hand. As the English barons are frequently embroiled in disputes and quarrels with their sovereign and each other, they take the precaution of building strong castles for their residence, surrounded by deep moats and high turrets and strengthened with drawbridges, posterns and portcullises. And further, to enable themselves to hold out for a considerable length of time in case they should happen to be besieged, they make a provision of victuals, arms and whatever else is necessary for the purpose.'

Geoffrey de Mandeville

Soldiers looting Hall

Of Sir John Barry, builder of Dudley in early C14, a contemporary report says:

'He has obtained such mastery in the County of Stafford that no-one can obtain law nor justice therein; that he has made himself more than a king there; that no-one can dwell there unless he buys protection from him either by money or by assisting him to build his castles, and that he attacks people in their own houses with the intention of killing them unless they make fines for his protection.'

ROOFS

Usually timber framed and covered with various materials depending on resources, but including thatch, oak shingles, slates, stone flags, clay tiles. The former were susceptible to fire which was an inevitable concomitant to war, nevertheless thatch persisted into C13 (e.g. Marlborough). When the owner could afford the great expense, lead was used because it was less combustible as well as being water and wind proof. Sand was sometimes laid beneath the lead to dissipate heat and improve fire resistance. Vulnerable roofs were protected by screen walls or being placed close behind curtain.

Roofs of rectangular plan are usually single or double gables while circular ones usually develop into a cone or dome-shape. Flat roofs were exceptional and stone vaults on uppermost storey are rare. Roof-beams were located in a groove, holes in the masonry or carried on corbels.

They were drained by gutters along the cross-wall (if double gabled) or by side gutters emptied by spout holes or gargoyles issuing beneath rampart walk.

The occupation of the roof for defence was a later development and originally limited to a rampart walk (c. 4 ft wide), sometimes with a rear wall. The field-wall or parapet was sometimes as much as 8 ft high (e.g. Rochester) to protect the vulnerable roof. On great towers angle-turrets provided platforms for observation and their sometimes solid construction may have permitted the mounting of war engines.

ROSS AND CROMARTY

Eilean Donan, Kinkell (Conon Bridge) and motte at Dunscath are worthy of mention.

ROXBURGHSHIRE

Besides remains in the county town there is the famous Hermitage and the less well-known Smailholm Tower. Some motte-and-baileys e.g. Hawick.

Hermitage, Roxburghshire

ROUND TABLE

A chivalrous form of tournament intended to replace the gang melée and its attendant hooliganism by a highly structured entertainment, exhibiting a variety of knightly skills and accomplishments, of which the central feature was a passage of arms between two knights at a time, armed with blunted weapons and governed by conventions which were intended to limit the number and nature of injuries. The whole was set within ritualised forms, accompanied by splendour and involving feasting, music and softer recreations.

Even these entertainments could be lethal and lead to spectator involvement which might end in mass turmoil. Edward, who had introduced the Round Table in imitation of Arthur who was believed to have held court at Windsor, passed a statute (1267) limiting the number of attendants allowed to participants and specifying the weapons which might be carried on these occasions by knights, squires, grooms, footmen, heralds and spectators. There seem to have been no casualties in the tournaments held under his supervision.

Round Table, Winchester
(King Arthur at top, names of knights round perimeter)

ROYAL CASTLES   see Tenure.

Not merely for external defence or internal order but also centres of administration, provincial treasuries and prisons. They provided official residences for sheriffs

Arms: Henry II

153

(who were often constables) and for bailiffs and thus were centres of local government. They were also royal residences, stages for progresses, centres of regal work and recreation.

Nevertheless, they were pre-eminently fortresses in the four centuries in which warfare hinged on and was dominated by the castle. Mediaeval military campaigns consisted largely of sieges and the approach of war is indicated by the stocking, garrisoning and readying of royal castles. They were not only defensive strongholds but bases to command areas and lines of communication. When armies were small and their cohesion brief, command of a territory depended on possessing its castles.

Plantagenet (Conisbrough)
Edward III, Richard II,
Henry IV

Castles expressed both the symbol and reality of temporal power, or lordship 'in castle and tower', it not only conferred prestige on its possessor but was a potent reminder of his existence. They were a visible embodiment of the royal power, flying the king's standard and displaying his arms and badges. Contemporaries described them as 'the bones of the kingdom', providing structure, frame and security. When the royal accounts show expenditure on frontier fortresses it is a sign of external threat as much as spending on internal castles indicates a threat to internal stability.

Henry III was, in 1227, master of nearly 60 castles though the number was reduced to 47 at his death due to gifts, especially to his brother.

RUBBLE

Coarse, and uncoursed, material used for infilling. It was made from the chippings of masoned stone and stones too small to use as ashlar bonded together with a lot of mortar. Occasionally it was used, without ashlar facing, as a wall material. In this case it was held in place with wooden shuttering until the mortar set.

RUTLAND

Only two castles have been listed from this tiny county: Oakham with its magnificent hall and Burley of which only earthworks remain. There may have been a castle at Essendine, there is a gatehouse at Tolethorpe Hall. A former palace of the Bishops of Lincoln at Lyddington was converted into a Bede House in C17 but it retains its watch-tower.

Oakham, Rutland

SALLETS

The armour of archers and 'middling folk': consisting of tough leather coats and helmets, the latter probably made from 'cuirboulli' (boiled leather) which was malleable immediately after boiling but dried very hard and strong.

SALLY PORT

Sometimes used as synonym of postern (q.v.) but usefully distinguished. A gate which allows the besieged to make a sally or sortie (q.v.). It sometimes gave access to neighbouring town, river or sea (e.g. Denbigh). In its fully developed form it became a considerable gateway (e.g. Chepstow, Helmsley, Kidwelly) or a gatehouse which was almost indistinguishable from the great keep gatehouse itself (Beaumaris, Caerphilly).

Sally Port at Bodiam

SALT

An important commodity which had to be carefully looked after. 'Ready-use' salt kept in salt-box in chimney recess (survivals in Scottish tower-houses). Later it would have, in great households, a worthy table-container called 'the salt' which acted as a social demarcation point at a banquet. (Hence 'below the salt'.).

Apart from the flavouring, salt was an important preservative (others were pickling and smoking). Because of the problems of winter feeding much stock was killed off and preserved either by dry-salting (buried in bed of salt pounded to fine powder) or brine-curing in strong salt solution.

SANCTUARY

A castle chapel or church would be assumed to have normal spiritual protection and privilege. This was not always observed: Bruce slew his enemy Comwyn in church and William 'the Lion' indiscriminately massacred 300 refugees sheltering in St Lawrence's minster when he took Warkworth castle (1173).

SANITATION   see also Lavabo, Privy.

Rochester's surrender in 1088 was brought about by absent sanitary provision. Privies were subsequently cut in the walls of stone keeps and later they were provided for individual mural towers and other accommodation (usually crude vents voiding into ditch or shafts emptying into cess-pits).

Henry III was much concerned with this convenience and necessity ('necessarium') and frequently demanded of a constable that he should improve unpleasant aspects of sanitation as he 'values his life and liberty'. In the case of the Tower he wrote:

'Since the privy chamber of our wardrobe at London is situated in an undue and improper place, wherefore it smells badly, we command you on the faith and love by which you are bounded unto us, that you in no wise omit to provide another privy chamber to be made in the same wardrobe in such more fitting and proper place as you may select there, even though it should cost a hundred pounds.'

For its military importance we might cite the case of the high-spirited defenders of Kenilworth (1266) who gave in after six months on account of dysentery.

Sap

SAP

The process of undermining a wall or defensive work; the process of constructing covered trenches in order to approach a besieged place surreptitiously, the trench constructed for such purposes. The most advanced portion of a sap is called a sap-head.

SAPPERS

Strictly should be distinguished from the miners: the sap is the approach trench or tunnel, the mine is the chamber beneath the objective whose firing is designed to wreck the point attacked. Mining is more skilful and technical than sapping. Both sappers and miners were often protected by movable shelters: mantlets or pavises (q.v.) which gave forward cover, or a sapper's tent similar to that used by other assault parties with a strong roof against heavy missiles and covering against incendiaries (usually damped raw hides). Sapping operations were

Sappers' Tent

assisted by diversions and by covering fire from bowmen in forward positions, similarly protected by mantlets.

SCALING LADDER (Sambuca)   see also Escalade.

The necessary utensil for escalade, assault over or on to walls. Sometimes two were carried by the assault party so that one could be used for descent on other side. Some consisted of a single pole with foot-holes or projecting pegs, others were a form of 'rope-ladder' made of leather thongs and equipped with grappling hooks. The development of high curtain walls must have made their employment even more hazardous if not entirely impractical but they persisted thoughout the castle period and took a variety of ingenious forms including 'belfries' and 'lifts'.

The outer defences of Devizes were captured by use of scaling ladders (1140), after which the defenders held out for a time in the keep.

Scaling Ladder in use (from C15 m.s.)

SCARP

The inner face of a ditch (i.e. that which faces field), also used of the steep slope before a wall or tower. 'To scarp' is to cut away earth or rock so as to produce a more precipitous face towards the field.

SCORPION   see Catapult.

SCOTLAND

It is estimated that there are over a thousand castles
and fortified houses with concentration in counties of
Berwick, Dumfries, Kirkcudbright, Peebles, Roxburgh,
Selkirk and Wigtown, of which a high proportion are
still inhabited. About 30 of these latter are open to
view. In addition there are some 50 motte-and-baileys
and a score of ruins which should not be ignored by the
serious castle explorer, including Borthwick, Bothwell,
Caerlaverock, Cawdor, Craigmillar, Doune, Dunottar,
Inverlochy, Kisimul, Rothesay, St Andrews, Tantallon,
Urquhart.

There are significant differences between Scots and
English castle-building which include French influence
but is most affected by the different states of the two
countries.

Fore-Tower,
St Andrews, Scotland

'In England, during the era of settled Tudor
government, the castle as a defended house ceased to
exist. It was replaced by an architectural type
unmistakably domestic. In Scotland, however, there was no such period of
prosperity. Local disturbances succeeded national warfare. The country was
impoverished, its culture backward, and the castle idea long survived, albeit
with ever-increasing concessions to comfort and convenience. Thus there is to
be seen today in great numbers throughout Scotland, the 'Keep' or
tower-house of the late Middle Ages, a gaunt reminder of unsettled times in
an unkindly soil.' (S. Cruden).

SCOTTISH ARCHITECTURAL TERMS

Check : rebate for door, window etc.
Entresol : intermediate storey between two principal floors (mezzanine)
Garner, Girnal House : granary
Ingo : recess c.f. Inglenook
Pend : vaulted passage
Raggle : grooving in wall to receive timber
Roundel : round turret, usually at corner
Scale stair : 'ordinary' stair as opposed to spiral
Shot-hole : gun-loop, often decorated or cut in decorative shape such as
quatrefoil, sometimes closed by internal shutter
Skew-put : English 'put-hole' (q.v.)
Transe : passage
Turnpike stair : spiral stair – also wheel stair
Woman-house : laundry

SCOTTISH CASTLES

Required for two centuries and more longer than English (other than Border)
castles. There was long lack of strong monarchy (from C15 to C16, the only
king who died in bed perished of a broken heart), ancient and continuing

tribal feuds and the nature of the Reformation was more violent than in England. Consequently every laird's house was necessarily a stronghold and all are or were equipped for arquebus defence.

SCOTTISH KEEPS

The great stone tower was rare in England compared with the number of timber halls and towers. Its survival in Scotland is an even rarer phenomenon as it did not penetrate so thoroughly and was probably seen as a mark of alien influence to be reduced whenever possible. There are remains at Castle Sween(?) and Wyre, Orkney (Norse).

SCOTTISH LEGAL TERMS

Barony : land-holding and associated rights granted by royal charter. Could be simple barony, burgh of barony or barony of regality according to the nature and extent of rights involved

Bordland : 'terra mensalis' – the home farm of the castle and source of its normal provisions

Capital messuage : principal dwelling-house of barony, comparable with English manor-house

Conjunct Fee : right (usually land-holding) granted in favour of two persons jointly

Demission : surrender

Escheit : forfeiture

Horn, put to : outlawed

Intromission : assuming possession and management, legally or illegally, of someone else's property

Justice Ayre : circuit for the execution of justice, taking place at intervals of between six months and several years

Poinding : confiscation of debtor's movable property

SCOTTISH MONEY

The Scots £1 was worth about $1/12$ of the contemporary English pound sterling.

SERJEANTY

A variety of tenure (q.v.) by which other than knight-service (q.v.) was required. In serjeanty a fief might be required to furnish auxiliary troops, horses, arms or other useful material (e.g. ballista).

SERPENTINE

Brass cannon of late C15, about twice as big as a 'falcon' and firing a ball of four-five lbs weight.

SCREENS

Wooden partition at lower end of hall to limit draughts (and noise ?) behind which lay the screens passage leading from the entrance and separating screens from kitchens, serveries etc. Screens had three openings, of which two were sometimes mere hatches from bottlery (buttery) and pantry

Screens

(bread store) while the third (usually central) led to the kitchen. The central door might be double for the entrance and exit of servants carrying food to dining tables. The screens often supported a minstrels' gallery facing towards dais and high table at upper end of hall.

SELKIRKSHIRE

Possesses, inter alia, Dryhope Tower (St Mary's Loch) and Yarrow. There is a motte-and-bailey near the county town.

SERVANTS   see also Household.

Great castles supported a multitude of servants: scullions, cooks, laundresses, brewers, bakers, grooms and pages, falconers and huntsmen, doctors and clerks, masons and carpenters, plasterers and painters, smiths and such superior servants as the butler, seneschel, and marshal who were departmental heads.

SHELL-KEEP

Masonry building completely surrounding the summit of a motte or revetted against its lower slopes. The walls varied in height from 20-25 ft and were from 8-10 ft thick, strengthened by buttress and, sometimes, wall-towers. The interior was treated variously: Carisbrooke – a small open court in centre with surrounding pent-house buildings backing on to wall; Lincoln – interior entirely floored over (apart from light-shaft in centre?); Berkeley – two-storeyed buildings around central court with interior of shell crossed by wall supported on arcade.

Shell-Keep, Restormel

Originates as replacement of wooden palisade crowning motte by fire-proof wall. It is hollow because mottes were not strong enough to bear the weight of a solid tower. The domestic buildings of the lord were usually placed within this circular enclosure. This replacement had generally taken place by C13 which often saw the addition of a small gatehouse fore-building. Interesting examples include Lewes (c. 1300) with semi-octagonal wall-towers; York (c. 1312) quatrefoil with rather thin walls and later gatehouse (the idea may have influenced 'keep' at Stokesay); Sandal (c. 1320) with two wall-towers and gatehouse may have provided the model for the (also destroyed) Queenborough (1361). There is a suggestion that the four-lobed tower at York may have influenced other towers with protuberances e.g. gatehouses at Barnwell, Kidwelly, Leybourne.

Other surviving examples at Arundel, Berkhamsted, Brecon, Cardiff, Clare, Durham, Eye, Launceston, Pickering, Plympton, Restormel, Tamworth, Tonbridge, Totnes, Trematon, Warwick, Wigmore, Windsor (all in top of earlier motte).

Examples of revetment: Berkeley, Carmarthen, Farnham, Tretower. Foundations only at e.g. Haughley, Ongar, Tutbury.

The monstrous shell-keep at Acre was 160 ft in diameter.

SHETLAND

Both Muness (the most northerly castle in Britain) and Scalloway present interesting features.

Muness, Shetland

SHIELD   see also Pavise.

A defensive arm which developed from the kite-shaped form of the Normans to the popular 'heater' shape in C13 which broadened in C14 and C15 and then tended to disappear except in heraldry and even there the shape became grotesque.

SHOCK WEAPONS

Include spear, lance, sword, dagger, axe, martel, mace, hills and pikes.

SHOT-HOLES   see Scottish Architectural Terms.

SHROPSHIRE

Shropshire is a border county and therefore had its fill of castles but expectation may be disappointed. Its greatest ruin is Ludlow with some important remains at Shrewsbury. There are keeps, more or less dilapidated, at e.g. Clun, Hopton, Lea, Oswestry, Ruyton. Scant remains at Bishops Castle, Bridgnorth, Broncroft, Caus, Hawkestone, Holdgate, Knockin, Shrawardine and rather more at Moreton Corbet, Wattlesborough, Whittington. There are two very important manor-houses (Acton Burnell, Stokesay) and earthworks at e.g. Bryn Amlwg, Ellesmere, More, Pontesbury.

SHUTTER

Movable device for closing the crenel or opening in wall and thus giving added protection to defenders. Sometimes it was in two parts which could be opened or closed independently. Shutters could be fixed open or allowed to drop back into place after observation or firing. They were hung on iron axles fixed in the outer face of the wall or suspended from trunnions fitted in grooves or holes in adjacent merlons. There are traces of fixing at Alnwick, Maxstoke, Stokesay, Warwick, York walls. The shutters at Alnwick and Corbridge were fixed by a groove at one side and a slot at the other thus ensuring speed in their fitting. At Conway Eastgate there are right-angled stone slabs built into the return of the parapet to give gateway-defenders protection from the field.

Shutter

Apart from crenel shutters, windows were normally closed by shutters especially in their lower portion. These shutters were often bound with iron.

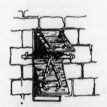

Double Shutter

SIEGE

Mediaeval history is filled with sieges and royal castles, together with any situated on communication lines, were particularly prone e.g. Pevensey was besieged by Rufus, Stephen, de Montfort and again in the reign of Henry IV; Bamburgh was besieged in 1095, 1123, reign of Edward III, 1462, 1464. Alnwick similarly suffered, among other occasions, in 1405, 1462, 1464. Nevertheless, even the most beset fortresses had long periods of domestic quiet and entire generations could live in a castle without ever seeing it put into a state of war-readiness.

The fundamental purpose of besetting, besieging or sitting about a castle was to prevent the reinforcement of men and/or supplies and thus cause its surrender through failure of resources, especially food and drink (but ammunition was important) and thus avoid direct assault. From C13, the besieged began to take a more active role – symbolised by omitting the keep in new castle plans, development of sally ports, moving command to vulnerable point etc. The aggressive tactics of the garrison of Kildrummy (1306) so harassed the besiegers that they were on the point of withdrawal when the castle was fired by a traitor.

A siege was necessarily a long drawn-out process, especially against an adequately armed and provisioned castle. A castle husbanded its resources by collecting and returning usable missiles (Richard I was killed by a returned English bolt). Consequently a formal siege was preceded by attempts to gain speedier submission. It seems that only a minority of sieges were carried through to the bitter end. Most seemed to have been abandoned on the initiative of one side or the other. The besiegers might be outfaced by the massed might of the attackers or the threat of their engines and ask for a truce (q.v.). The besiegers might despair in face of the impregnable strength of their objective or the resolution of its garrison (particularly if they lacked a siege-train).

First, heralds asked for honourable surrender in the face of a vastly superior force. If these overtures were rejected they were followed by a bombardment followed by repeated demands for surrender. If these failed, then a close assault was attempted. These two stages, though theoretically distinct, were in practice usually complementary.

On the one hand, the full-scale investment

Siege

Siege – Desperate Defence

161

and costly assault on a strong position were not undertaken lightly and, on the other, to surrender to a superior force when there was little hope of eventual success or relief was not regarded as dishonourable. The compromise of some sort of truce with agreement to surrender if relief failed to arrive within a specified time was usually acceptable to both sides. War 'a la outrance' was rare and usually the result of highly charged emotion. Yet if a garrison refused all offer of terms and inflicted heavy casualties on the besiegers it seems that it could expect no quarter if the castle was eventually taken.

C12 Siege Warfare from Contemporary m.s.

Further considerations included the facts that feudal levies only owed service for 40 days, that mercenaries were costly and unreliable if not paid promptly, that siege works themselves were costly in men (specialists), materials and transport, that the besieged were vulnerable to supply-failure and besiegers to rear attack by relieving force.

SIEGE OF BEDFORD

A contemporary account gives a vivid picture of a mediaeval siege, resulting from Henry III's determination to crush the rebellious Falkes de Breauté (1224) who had retreated to his castle and offered defiance.

'On the eastern side was a stone-throwing machine and two mangonels which attacked the (new) tower every day. On the western side were two mangonels which reduced the old tower. A mangonel on the south and one on the north made two breaches in the walls nearest them. Besides these, two wooden machines were erected. . . overlooking the summit of the tower for the use of crossbow-men and observers.

In addition there were very many engines positioned which concealed both crossbow-men and slingers. There was also an engine called a 'cat' under whose protection underground diggers, called miners, . . . undermined the walls of the tower and of the castle.

Now the castle was taken through four assaults. In the first, the barbican was captured where four or five of the outer guard were killed.

Assault on Gate

In the second, the outer bailey was taken where there were more casualties and in this place our men captured horses and their harness, hauberks, crossbows, oxen, bacon, live pigs and other things without number. But they burned the buildings stocked with grain and hay. In the third assault, thanks to the work of the miners, the wall near the old tower fell and our men forced an entry through the rubble and occupied the inner bailey at considerable risk. Many of our men perished while achieving this and a further ten who tried to rush the tower were trapped and held prisoner there by the enemy. At the fourth assault, which took place about vesper-time on the Vigil of the Assumption, the miners set a fire under the tower and smoke broke through to the tower room occupied by the defenders and the tower subsided and cracks appeared.

Then the enemy, giving up hope of their safety, allowed Falkes' wife, all the women with her and Henry (de Braybroke), the king's justice (whose capture by Falkes' brother had caused the siege) with other knights whom they had previously imprisoned, to go unharmed. They then made their own submission and hoisted the royal standard to the top of the tower. Thus they remained, under the king's custody, on the tower for that night.

The following morning they were arraigned before the king's tribunal and having been absolved from the excommunication they had incurred by the bishops present, they were condemned by the king and his justice and more than eighty of them were hanged on the gallows.

At the petition of the commander, three Templars were spared by the king on condition that with their Order they should give their service to Our Lord in the Holy Land. The chaplain of the castle was bound over by the archbishop for future trial in an ecclesiastical court.'

End of Siege of Bedford

Falkes himself escaped with his life on condition that he took the Cross and he was allowed to leave the country. His mighty castle which had held out for eight weeks against all the resources of the king was dismantled except for some living quarters in the inner bailey and the stone of the keep, the tower and the outer bailey was given to local churches whose masonry had been robbed by Falkes to strengthen his castle.

SIEGE CONDITIONS

Odericus Vitalis gives a vivid account of the conditions inside Rochester resulting from its protracted siege (1086).

'Innumerable flies were engendered in the excrement of men and horses, and being nourished both by the heat of the summer and the atmosphere caused by the breath of so many inhabitants closely pent up, their swarms horribly infested their eyes and nose, food and drink . . . that they could not eat their meals either by day nor night, unless a great number of them were employed in turns to flap them away from the faces of their comrades.'

During the siege of Kenilworth (1264), the garrison was reduced to living on the flesh of their mounts and became ravaged by dysentary. When the royal forces eventually took possession after the castle's surrender, they were almost suffocated by the stench from the ordure and dead bodies of men and beasts.

SIEGE ENGINES   see also Artillery, Belfry, Cat.

For the great siege of Bedford (see above),

Henry caused siege engines to be carted from Lincoln and Northampton across Oxfordshire while others were built on the spot by carpenters who had ridden post-haste by day and night from the royal stronghold at Windsor. Rope and cables came from Cambridge, London and Southampton; hides for their slings and to protect them from fire from Northampton and tallow for their lubrication from London.

Lack of a siege-train could cause a field force to abandon its attack on a strong and resolute castle (e.g. William the Lion's withdrawal from Newcastle in 1173).

Multi-Purpose Siege Engine

Siege engines and their operators were a special target for the crossbows and engines of the defenders and there could be heavy casualties around them. Apart from this, there could be dangerous misfires e.g. at William the Lion's siege of Wark where such an accident caused the death of one of his knights and the consequent abandonment of the siege. (Perhaps William lacked competent professionals to operate his engines.).

The 'Malvoisin' at the siege of Bamburgh (1095) was sited so close that the castellan (de Mowbray) could shout threats and reproaches at his retainers who had been forced to man it against their overlord.

Siege Engines

SIEGES, NOTABLE

Rochester (1215) was the greatest single military event in civil war which closed John's reign and Magna Carta was among the peace terms. It exemplifies the resistance that a single fortress could offer to royal forces, the effectiveness of mining to reduce keep and the unique use of its cross-wall as a further defence. The fall of such a stronghold produced a temporary loss of confidence in castles.

Dover (1216) is notable for the spirited defence and the elaborate offensive plan for mining which was thwarted by timely relief but produced the building of Spur to stop a similar mine in future.

Bedford (1224), see above. Another example of the concentration of royal military might against a recalcitrant subject. A text-

Besiegers using Cannon and Incendiary Bolts

book case of overcoming defence in depth culminating in successful attack on shell keep and its enclosed tower (similar to Launceston). The garrison, having resisted in spite of excommunication, were hanged.

Kenilworth (1266) where a band of de Montfort's supporters endured for six months against the skill and power of Henry III and the Lord Edward. Mining was impossible because of the broad water defences and it was only through lack of food that the garrison eventually surrendered with the honours of war, after having asked for the conventional truce.

Berkhamsted (1217) against Louis, Dauphin of France, who was still preparing his siege lines when the garrison made a vigorous sally and captured much baggage and equipment. Next day they were assaulted with showers of stones but replied with devastating effect. After a protracted siege, Henry III ordered his constable to surrender (presumably on humanitarian grounds).

When their day was thought to be over, castles suffered long sieges in the Civil War e.g. Corfe (May 1643 – March 1646) and Pontefract (1648 etc.).

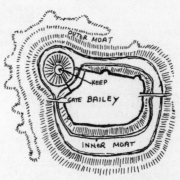

Berkhamsted Showing Siege Works

SIEGE-WORKS

'Stephen's rings' near Corfe were thrown up during his siege (1139) and later (1144) nearly 80 of his workmen were killed while constructing a siege castle against Lincoln, occupied by the rebellious Earl of Chester.

There are also remains of siege-works across the river from Wallingford and a motte-and-bailey out of arrow-range of Huntingdon (1174). The earthwork ½ m. N. W. of Pickering probably represents a siege-work and the emplacements for Louis' trebuchets in the siege of

Corfe in 1643 Siege

1217 can still be seen outside Berkamsted.

In the siege of Hereford castle (1140) the cathedral tower was occupied as a position for archers and catapults. The wall and ditch W. of cathedral might be a siege-work of this date. The mound at Oldbury is probably site of siege castle erected by Henry I at siege of Bridgnorth.

SINKS   see also Lavabo.

Kitchen sinks survive at e.g. Aydon, Compton, Warwick.

SITE

Rational use was made of natural defensive features: island (Kilchurn, Tintagel), peak (Peveril), natural mound (Dumbarton, Kendal), river loop (Durham), promontory (Ludlow, Pembroke), cliff (Carreg Cennen, Kidwelly, Llanstephan), cliff and ravine (Barnard, Dunscaith, Norham).

A high site is characteristic of earlier castles but the ever-present fear of mining led to many later castles being located where a moat or other water defence could be utilised, the only sure defence which would flood any gallery driven towards walls.

Because bridges were few, castles frequently guard river lines e.g. Trent (Nottingham, Newark, Lincoln), Don (Conisbrough, Tickhill) Calder (Sandal), junction of Calder and Aire (Pontefract), Wharfe (Harewood), Ouse (York), Nidd (Knaresborough), Ure (Middleham), Swale

Coastal Defence

(Richmond), Tees (Barnard), Wear (Durham, Brancepeth), Tyne (Prudhoe, Newcastle), Tweed (Norham), Alne (Alnwick), Wansbeck (Mitford), Coquet (Warkworth), Derwent (Pickering, Malton). Similarly, Cleveland had Castleton, Helmsley, Rydale and Skelton while the coast is protected by Bamburgh, Dunstanburgh, Scarborough, Skipsea.

SITES, RE-USED

A number of castles occupy previously fortified sites, occasionally prehistoric. William and his followers sometimes set their castles within Roman fortifications e.g. Lancaster, Lincoln, London, Pevensey, Portchester, Rochester (where the Roman walls bounded the bailey or part of it). In other places they re-used Roman materials (e.g. Colchester, Newcastle). More rarely, they occupied Anglo-Saxon strongholds (Bamburgh, Dover).

SLING

Besides the great siege-engines (q.v.) sometimes called slings there were hand-slings. Pictures of slingers occur in many mediaeval representations of assaults on castles.

SLIT

Narrow vertical aperture in wall, splayed within to give light but prevent entry of people or objects.

Slinger with Staff Sling
(Fustibal) C13

166

By no means all slits are loops (q.v.) for bowmen. An arrow slit must provide stance and considerable depth and some falsely so-called are light and ventilation shafts.

SMITHS

Responsible for the forging and repair of domestic and military iron-work which could vary from kitchen utensils to plates for siege engines and fetters for prisoners. They also sharpened easily blunted tools and weapons, knocked out dents in armour and removed damaged helmets from their owners' heads. Some metal-work e.g. the making of weapons and armour was highly specialised and much was imported.

Smiths mending Armour

Smiths could be required to make weapons, hooks, hinges, screens, bars, window frames, iron doors and portcullises, chains for drawbridges, fire-irons and candelabra, masonry clamps and crampons.

SOLAR

Originally 'solar' or 'soller' seems to have been used indiscriminately of any room, gallery or loft above the ground-level of a building. It more precisely refers to a well-lighted parlour facing south, irrespective of floor level. In general it is a comparatively small room adjacent to the upper end of the hall functioning as a private withdrawing-room for the lord and his family. In keeps it is usually located on a protected side so that it can have windows instead of slits and take advantage of the sun. Sometimes this apartment was the preserve of the lady of the castle (see Bower).

War Preparations. Sword Sharpening

SOMERSET

The noteworthy towers of this county are those of churches, for it is poor in military architecture. The only castles of significance are Nunney and Farleigh Hungerford. After these are Bridgwater, Bristol, Dunster, Newton St Loe, Stogursey, Sutton Court (Stowey), Taunton. We have also included Castle Cary, Neroche, Hether Stowey and Wells, but not the earthworks at Crewkerne, Harptree, Locking, Montacute or Puriton.

SORTIE (Sally).

A sudden attack of the besieged upon the besiegers, usually directed against some particularly menacing work or engine or to relieve pressure upon part of defences. The investing forces had to be always aware of, and provide defences against this possibility since the short internal lines of communication within a castle made rapid concentration easy. Late castles provide large gates to allow considerable force to emerge rapidly and always a large proportion of garrison was mounted.

Sortie

SOW

Like 'cat', a name sometimes given to the protective pentise of a ram or sapping party.

SPIRAL STAIR   see also Stair, Vice.

Many advantages in a military situation: economy of space, could be fitted into thickness of wall, provided constricted and steep access and therefore easily defended. Many stairs are designed to ascend clockwise around the central newel giving an advantage to the defenders by making those ascending the stair expose more of their body in order to use the sword in their right hand.

SPLAY

An aperture which widens as it progresses inwards. Castle windows, particularly loops (q.v.), have usually very broad splays so as to give maximum light with minimum of vulnerable opening. Very wide splays sometimes provided accommodation for more than one bowman while still presenting a very narrow slit towards the field.

Spiral Stair

SPRINGALD (Springal, Springle).

A war engine, projecting heavy dart or lance, which came into general use in C13. It derived its power from a vertical spring-board, fixed at its lower end. The lower end was drawn back by a windlass and, when triggered, punched the after-end of projectile which had been loaded into support in front (like flicking pellets with knife or ruler). Another form was equipped with an even more springy arm which could be drawn down to a horizontal position and a projectile placed in a depression at its end or in an attached sling (see also Mangon).

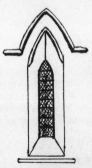

Splay Window

Edward I's engineer, Reginald, added four springalds to the towers of Chepstow, one of which was mounted on the roof of the keep.

SPUR

(a) An important accessory of a mounted knight and almost a badge of his status (c.f. 'winning his spurs') for they were only worn by knights during the Middle Ages. The earliest form (prick spurs) was a long pointed goad, rowels (small wheels toothed with sharp points) came into use from late C13.

Springald

(b) A pointed masonry projection from a tower towards field. Characteristic of French towers but rare in this country (e.g. Barnard, Chepstow, Denbigh, Goodrich). It acted both as a strengthening buttress and a deflecting surface against the impact of projectiles. The word is also used of a wall or earthwork projecting sharply from main defences (e.g. Chester, Dover, Southampton).

SPYING   see also Belfry.

Apart from the 'squints' in chapels, there were sometimes 'peepholes' from the chamber or solar to the hall e.g. Beverston, Broughton, Great Chalfield, Penshurst, Stokesay. At Winchester there was a primitive kind of speaking tube from solar to hall called 'the king's ear'. McLellan's has a spy-hole in the fireback and there is 'the Laird's Lug' at Fraser.

Clothing a New Knight

SQUIRE

Knight-training began in infancy and sons of noble households learned to ride and use arms almost as soon as they could walk. At seven or eight they were usually sent to the court of a superior lord where military and social training continued as a page or 'valet' when his tasks could include mucking-out stables, currying horses, polishing armour or running errands for ladies. At about fourteen he was promoted to squire (shield-bearer)

Squire receiving Accolade on Battlefield

when he was attached to a particular knight as a body-servant, armourer, carrier of spare weapons and leader of his spare horse. He was expected to defend his knight in battle, rescue him when dismounted or wounded and take charge of any prisoners. Thus he not only learned the brutal business of war at first hand but also received practical education in the courtly arts – the education of a gentleman. These included not only the management of horses and weapons but the rules and conventions of knighthood, genealogy and heraldry, social skills and graces (including dancing and some literary and musical training).

Squire Serving Table

He also acquired some knowledge of the customs and duties involved in a great household, acted as a body-guard to his knight at all times and often slept at his feet or outside the door of his chamber. When this apprenticeship was completed and he came of age the squire could seek knighthood (q.v.).

STABLES

Castles provided accommodation not only for the great destriers of the knights and mounts for infantry but they also sheltered hunters, palfreys for the ladies, and transport for messengers. Each knight may have had three horses for his own use and sometimes castles were centres of horse-breeding. The stables were part of the responsibility of the marshal (q.v.)

Foundations remain of the very extensive stables at Pickering (240 ft × 18 ft × 18 ft) with three rooms above, and John of Gaunt (1399) had large stables at either Pickering or Pontefract. Other examples at Corfe, Goodrich, Kenilworth.

STAFFORDSHIRE

A comparatively large county both in area and population but has few castles, perhaps because of its remoteness from frontiers and centres of power. It has traces of about a dozen castles of the earliest type and some C14 remains e.g. Alton, Caverswall, Chartley, Eccleshall, Heighley, Newcastle-under-Lyme, Pillaton, Stafford, Tamworth, Tutbury.

STAIRS   see also Spiral Stairs, Umbrella, Vice.

Many stairs in castles would consist of open wooden ones or even movable ladders. Masonry stairs are found mainly in walls and towers and ascend either in straight flights in the thickness of the wall or rise spirally within a containing tube. Their provision was a compromise between convenience and security, and this is particularly noticeable in keeps. The great stair or main access was originally from the ground outside to the level of the first

Stairs to Wall-Walk, Beaumaris

floor by means of a ladder or a permanent (but inflammable) wooden staircase ending in a drawbridge. When this stair was stone it usually was protected by a forebuilding. Interior communication may have involved two staircases; one privy, the other public (usually newels and often placed in the corners of the tower). As corner location weakened an already vulnerable point, stairs might be placed in the middle of the wall (e.g. Scarborough) or in special stair turrets.

Access to the basement from the first floor was usually by trap-door and ladder but occasionally by a vice which began in chamber and not on first floor in order to safeguard provisions and stores from unauthorised access. The upper floors were attained past a number of safety devices which might involve traversing intermediate floors, discontinuities, cul-de-sacs, guard-rooms etc. Changes in the mode of access often take place in the castle's history.

The first spiral stairs were laid on concrete vaults but from early C13 they were normally composed of specially cut slabs which fitted into containing wall and composed newel as they rose. Examples of vaulting at Caerphilly, Kirby Muxloe, Newport; of slabs: Alnwick, Belsay, Warkworth. Most ascend clockwise on assumption that attackers are ascending but later castles do not make this assumption e.g. in inner bailey of Caerphilly seven ascend clockwise, two anti-clockwise; at Conway the respective numbers are seven and one; at Beaumaris, six and four; at Caernarvon, seven and four.

Access to the wall-walk seems most commonly to have been gained by temporary ladders or wooden stairs, though occasionally stone steps were provided from the bailey which ascended the inner face of the wall. In later castles access was often through independent wall-towers.

STEPHEN (1135-1154)   see also Anarchy.

This reign saw the breakdown of royal authority in the face of over-mighty subjects. The land was filled with unauthorised and uncontrolled castles (see Adulterine). Many royal castles passed into the hands of his adversary, the empress Matilda, or into the control of great barons who took the opportunity to increase their own estates and power. Yet Stephen was no military incompetent and he captured castles at Bedford, Carisbrooke, Devizes, Ely, Exeter, Malmesbury, Newark, Salisbury, Sherborne, Shrewsbury,

Barons Attack a Royal Castle

Sleaford. His attempt to build a castle at Beverley (1149) was frustrated by the alleged intervention of St John of Beverley.

STIRLINGSHIRE

Besides the famous and important castle of Stirling itself there are lesser but interesting examples at Castle Cary, Duntreath and Fintry.

STORAGE

The principal store was the basement of the keep which provided both room and security for magazines, both of provisions and arms, within a confined space leaving the muster-ground in the centre of the bailey as clear as possible. Additional storage was provided in bailey buildings.

At Newark the large vaulted basement provides both a level site for the hall and storage accessible from the river. At Carew there are storage cellars occupying the entire space beneath the lesser hall and adjacent buildings. At Pembroke a large natural cavern beneath the hall and with access from the water-side was used for storage.

STORES   see also Provisions, Supplies.

Stores particularly susceptible to pilfering were usually kept in the basement of the keep. Sometimes it could be entered only from the lord's chamber and its keys were the responsibility of the watchman. Temporary stores, as distinct from reserves or siege stores, were provided in outbuildings. The basement store under the hall was so important and traditional that new halls were often cut out into the rampart-scarps in order to

Stores

accommodate them instead of a more obvious and natural location (e.g. Helmsley, Newark).

Records do not give much evidence of the stocking of arsenals (Evreux [1198] was stocked with 6,200 bolts and 4,000 arrows.) Some weapons may have been permanently stored in the castle, some could be made on the spot from raw materials, other could be gathered from a centre while many were the personal property of the garrison. However, Henry II's stocking of Salisbury (1173) included: iron (16s), charcoal (6s 8d), four hand mills and their equipment (8s), '500 engines', 12 iron hooks and one chain for the bridge (13s 6d) and one large cord for the castle well (13s 4d). In the same reign the stores collected at Newark in readiness for a possible siege were valued at 110 lbs of silver.

STRATEGIC SITING   see also Site.

Overall, there was no strategic plan in the location of castles. There may have been some tactical consideration but, by and large, their positioning was 'ad hoc' in the first instance. Perhaps the commonest aim was 'to protect a gang of adventurers trying to carve out a land-holding for themselves in debated country or to provide a Norman earl with a suitable headquarters to govern his lands.' (Renn) This does not mean that individual

Scarborough Keep and Barbican. Guarding a Harbour and stretch of Coast

castles did not control a river crossing, help
to defend a frontier, block a pass or highway,
overawe a town or guard a stretch of coast.

STRENGTH

Purpose of castles was to allow a small
garrison (q.v.) to maintain a defensive
position, hold up larger bodies etc. e.g. a
pele-tower in Redesdale resisted the assault
of 300 knights and 2,000 Scottish
foot-soldiers (1388) but conversely ten years
earlier it was captured by seven Scots who
later, augmented to 48, held out against

Skipton which commanded Aire Gap

10,000 English troops. Early in previous century, the tower at Odiham,
manned by three knights and ten sergeants, held out for eight days against
Louis and his army (1216). Similarly, it took Richard I and an up-to-date
siege train to bring the rebel garrison of Nottingham to terms in 1194. An
ill-prepared garrison in Rochester held out against King John and all the
power he could muster for seven weeks (1215). The next year, Louis with the
latest engines of war was not able to reduce Dover.

In late C13, Stirling (with garrison of 30) held out for three weeks against
English army led by Edward I and equipped with most advanced
siege-engines.

SUB-INFEUDATION

The practice of sub-letting portions of a fief
(q.v.) to sub-tenants in return for
feudal service. See also Fee, Knight's.

SUFFOLK

Little Wenham, Suffolk (1270–80)

One of the richest treasure-houses in England
for the amateur of mediaeval churches and
furnishings but little to offer of memorable
military architecture. Perhaps the outstanding
castle is Framlingham and the only keep of
national importance is Orford. There are
earthworks at Pytches Mount (Groton Park), a
moated site at Offton and sparse remains at
Lindsey and Milden. Worth visiting are
Bungay, Clare, Eye, Haughley, Lidgate,
Mettinghan, Wingfield and the very important
fortified manor-house at Little Wenham.

SUPPLIES   see also Stores, Provisions.

Food at Orford seems to have been mainly bread,
pork, beans, cheese and eels. (Diet seems to have
been affected by location e.g. castles in forests had
venison, castles with sheep had mutton.) Pipe rolls

Orford, Suffolk

shown purchase of hand mills for corn-grinding, cables for engines, cords for crossbows, salt and coal.

The complexities of supply on a massive scale can be seen in the Edwardian organisation for the building of Welsh castles but even in the earlier reign of Henry III, his determination to crush Bedford castle involved marshalling men and materials from some ten counties.

Castle logistics had become sophisticated by C13 and food supplied could be purchased from general contractors (e.g. Henry III's constable at Rochester, provisioning his castle in June 1266, ordered from one man [John Husting]: 251 herrings, 50 sheep, 51 salted pigs and quantities of rice, figs and raisins). More usually, large quantities of a particular commodity were bought from specialist suppliers e.g. the same constable (Roger Leyburn) bought fish from fishmongers in Northfleet and Strood; oats from merchants in Leeds, Maidstone, Nessindon; rye from Colchester and wine from vintners in London and Sittingbourne.

Posterns, many of them near kitchen, seem to have been located with eye to convenience of delivery. Some have access to water-born traffic (e.g. Scarborough) and many castles by sea or river have a water-gate and sometimes facilities for docking (Beaumaris, Caister, Harlech). The foundations of the bridge to the postern at Bodiam are stronger than those of the bridge leading to the main gate, probably because the former carried the heavy supplies from the harbour basin in the River Rother.

SURREY

'A history of English mediaeval architecture could be written without once mentioning a surviving Surrey building.' What is true of mediaeval architecture in general is true of its military architecture in particular. The county possesses no significant castles but Farnham and Guildford rate a mention and there are plenty of primitive motte-and-bailey sites some of which survive to a greater or lesser extent e.g. Abinger, Bletchingley, Reigate, Rudgewick.

Town Gate, Rye.

SUSSEX

The county has examples of most kinds of castle from the primitive motte-and-bailey to the nostalgic and romantic perfection of Herstmonceux in the new material of brick. Perhaps the special interest of Sussex lies in its coastal fortifications, particularly the mediaeval defences of Lewes, Rye and Winchelsea. Bodiam together with Pevensey must take the lead among castles, and we have also listed Aldingbourne, Amberley, Arundel,

Arundel, Sussex

Bramber, Camber, Chichester,
Hastings, Knepp and Midhurst.

SWING BRIDGE see Turning Bridge.

SWORD

As a weapon, the sword in castle
times began as a cutting weapon but
by C15 it had become longer, tapered
and furnished with a long grip
adapted for both cut and thrust. A
later development was the heavy
two-handed sword (often 5 ft long)
designed for a whirling cutting action
and assuming wide clearance.

Sword (C14)

As a symbol it has represented
justice, sanctity, peace and war. It was
particularly apposite as a sign of knighthood and the handing over of the
sword was the central moment (tap on the shoulder replaced buffet). The
participants were aware that the sword was cross-shaped – swords were
blessed and named, e.g. 'Mongley' at Arundel and sometimes the hilt or
pommel contained a relic.

Sword and Buckler Practice

TALUS see Batter.

TENANT see also Feudal System.

Holder of estates. Tenant-in-chief, direct from king; tenant-in-mesne,
holding from another lord.

TENANCY OF CASTLES see also Licensing.

Castles were legally held of the king in fee (given as part of fief) or they were
royal castles governed by a constable. In the latter case, the grant was only of
'custody' i.e. of the office of constable or castellan.

A castle held 'in fee' was normally only lost through actual or suspected
treason whereas a constable's tenure was at the royal will though in some
cases the office became hereditary.

Baronial castles could revert to king's hands through minority of heir or
lack of heir, and episcopal castles could revert during a vacancy in see.

Tenure

'It was round the great castles of C11 that the
politics and warfare of feudal England were
to revolve. They dominated the principal
towns of the kingdom, and they formed the
military and administrative centres both of
royal government and the great baronial
estates.'

Building a Royal Castle

In C11 king and barons had the common
cause of maintaining their hold on a
conquered nation but once the conquest was
secure mutual support was less necessary.
However, kings had support of most of their
barons most of the time since they remained
bound by service and loyalty, common interests,
community of class and race and, not
infrequently, by blood relationship.
Nevertheless, interests did not always coincide
and it was always in the Crown's interest to
prevent the exclusive control of a large district by baronial castles, to ensure
that strategic fortresses were in trustworthy hands and to arrange that the
placing of royal castles expressed and upheld royal authority as well as being
at convenient travelling distances.

TENURE

In spite of the legal niceties enshrined in the Feudal System and later law, the
ultimate right was that of might – the might by which William the Bastard
acquired the entire land of England in 1066 and a Welsh adventurer acquired
it in 1485. It is explicit in the celebrated boast of John de Warenne, castellan
of Conisbrough who, when asked to produce his title to his lands in the reign
of Edward I, flourished his sword and cried:

'With this my ancestors, who came with William the Bastard, conquered their
lands and with this will I defend them against all who desire to seize them. For
the king did not conquer his lands by himself but our ancestors were his
partners and helpers.'

'Barony by tenure implied that the owner had got it by the sword, or in reward
for bravery, and what he had got by the sword he would hold by the sword.
Title went with lands; but the last time this was recognised was in 1433, when
Sir John FitzAlan, holding the town and castle of Arundel, claimed to be Earl
of Arundel by such tenure, and the claim was admitted, though only, it seems,
through a special Act of Parliament.' (Finlason).

TENURE, CLASSIFICATION BY   see also Tenancy.

Whether a castle is royal or baronial has some effect on its position, character
and purpose. Royal castles have political and national significance, they are
designed to overawe potential centres of revolt, to defend frontiers

and to cover strategical points within or on the perimeter of realm. They are often placed within walled towns (e.g. Cambridge, Colchester, Exeter, Gloucester, Lincoln, London, Salisbury, Worcester). Castles which were extra-mural seem to imply suspicion of loyalty of adjoining town (Chester, Hereford, Norwich, Winchester, York). Intra-mural position sometimes suggests unity of king and town against common external enemy (Caernarvon, Conway), but it may represent an attempt to overawe turbulent subjects. Strategic location of royal castles includes coastal sites (Dover, Hastings, Orford, Pevensey, Portchester, Scarborough, Southampton) and covering lines of communication: river-crossings (Newcastle, Wallingford) or passes and defiles. When a baronial castle occupied such a position, the king usually tried to acquire it (Corfe, Newark).

Surdeval (Skelton)

Baronial castles were centres of their fief, a place of personal security, tactical rather than strategical (though they were sometimes placed in mutual support in Marcher country). They tended to be built on the most eligible site within demesne, determined by natural strength or geographical convenience (and sometimes both), e.g. Carreg Cennen, Dunster, Peveril, Tintagel, (precipices); Acre, Kenilworth, Tonbridge (water). If neither high site nor water defences were available through nature, they were provided artificially by building a mound or by damming streams

Richard III Conversing with Noble

(Broughton, Caerphilly, Leeds, Shirburn) or by a combination of natural defence and human work, commonly by isolating spur or promontory by a ditch (Chepstow, Morpeth, Okehampton).

THICKNESS OF WALLS   see also Keeps.

Enormous depth of masonry is defence against pounding of petraria (q.v.) and assault of ram or bore. Conisbrough curtain is 7 ft thick, Bolton from 7-10 ft; C11 curtain at Corfe varies from 10-12 ft; Chepstow up to 20 ft; Brough 11 ft; Knaresborough 11 ft; Richmond 9 ft. Keep walls: Bamburgh 11 ft; Brough 10 ft; Carlisle 15 ft; Dover 12 ft; Kenilworth 14 ft; Newcastle 18 ft; Norham 15 ft; Pontefract 18 ft; Portchester 7½ ft; Richmond 12 ft; Rising 7+ ft; Tattershall 14 ft.

TILTYARD   see Tournament, Lists.

Yard, field or enclosed space for tilts and tournaments and the preparatory and training exercises. A tilt was a combat for exercise or sport between two mounted knights armed with lances who rode at each other on opposite sides of a barrier (tilt) and who scored by 'attaints' or lances broken. There was usually a

Tilting

tiltyard within or in the neighbourhood of later castles, either a space which could be suitably equipped or a permanent provision. Tilts also took place on water.

TIME, BUILDING

Building was seasonal and usually excluded the winter months. The time involved in the erection of a castle could vary from the few weeks required for an earth and timber one to the same number of years in the case of a masonry structure. In the case of keeps, Renn has related heights to building seasons in the rough ratio of ten to one e.g. Bowes: five seasons, 50 ft, Chilham three, 35 ft, Dover nine, 80 ft, Newcastle eight, 80 ft, Odiham five, 50 ft, Orford seven, 65 ft, Scarborough, ten, 90 ft. Foundations took one season unless the building was directly on earlier masonry (e.g. Bowes, Chilham).

TOOLS

For building or repair were made from iron and wood and most of them could be made or renewed on the premises. Shovels and spades seem usually to have been made of wood and in other cases where we would use metal (barrows, buckets and other containers), the mediaevals had to make do with less enduring wood including wicker and basket-work. Most mediaeval tools had changed little in design from Roman times (as they have changed little until recently) but it is worth remembering that the only materials available for their fabrication were wood and iron. In the case of cutting tools it was often only the edge that was made of iron or primitive steel. A good deal of time must have been taken up in constant resharpening and frequent replacement.

TORMENTA

A frequently used term in mediaeval mss. for war-engines. It applies to those which gained their projectile power through twisting ropes of fibre or hair (see Mangon).

TORTOISE

A name (alternative to 'cat') for the slow-moving assault pent-house sheltering a mine, sap-head or the activity of a bore or ram. Also used of the temporary shelter afforded by locking together heavy shields (or pavises) to protect a storming or assault party.

TOURNAMENT   see also Joust, Round Table, Tilt-yard.

Aristocratic entertainment and display. Its principal feature (up to C14) was the mock-battle or melée (q.v.). Individual jousting or tilting only developed in later C14.

Tournament

There were national tournament centres and individual castles also often had 'lists' or greens, usually in the outer bailey or just outside the castle where galleries and platforms for spectators, a field for the events and space for the competitors' pavilions could be provided. Sometimes the provisions included permanent facilities and even a chapel and chaplain for spiritual preparation 'in periculo mortis'. Their conventions were much affected by the cult of 'courtly love' where knights battled for their lady's favour (q.v.) and wore her token (often a sleeve). They were accompanied by much display and had a great effect on the development of heraldry. There were supporting attractions and the accompaniment of music, feasting and revelry.

Tilting Lances (C16)

The heart of these magnificent and popular occasions was the imitation of battle-conditions, with their accompanying dangers, giving a knight the opportunity of showing his skill and valour, make some money and proclaim the merits of his lady. There were fundamentally two kinds of combat: the team or melée and the individual competition or joust (q.v.). The origins of the tournament may go back to the pagan and classical times (e.g. Game of Troy) and they were frowned on by both church and state for a variety of reasons. When it proved impossible to suppress them, attempts were made to civilise the occasion by rules about blunted weapons, procedures and numbers. They remained popular even when their military purpose had been vitiated by changes in warfare.

TOWER   see also Keep, Wall-tower.

Large tower took about a season to raise 10-12 ft at a cost of at least £100 p.a. Their plan developed from the square or rectangle to a polygonal or circular one. Mural towers often retained the square shape within the wall and presented a semi-circle to the field (D-shape) thus adding the advantages of space to the improved military design. The changes towards the field had two motivations: it improved the field of fire and eliminated dead ground in which assailants could work. It was less vulnerable for a variety of reasons: its lack of salient angles demanded a larger excavation for it to be mined effectively, its shape was more likely to deflect large missiles than receive their full impact, its masonry was more resistant to battering or boring since the joints were no longer parallel but radiating and thus more difficult to force out individual stones.

Later wall-towers combined the function of miniature keeps as well as flanking the walls and dominating the allure e.g. Rosamund's Tower, Pickering, had a postern passage, facilities for small draw-bridge, chambers on two levels with access to wall-walk from upper (c.f. Diate Tower in same castle). Often such wall-towers provided a prison in their basement (e.g. Mill Tower, Pickering). 'Independent' towers are characteristic of C15 probably related to Bastard Feudalism (q.v.) e.g. Ludlow, Raglan, Warwick.

In the early days of fortification a single tower was often multi-purpose e.g. tower at Oxford served as keep, church tower and town belfry and St Leonard's, West Malling, was similarly used.

TOWER-HOUSE

A complete fortress-residence, independent of curtains or baileys and often dispensing with them, which developed in C14-15 e.g. Ashby (1474-6), Dudley (c. 1320), Dunstanburgh (c. 1380, by remodelling, c.f. Llanstephan), Nunney (1373), Tattershall (1433-43), Warkworth (c. 1390). The name is also given to the integrated and compressed C14 rectangular castle with its high curtain, angle-towers and domestic buildings built into the curtain, sometimes with a central courtyard (Bolton, Hylton, Lumley, Raby, Witton) but this seems to represent a different solution to the same problem.

Mill Tower, Pickering

The (true) tower-house is characteristic of Scotland and northern England, rather less than a real castle but a very strong residence (see Pele Tower). Originating in rectangular blocks, later designs added a small wing at right-angles (L-plan q.v.), and later still, projecting turrets were built at opposed corners of the rectangle (Z-plan q.v.). Scottish tower-houses open to public include Cardoness, Clackmannan, Claypotts, Glenbuchat, Greenknowe, Loch Leven, Orchardton, Threave.

TOWER, SIEGE   see Belfry.

TOWER-WALL   see Wall-tower.

TOWN AND CASTLE   see also Bastide, Tenure classification by.

The earliest castles seem to have been designed to control neighbouring town rather than to protect it, though the latter purpose seems to have developed with time and sometimes a settlement grew up in the shadow of a castle where there had been none before. This was especially true in Wales when the castle often protected a 'colony' against nationalists e.g. Brecon, Caernarvon, Cardiff, Flint, Montgomery, Pembroke.

Castellans had right to levy tolls on goods entering or leaving the town and to extort heavy contributions from citizens for maintenance of castle and its occupants. At Norwich the whole town was subject to the constable. At Rochester and Salisbury the military and ecclesiastical authorities were frequently at odds and in the latter case conflict with the garrison caused the cathedral (and eventually the city) to separate from the castle site. There were also frequent disputes

Town and Castle, Conway

between the constable of Dover and the Wardens of the Cinque Ports.

Even when a town had freed itself from thralldom to the castle, the latter retained an independent jurisdiction or 'liberty' (q.v.) Jews could only be called to account before royal justices or the constables of royal castles because of prejudice and in 1189 the Jews of both Lincoln and York sought refuge in the castle against town mobs. The same happened at London (1262).

Old Sarum (Salisbury). Town and Castle

Royal castles often had the sheriff as constable and included gaols for common criminals from the town and surrounding district. They retained this prison function for centuries after their military use had ended.

TOWN DEFENCES

Designed to resist the same kinds of attack as those to which castles were subject and adopted much the same means (e.g. Sandwich). They tried to provide themselves with a secure perimeter by walls, ditches and/or water defences. The walls were protected by flanking towers and their gates with barbicans and portcullises. There was a rallying point in the centre (usually market place or town square – c.f. French Bastides). Easy access to threatened points was provided by a continuous wall-walk with battlements and a pomerium (q.v.) immediately behind walls. Houses within towns were sometimes fortified and there are rare examples at Norwich (e.g. Bishop's Palace, Music House).

The best preserved and most complete town fortifications are Caernarvon and Conway (late C13) followed by Chester and York (largely C14). Not much remains of Norman town fortifications but there are bank and ditch enclosures at Abergavenny, Acre, Longtown, Ongar, Pleshey, Radnor, Rhuddlan, Wigmore. Southampton Bargate may have remains of 1203 and the gatehouse at Acre may be Norman but this is a little in comparison with e.g. the walls of Avila in Spain (1099).

Towns were usually sited on one bank of a river and the crossing bridge was defended by a 'tete du point' (Kenilworth) or the bridge itself fortified (Monmouth). When a river bisected a town there were usually arrangements to close its passage by booms and chains (Bristol, York).

TOWN DITCH

An essential and integral part of town defences. Often (with a palisaded bank) it was the earliest and sometimes the only defence. It not only required digging (the 'fossores' at Conway [1285-6] were paid between £1.9.0 and £2.2.0 a perch length) but regular cleaning as it provided a natural dump for rubbish and privies often emptied into it.

TOWN GATES

Provision varied according to
whether a town was a
thoroughfare on lines of
communication or a cul-de-sac.
York is an excellent example of
the former situation and it has four
great gates or bars; Bootham
blocking the road from Thirsk and
Easingwold; Micklegate, the road
from Tadcaster, Monk from
Scarborough, Walmgate from Hull
and Beverley. All have
rectangular gatehouses, dating
from C12, with upper stages (from
C14) with bartizans and
'defenders'. All originally had
barbicans but only that at
Walmgate survives. *Conway* is a
cul-de-sac, one gate leads to the
quay, another to town and castle
and the third to the castle-mill.
This last (1286) cost £150
excluding cost of stone and wages
for quarrying, cutting and carting.
Caernarvon is similarly placed and
had only a main gate on the East
and a postern to the quay.

Alnwick Town Gate

Town Gate with Barbican

Chepstow has only one gate (N.W.) *Southampton* had five: and most complex
town gate in Britain, Bargate, the main gate to N. (C12, with C14-15
additions), Eastgate (vanished), Watergate, Westgate and S.E. gate to quay
with spur-work.

There are fine remains of the Westgate at Canterbury and of the brick
North Bar at Beverley while the Landgate, Rye, has round towers,
machicolation and portcullis grooves. C14 gatehouses were flanked by drum
towers (Canterbury, Conway, Winchelsea) but the sense of military need
seems to have diminished during the century: Lincoln Stonebow served as
little more than a gate-hanger while elsewhere churches appear over gates or
on adjoining wall (St John's Gate, Bristol, West Gate, Warwick). However at
Tenby (walls begun in 1328) the West gate was protected by an almost
semi-circular barbican (the openings producing the 'Five Arches' are much
later and alien to original design).

TOWN WALLS

Fortified towns antedate castles in England, not only in the late Roman towns
but also in the Anglo-Saxon 'burhs'. In Norman times some towns and villages
were provided with an enclosure of ditch, bank and palisade but by C13 they
were being enclosed within stone walls or older stone defences were

strengthened. There are remains of town walls at Caernarvon with eight towers and two gatehouses at Conway with 22 towers and three gatehouses. Their English rivals in completion are Chester and York, while there are greater or less fragments at Chepstow, Denbigh, Durham, Exeter, London, Newcastle on Tyne, Norwich, Oxford, Rye, Southampton, Tenby, Winchester.

Newcastle Town Walls, exterior (Reconstruction)

Town walls were perhaps most developed in settlements of Edward I designed as part of his plan to unite England and Wales. The towns were planned on a grid system where the squares were sub-divided into lots to which settlers were attracted by low rents and perhaps other privileges. The walls of these places seem to have been designed as a complete perimeter defence of which the castle, so to speak, formed the inner bailey. It was completely battlemented, served by a continuous wall-walk (except where it joined the castle), between five and six ft thick, 20 ft high and protected by flanking towers at regular

Newcastle Town Walls, interior

intervals (150 ft approx.) The gates were naturally protected by powerful gatehouses usually including a pair of drum towers.

The cost of the whole southern (and most substantial) stretch of Conway (Feb.-Sept. 1286) including twin-towered gate and six wall towers was about £400. Ordinary wall 16 ft high @ £1 linear foot. Battlements were extra and cost rather more than £1 per linear foot and their 'daubing' £3 for 98 ft. ('Daubing' = lime-washing and/or rendering.)

The towers which flanked town walls were usually open-gorged so that, being set towards the field, there was no structural continuity with the wall-walk. The gap was bridged by a temporary wooden bridge or plank which could be removed to impede the advance of an enemy who had gained a section of the wall-walk. At York the circuit is only impeded by the great gatehouses, the flanking towers do not rise above wall-walk level and the access to their interior is from below the level of the wall-walk.

Some town walls provide an extended outer bailey of which the castle is the 'keep'. Others are entirely independent and represent the later castle (castle of enceinte) where the whole site is the fortress.

Transport

The development of town fortifications is possibly a visible indication of the economic shift from the private stronghold of the great landowner to the corporate mercantile entity of the town.

Mediaeval Walled Town

TRANSPORT

The records are full of details of the vast transport organisation involved in the King's Works, especially the stupendous Edwardian castles. Transport costs have been estimated at 25 per cent of the total involved and worked out at about 3s 6d a ton-mile. Consequently materials were gathered from as near as possible and stone was quarried on the site if at all usable. Water transport was cheaper and more convenient

Transport

for heavy material and thus far offset the distance involved. Pack-horses were sometimes used, hence the small size of building units (about one foot cubes).

The building of Bolton involved the conveyance of timber from the Cumbrian forest of Engleby and relays of oxen were supplied to ensure its continuous and speedy transport. On-site carrying was by sledges, two-man stretchers, baskets, wheel-barrows, bags, tubs and barrels.

TREBUCHET, Trebucket (Trip – or Trap Gate).

A great and much improved siege-engine introduced to England in C13 to great consternation of castle garrisons because of its longer range, larger missile, higher trajectory (producing a mortar-like effect over even the highest curtains) and more accurate ranging. The machine is first mentioned at the siege of Piacenza (1199). It was introduced into England by Louis of France. (One of his ships was carrying such a machine when it attempted to enter Thames (1217) but its weight brought the ship so low in the water that its decks were almost awash.) Its effectiveness lay very much in the accuracy with which it could be laid since it had calibrations relating counterweight to range. It could hit repeatedly the same fixed

Trebuchet

target in the same place. (One, at the siege of Montsegur (1244), hurled a succession of 88 lb missiles, day and night at 20 minute intervals, at the same point in the walls until it battered an opening.)

The basic design (of which there were many variations and modifications) was a long arm pivoting on an axle at the summit of a high frame. One end (the shorter) carried enormous containers of earth and rubble weighing many tons and lead was also used for counterweight. Edward I robbed lead from church roofs around Stirling for his engines. The longer end, called the 'verge', was winched down to ground level against the pull of the counterweight by a system of winches. This end carried the projectile in either a spoon or sling which, when 'sprung' or triggered, hurled its charge in a high trajectory to a range which could be adjusted by a sliding counterweight on the longer arm (similar to the effect of the 'slide' on medical scales). Accuracy was also increased by the use of standard 'shot', specially cut stones of a known weight which could be up to three cwt or over 300 lbs. Stones weighing 240 lbs have been found at Pevensey and one of Edward I's trebuchets at the siege of Stirling is reputed to have cast stones weighing three cwt.

Extreme range seems to have been about 500 yards and this, together with the weight of missile and its high parabola, could cause a garrison to surrender at the mere sight of this terrifying engine. Missiles aimed to clear walls could burst with the effect of shrapnel on stone courtyards or against an inner wall with devastating anti-personnel effects. There are records of three fully armoured knights being killed by one burst and of garrisons complaining that a small fragment could either 'kill or spoil a man'. Its standard ammunition was stones weighing either 60 or 100 lbs of which ten could be produced in a day by a single stone-cutter. But it was a flexible weapon and missiles known to have been fired from it include human heads, mill-stones, paving stones, pots of quick-lime, bars of forged iron, dead horses and other carrion.

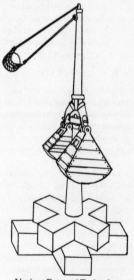

The emplacements for the seven trebuchets, including 'La Malvoisine', with which Louis assaulted Berkhamsted can still be seen and Pickering seems to have been extensively damaged by such a weapon, judging by the repairs necessary in 1218.

Variant Form of Trebuchet

Defenders adopted this machine when they could. The North tower at Criccieth was specially strengthened to support an engine on its roof and centuries later the hard pressed garrison of Pontefract during the Civil War was operating a 'sling' effectively over distances in excess of a quarter mile.

It is pleasant to record that in times of peace a trebuchet was used to bombard ladies with showers of roses in the Tournament of Love.

Truce

TRUCE   see also Siege.

Sieges were long and therefore costly affairs so before settling down, the besiegers' heralds asked the garrison to surrender honourably in the face of vastly superior forces. The besieged could ask for a truce – 40 days cessation of hostility during which they could communicate with their lord asking for relief or permission to surrender or they could reject the overtures with defiance. In the latter case bombardment would begin with repeated demands for surrender (e.g. when a breach was made). If the besiegers were forced to an assault either after the 'quarantine' had elapsed or after rejection of subsequent appeals they might grant no quarter when the castle was reduced.

In 1271 e.g. the garrison of Berkhamsted, after a few day's bombardment by trebuchets (q.v.), asked for a truce and communicated with their lord who gave them permission to surrender, which they immediately did.

TURRET

A small tower. Sometimes placed on top of a larger one to provide a lookout-point and also to cover the stairhead (e.g. Warwick). Such watch turrets, sometimes called 'garrites' were characteristic of Edwardian and C14 castles (e.g. one in Pickering curtain wall to control access from wall-walk).

Turrets on Gatehouse

TURNING BRIDGE

A wooden bridge pivoted on a central axle or trunnion (like a see-saw). The end nearer the gateway was counterpoised by weights which allowed it to sink into a pit. When the bridge was level it connected with a fixed wooden bridge crossing the ditch which ceased at the edge of the deep pit formed between the flanks of the gatehouse towers. When its forepart was raised it provided an extra barrier in front of the gates. The axle on which it turned was located in the projecting masonry in front of a gatehouse or barbican and was probably wood, square in section except at the ends. It was usually operated by withdrawing heavy pegs which supported its rear end through holes in the flanking walls and the counterbalances would effect an easy and quick descent to reveal the ditch which it formerly spanned. Returning it could be more leisurely and was probably effected by winches raising the rear end to the point when the 'pegs' could be reinserted. The curved slots for counterpoise arms can be seen at Bungay. A carpenter at Harlech (1324) was paid £10.18.4 for two

Types of Turning Bridge

turning bridges. The device was somewhat clumsy and tended to be replaced by more advanced form of 'drawbridge' (q.v.)

UMBRELLA VAULT

Sometimes forms the upper conclusion of a spiral stair. The newel is carried above the top stair to form the central column from which the ribs of a circular vault radiate (like the ribs of an umbrella). Examples at Alnwick, Belsay, Cockermouth, Warkworth.

Umbrella Vault

UNDERGROUND PASSAGES

Most underground tunnels are drains but concealed passages do exist: underground at Ashby, Carlisle, Dover, Herstmonceux, Knaresborough, Lincoln, Pontefract, Salisbury (two) through rock beneath Nottingham and Tintagel and in walls of Tower of London.

USE OF CASTLES   see also Residence.

Not only strongpoints commanding an area and neighbouring lines of communication but also centres of aggression, havens for field forces, a resource for quick mobilisation, a munitions storehouse or armoury (e.g. quarrels at Corfe, siege engines at Tower).

'In the last resort the land could be neither won nor held without the castles, and the castle dominated during the warfare of the Middle Ages because it dominated the land.' (Brown).

White Tower, London

VASSAL

One holding lands from a superior on conditions of homage (q.v.) and allegiance, a feudatory or tenant-in-fee. The apprentice-knight was called a valet which means 'a little vassal'.

VICAR'S PELE   see also Abbeys, fortified; Churches, fortified.

A pele-tower which was also the parsonage e.g., Corbridge, Elsdon, Embleton, Ford, Ponteland, Whitton. At Ancroft an entire fortified manor-house was built into the W. end of the church (C13 or C14).

Vicar's Pele, Corbridge

VICE   see also Umbrella Vault.

A spiral staircase occupying the whole interior of a turret.

VILLAGE   see Manor.

VILLAGE ENCLOSURE

Sometimes an earth bank, like a second or third bailey (and frequently still enclosing the church), provided some protection for a settlement near a castle. This might be considered as an early and primitive form of the great bastides of Caernarvon and Conway.

Chamber, Pele-Tower, Corbridge

VILLAGE, FORTIFIED

A deserted village, called Evistones, on the Northumbrian moors near Horsley, seems to have consisted of half a dozen bastle-houses (q.v.) within an enclosing wall. (Graham)

WAGES   see also Building Costs, Employees, Professionals, Workmen.

Masters generally received 6d per day when working and a retainer of 3d per day and a gown allowance. Exceptional individuals were paid rather more and also might receive ex gratia payments and gifts of land. Ordinary craftsmen, such as carpenters and masons, had a daily wage of 4d, quarrymen and miners, of 3d. (C13). They could also be paid for piece-work ('task') e.g. a mason received 25s a 100 for producing dressed ashlar blocks measuring 2 ft × 18 ins × 12 ins.

In C12, 'servants' i.e. ordinary foot-soldiers were paid 1d a day (the royal pikemen [Flemings] received the same). By the time of Henry III (beginning of C13), 'common soldiers' in the royal castles were hired for 2d a day. A crossbow-man (Rhuddlan 1281) was paid 4d a day and an archer half as much.

The garrison of Beaumaris (1296) was paid as follows:

10 mounted men-at-arms, 7s a week (1s per day)
20 crossbow-men, 2s 5d a week
100 foot-soldiers, 1s 2¼d per week

WAINSCOTTING

Walls of living rooms were sometimes masked by simple vertical panelling (usually Norwegian fir), generally painted white. This treatment began at (and often did not proceed beyond) the dais end of the great hall.

WALES

The land of castles par excellence, possessing not only the strongholds of its native and Norman invaders but also the prince's mighty fortresses of Edward I, perhaps the finest collection of castles in these islands.

WALL CONSTRUCTION

Where possible, foundations went down to bed-rock quarried flat to receive footings. Otherwise, trenches wider than wall were dug and filled with rammed rubble or

Pembroke

oak stakes were driven into sub-soil by a crude pile-driver made from a weight slung over a pulley. The foundations of C11 curtain at Richmond required the removal of 9 ft of upper clay after which a raft of holly and birch piles was driven into lower clay. Convenience sometimes led to the re-use of earlier foundations, sometimes supplemented by a broader timber raft laid above them.

The walls themselves could be made of rubble which was framed by wooden shuttering until the mortar set (so at Pickering where evidence of the shutters being made of notched and overlapping timber framework was found). More frequently, they were ashlar-faced with a rubble core (sometimes strengthened with wood or metal 'ties'). The ashlar was usually worked on the site and the chippings and odd-shaped stones were used for rubble infilling. The ashlar was laid in carefully fitted horizontal rows called courses and sometimes a course of slate was laid to provide a more precise horizontal level for continuation (see also Herringbone).

When the wall height got out of reach, scaffolding was erected to carry both men and materials. This consisted of stripped trees, standing in holes or tubs, lashed together with rope and the inner end of horizontal members lodged in put-log holes (q.v.) The flooring was of planks and access was by steep inclined planes or simple hoists and pulleys ('engines'). At the appropriate height, the wall was levelled off to provide allure and receive parapet and parados. Making of merlons and loops seems to have been a specialised job. Rarely, a stone staircase was built (parallel to wall) to provide access to battlements where there might also be gutters and spouts, latrines,

Wall Construction

corbels, machicolations, finials, mouldings, location holes and slots for hourding, shutters etc. The finished wall was coated with plaster and whitewash and was then painted (often with thin red lines imitating regular masonry joints). Sometimes large specially painted shields of arms were hung on the outer face.

In a fully developed castle such as Beaumaris or Harlech, the outer curtain would be some 20 ft high, 8 ft thick and some 1,200 ft long. The overtopping inner curtain would naturally be shorter but perhaps 15 ft higher and 2 ft thicker. Mural towers on outer curtain would overtop wall by 10 ft and on inner curtain by 15 ft. (See also Curtain, Mantelet, Town Walls.)

WALL GALLERIES

Fighting platforms in the thickness of the walls. They occur in some great towers but are rare in English curtains. Good examples at Caernarvon and Beaumaris. At Caerphilly the gallery in south wall, between hall and moat, solves a problem of defence occasioned by the crowding of domestic buildings.

WALL TOWERS   see also Cavalier Towers.

Towers at the angles of enclosure were built throughout the Norman period but some projected internally, as though to keep people in rather than out, and thus missed the point of flanking (q.v.) It may be, as Renn suggests, that this positioning was designed to protect them from direct assault by an enveloping wall or to enfilade attackers who had penetrated curtain. Before end of C12, mural towers are rectangular but occasionally (as at Ludlow) their corners are chamfered to reduce dead ground and danger of mining.

Later wall towers tend to be round but there was something of a fashion for polygonal ones in late C13-14 (e.g. Caernarvon, Conway, Raglan, Warwick).

Developed wall towers served a double purpose:

(a) They flanked the wall so that each pair covered the entire face of the intervening wall.
(b) They commanded the rampart-walk so that a successful escalade was both exposed and confined.

There are three types of wall towers:

(i) Open: where the tower is merely a 'kink' in the curtain and has no masonry on the side facing inwards (e.g. Framlingham).
(ii) Closed: a complete masonry tower which might be a solid bastion, capable of mounting an engine (e.g. Conisbrough), or a miniature keep with accommodation on several floors (e.g. Pevensey).
(iii) Open gorged: i.e. closed up to level of wall-walk and then becoming open at parapet level. Wholly or partly open towers were common in town walls (Caernarvon, Chepstow, Conway, York) but rare in castles.

Closed mural towers are usually of two or three stages: basement and upper guard-rooms. The former is sometimes vaulted (Alnwick, Pevensey) and occasionally possesses a fireplace (Kenilworth). Upper rooms frequently have fireplaces and latrine (latter usually at junction with curtain and corbelled out (Portchester, Southampton town walls)). Some mural towers are entirely given over to sanitary purposes (Coity, Framlingham, Manorbier). Others accommodate prisons, or chapels and chaplains (Carew, Richmond) while one at Warkworth was the emplacement of an enormous crossbow. Some protect access to curtain and others guard a postern (Chepstow).

WALL-WALK   see Allure.

WAR FOOTING

Castles were not permanently maintained in a state of war-readiness. This would have been neither convenient nor economic. At most, they were held on a care-and-maintenance basis. If war-clouds gathered there had to be a strengthening of defences (perhaps including deepening of ditches, clearing fields of fire etc.), the fitting of hourds and shutters, refurnishing and testing of arms, increasing strength of garrison, stocking of adequate food and ammunition.

Fixing Hoarding (War-Footing)

WARD

A guarded or protected area (hence Warder, Warden), often used of courtyard or bailey (q.v.)

WARD PENNY (Wayt-Fee).

The cash commutation of castle-guard (q.v.) The wayt-fee of a manor in Tivetshall was 20s per annum, payable to the constable of Norwich, of which 5s had to be paid on each of the four Ember days. At Rochester, ward-penny was due on St Andrew's Day (30th Nov.) and prompt payment was induced by doubling the arrears 'every time the tide swelled the Medway'.

Hoarding in Position

WARDROBE (Gardrobe).

A strong room which protected not only the precious robes of state but other valuable personal effects including plate, cash and treasure. The King's Wardrobe contained his personal treasury, which is why some accounts are paid from that source.

WARWICKSHIRE

One's expectations are not disappointed and the county is well represented, not least in quality. There are remains of typical motte-and-baileys and there are survivals which enrich the story of

Corfe with its three 'Wards'

191

military architecture : John of Gaunt's hall at
Kenilworth, Guy's tower at Warwick and C14
Maxstoke. To these we have added Astley,
Baginton, Beaudesert, Brandon, Brinklow,
Bromwich, Caludon, Coventry, Fillongley,
Kineton, Kingsbury, Oversley, Weobley.

WATCHMAN (Wakeman).

A permanent official of the castle, responsible for
security, doubtless assisted by a rota of
'look-outs', who gave notice of the approach of
friends, enemies or strangers by a variety of calls
on the horn which was his badge of office.
(Froissart, approaching a friendly castle, recounts
that when the watchman discerned their party 'he
sounded his horn so agreeably that it was quite a
pleasure to hear him'). Watchman also looked for
the movement of armies, fires and signals from
other castles and towers. He was often provided
with a sentry box and provision for signalling with
fire or lantern. His position was sometimes called
'the crow's nest' and he himself 'Jim Crow'.

Richard III holding Warwick.
Note Boar Badge

The siting of some castles is undoubtedly
affected by the distance that can be seen from its
towers e.g. Urquhart with view from Fort
Augustus to Inverness whose position is 'purely
that of an observation-post'. The motte of the
original castle at Rhuddlan is still called 'Toot-hill'
i.e. 'observation eminence'.

The watchman sometimes seems to have been a
sort of time-keeper or time-indicator for the
expenses at Caernarvon (1305) include 7d for the
horn which was used to signal the beginning and
end of workers' shifts. The watchman's
varied duties must have taken him to various
parts of the castle and the introduction of
'defenders' (q.v.) may have been designed to
cover temporary but necessary absences from
his post.

Watch Turret (Melridge Battle,
Northumberland)

WATER DEFENCES

Castles were often placed on the bank or at the
intersection of rivers and streams. Even early
castles produced artificial water defences by
damming the end of a river valley (Saltwood).
Some were planted on mounds deliberately
raised amid marshes or swamps (Knepp,
Skipsea).

Water Assault

C13 saw the development of the moated castle where new development allowed a low-lying site. The moat was the only secure defence against mining but the confining dam sometimes needed protection otherwise a besieger could break it and denude the water defences. The fortified dam at Caerphilly is the most striking feature of perhaps the mightiest fortress in Britain (1267). There were complex water defences in many places (e.g. Kenilworth) which have now been drained. In 1266 there was a water assault by night against Kenilworth using barges dragged overland from Chester.

WATER-GATE

Gave access to river or sea and thus to communications which were difficult to cut even during a siege. Most seem designed to facilitate provisioning but they could admit reinforcements or provide a means of escape. They sometimes communicate with a private wharf. There is a good water-gate at Newark, 'Traitors' Gate' is the water-gate of the Tower, Harlech has a hidden water-gate approached by a postern and a circuitous path. Pembroke has two – one via a cave beneath great hall and another in South side of outer ward. The water-gate at Leeds is tunnel-vaulted, while those at Chepstow and Rhuddlan led to quays.

WATER SUPPLY   see also Cistern, Well.

Water supply was critical and sometimes extremely sophisticated provision is made. A castle might hold a year's supply of emergency rations and supplies but men can only last a few days without liquid. In 1136 both wells at Exeter ran dry and though the garrison made do with wine and used it for baking, cooking and extinguishing fires, eventually they were forced to surrender and 'When they finally emerged you could have seen the body of each individual wasted and enfeebled with parching thirst, and once they were outside they hurried rather to drink a draught of any sort than to discharge any business whatsoever'.

Water supply should not have its origin outside the enceinte otherwise it could be cut or poisoned. Even where the source was inside the bailey, there was some danger of its being poisoned by treachery or accident and therefore the well was usually covered and placed within a strong and secured place in the innermost ward, beneath a gatehouse or keep. There is a well-chamber at N.E. of hall at third storey of Newcastle keep which gives access to a well lined for all its hundred feet. Water was

Waterworks under Construction

conveyed to this chamber by lead pipes to drawing places in other parts of the keep. There is similar provision at Dover (where the well is 350 ft deep and lined for about half its depth) and there seems to have been another well in the forebuilding. Middleham had two wells in the keep and there is a fine well-chamber in the keep at Richmond. Often there was another well in the bailey with its own well-house. Water was sometimes drawn by animal power. At Skipton water was gathered from the extensive roofs and piped into a cistern in Conduit Court, and Carreg Cennen has a complex system for gathering water.

WELL

An essential feature (e.g. in 1136 Carisbrooke surrendered because its water supply failed) and there may be more than one. Wells which now lie open in the courtyard were originally covered by a well-house, normally of timber, which was probably connected to a kitchen by a timber passage. There is a curious triple arched recess in the C14 well-head at Alnwick. Even in a keep, wells were conveniently placed near the kitchen which were otherwise provided with a convenient access to the well-shaft (Canterbury, Rochester). Some early keeps have them rather inconveniently in the basement (Colchester, Conisbrough).

Well-House, Alnwick

There is a particularly deep well in the bailey at Scarborough, one in the fore-building at Dover and at the east of the entry of Colchester's keep. When a well was placed in the basement, access was provided by a windlass running through trap-doors in the wooden floors above. When there are no remains of a well it is probable that it has been filled up. In more sophisticated arrangements the pipe of the well (a cylinder lined with ashlar) was often carried to the upper floors in the thickness of a wall, obviating a journey to the basement (e.g. Dover, Kenilworth, Newcastle, Rochester). Sometimes the water was drawn into an intermediate system from which it was channelled by pipes to various convenient local drawing-places or tanks (sometimes fitted with taps). In a draw-well water was raised by bucket and windlass and taken from a shallow well or cistern by dipping-wheel.

Some characteristic well depths: Bamburgh 145 ft, Carisbrooke 145 ft, Conisbrough 105 ft, Newcastle 94 ft, Pevensey 50 ft, Pickering 75 ft, Windsor 165 ft (6 ft 4 ins diameter and lined with ashlar for over 60 ft).

WEST LOTHIAN

Blackness is interesting as is Niddrie (Kirkliston), with its associations with Mary Queen of Scots, as has Linlithgow. Torphichen was once a preceptory of the Knights of St John. There are earthworks at Abercorn.

Blackness

WESTMORELAND

A border county whose abbeys and manors had to be fortified as well as its castles. There are lots of pele-towers of whom some (e.g. Askham, Godmond, Howgill, Preston Patrick) have not been mentioned, nor are some castles (e.g. Hartley) where the remains are scant. Our list contains Appleby, Arnside, Beetham, Bewley, Brough, Brougham, Great Asby, Hazelslack, Kendal, Levens, Pendragon, Sizergh, Yanwath.

WIGTOWNSHIRE

Has not much to offer to the castle explorer but perhaps Garlieston and Stranraer rate a mention.

WILLIAM THE CONQUEROR

'Castles he caused to be made, and poor men to be greatly oppressed.' (Anglo-Saxon Chronicle). William had a triple task: of keeping a conquered people in subjection, of repelling foreign invasion and of asserting his authority over Norman barons. His chief instruments were two: the mounted knight and the Norman castle. At every stage of the Conquest 'he founded, strengthened, established, placed and built' his castles, including three in London and two in York (see also Norman castles).

Groom bringing Destrier

WILTSHIRE

Possesses a rare survival of the Anglo-Saxon 'burh' at Cricklade but little of the important and favoured castles at Devizes, Ludgershall, Marlborough and Salisbury to which we have added Combe, Great Chalfield and Wardour. (There are additional more or less visible motte-and-baileys at Ashton Keynes, Downton, Membury, Oadsey, Somerford and Trowbridge.)

WINDOWS

Apertures for light and/or ventilation tended to be either loops (q.v.) or windows. Neither was entirely satisfactory for defending bowmen: slits rarely gave a view of ground and windows provided little cover (even the narrow crenels in parapets had to be supplemented by hourds and galleries).

The basement of a keep had either no windows or at most a few loops. Loops generally were provided with no closure apart from a coarse curtain. The first floor tended to have narrow loops with a wide splay, but the second floor often possessed quite large windows in deep recesses fitted with seats, forming light and private alcoves separated from hall or chamber by curtain (e.g. Conisbrough c. 1180). Similar provision was often made on the third floor and the windows were usually not superimposed in order to avoid weakening structure (naturally they were pierced on unexposed sides of military buildings). Richmond is an exception and its keep has been described as the 'darkest of C12 towers' but it was not designed as a residence.

Larger windows might be closed with shutters or with parchment (oiled sheepskin or goatskin) and were usually defended by strong external grilles embedded in the masonry. Glass was rare (though not unknown) in early windows other than those in chapels or oratories where they were painted or stained as in any other church. Later, the upper lights of hall windows were glazed and filled with heraldry of the kind still to be seen in some churches. Beneath the transom the windows were still closed with shutters for security.

Apart from the exigencies of defence, fenestration was affected by architectural fashion and gives useful clues for dating. Exeter gatehouse (C11) follows Saxon tradition of rectangular headed lights and unsplayed openings. Elsewhere there are many round-headed windows characteristic of the Romanesque style. Usually C11 windows above first floor were about 4 ft high and 12-18 ins wide. Their heads were round or flat and they were either splayed or set at the end of a tall and wide recess (e.g. Canterbury, Colchester – c. 1080, Pembroke c. 1200). They gave little light and even when their shutters were open, allowed little access to missiles. By late C12, there was a tendency to increase light by making two openings to one internal recess with window seats (Longtown, Pembroke, Conisbrough). Later developments produced the oriel (q.v.) and lofty hall windows on the bailey side. Basement loopholes were sometimes removed from reach of sappers or other enemies by being provided with a long steep shaft opening above the level of floor above (Canterbury, Skenfrith). Where the basement was a prison such a provision severely limited possibility of escape or signal to outside world.

WINE

Mediaeval England seems to have drunk wine as naturally as modern France. The records show vast quantities on the roads to royal castles. Some constables and castellans had right of 'prisage' (see Constable) and we know that 30 tuns were in the cellars of Portchester in 1205 – (a tun being 252 gallons) and that Exeter in 1136 had enough to use instead of water to extinguish fires in a siege. Bordeaux was part of the patrimony of English kings for much of the Middle Ages and had a brisk wine trade with England (fragments of Bordeaux wine pitchers have been found at Kidwelly).

Butler in Wine Cellar

WING WALL

A wall ascending the side of a motte and usually connecting keep or ring-work with bailey curtain (e.g. Carisbrooke, Pickering).

WOMEN, MILITARY CAPACITY OF

Matilda de Laigle held Bamburgh against William II until he threatened to blind her husband before her eyes (1096). Dame Nicholaia, the constable's widow, effectively defended Dover against rebel barons (1216). Another widow, Isabel de Fortibus, constantly improved and maintained Carisbrooke (1264-93). Isabel de Vesci held Bamburgh for five years in defiance of Edward II and Parliament (1370-5). Queen Phillipa beat Scots off from Bamburgh while her husband (Edward III) was besieging Berwick (1332). Lady Joan Pelham held Pevensey against the militia of Surrey, Sussex and Kent (1399).

This mediaeval tradition survived the Reformation and manifested itself frequently during the C17 Civil War.

WOODEN TOWER   see also Ardres.

The tower crowning earliest mottes was wooden and elevated on stilts and often called by some Latin version of 'brattice' or 'brettache', a word used later for quite a different structure.

William I apparently brought three such structures from Normandy in his invasion fleet – a kind of 'secret weapon' consisting of prefabricated forts which could be erected very quickly. As with palisade, the wooden tower persisted a long time and there was one on the mound at Shrewsbury as late as the reign of Edward I. (A number are illustrated in the Bayeux Tapestry.) Motte at York had at least three wooden towers; first destroyed in rising of 1069, second was burnt in pogrom of 1190, third was scattered to four winds by gale of 1228 when 2s was paid 'for collecting the timber of York castle blown down by the wind'.

WOODWORKERS

Besides carpenters (q.v.) and joiners, there were tradesmen called 'board-hewers' who apparently worked in the forest, producing joists and beams to standard sizes (e.g. 18 ft × 1 ft 6 ins × 2 ins) as well as bespoke pieces (some recorded as 32 ft long and 18 ins square). This was to reduce the cost of transport (q.v.)

Woodworkers

WORCESTERSHIRE

If one accepts that Dudley is in Staffordshire, one is faced with Pevsner's remark: 'Castles, it is strange to report, do not exist at all, except for the C14 tower of Holt castle'. Ham castle is only a name and Elmley (though listed) little more; only the moat marks the site of Hanley, the episcopal castle at Hartlebury bears few traces of its military past. There are only fragments at Harthill and nothing remains of Inkberrow. The great motte of Worcester was transmogrified in 1833 and its sandstone scattered.

WORKMEN

Included the quarrymen and rough-masons
who worked the stone from the quarries, the
free-masons who fashioned it for walls and
towers; the woodmen who cut out the timber,
the carters who brought it and stone to the site,
the carpenters who converted the rough
timber to floors, roofs and other furnishings.
There were miners who cut ditches and hacked
out cellars in solid rock, smiths sweating at
their forges, lime-workers at their kilns,
plumbers at their crucibles. There were
hodmen and barrow-men and innumerable
diggers. There were watchmen and soldiers to
guard the works and escort both men and
materials, clerks who checked material costs, piece-work and wages, and kept
the accounts. There were probably other clerks who saw to the spiritual
welfare of all on the site.

Masons' Tools

We have some knowledge of wages paid to those occupied on the king's
work: masons, 1s 2d a week, quarriers, 1s a week, smiths from 2s 8d to 2s 6d.
The daily rate for minor workmen (pick-men, barrow-men, hod-men) was
generally 1½ d. The clerks responsible for orders, accounts and payments
were paid about 2s 6d a week (C13).

It should be appreciated that there were considerable differences among
workmen, especially in the skilled trades, who were organised in a hierarchy
of masters, journeymen and apprentices. The master-craftsman was usually
accompanied and assisted by six assistants (apprentices) as the man-at-arms
was by his six 'servants'. It is probable that a mason's apprentices acted as
'layers'.

The large forces of workmen involved in the royal works in Wales were
organised on a near-military basis with knights in charge of large groups and
the clerks acting not only as book-keepers and accountants but as 'gangers
and keepers of the workmen' (so at Caernarvon in 1295 where in June there
was a labour force of 549.)

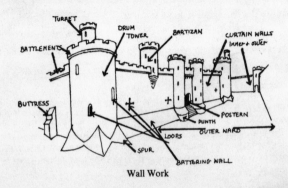

Wall Work

Workmen Building (c. 1250)

Yett

YETT (Yatt).

Door of iron bars crossing each other to form a long grille which seems to have replaced the portcullis in some areas as a reinforcement of entry door. It was common in Scotland and the North of England but there are few survivals (Burgh-by-Sands church, Cawdor, Dalston, Doune, Naworth).

This massive iron grille was hung on heavy hinges and secured either by draw-bars socketted into both sides of jamb or by strong bolts attached to the yett. In England it seems to have been incorporated in a wooden door, whereas in Scotland it was usually separate and the associated door could not be opened until the yett was released. There were also national differences in the structure of the yett itself. The Scottish pattern is arranged so that the bars alternatively penetrate or are penetrated by each other. This makes for a stronger forging but produces an open grille incapable of infilling. In the English form all the vertical bars pass in front of the horizontal ones and are rivetted or clasped alternately. The spaces between the bars were blocked by oak panels.

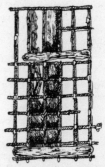

Yett. Bywell Northumberland
(inside)

YORKSHIRE, EAST RIDING

Apart from Wressle, there is no real castle in East Riding if we exclude remains of motte-and-baileys. Minor fortified portions of religious houses remain at Bridlington, Kirkham and Watton. If we include York, there is the motte of the Old Baile and the castle across the river with motte, Clifford's tower and other remains. Above all, there are the incomparable walls and bars. A tower-house at Paull Holme, fragments of a fortified manor at Flamborough, scant remains of the once mighty Percy stronghold at

Yett. Bywell, Northumberland
(outside)

Leconfield, the North Bar at Beverley and a selection of earthworks
(Aughton, Lockington, Skipsea) complete the tale.

YORKSHIRE, NORTH RIDING

Castles are an important part of the mediaeval monuments of this Riding with
important and representative examples from C11 to C15. Richmond has one
of the earliest stone halls in the country and a mighty tower (as have
Middleham and Scarborough). Bolton has been called 'a climax of military
art' and Bowes, Helmsley, Mulgrave and Pickering are not insignificant.
There are fortified manor-houses at Sinnington and well and
motte-and-baileys at Hutton Conyers, Kildale, Kirby Moorside, Leavington,
Northallerton, Pickhill, Yafforth. These last are not in the gazetteer but we
would like to draw attention to Sheriff Hutton and our other examples
include: Buttercrambe, Castleton, Catterick, Cotherstone, Cowton, Crayke,
Cropton, Danby, Gilling, Harlsley, Hornby, Kilton, Kirkby Fleetham,
Markenfield, Mortham, Nappa, Ravensworth, Scargill, Sigston, Skelton,
Snape, Topcliffe, West Tanfield and Whorlton.

YORKSHIRE, WEST RIDING

Not much remains of its most important castles: the Cromwellians left little of
mighty Pontefract after their siege, Sandal is but a mound and nothing
remains of Sheffield. Gatehouses (and little else) survive at Skipton and
Tickhill but if Conisbrough alone remained, the West Riding would have a
significant place in the history of military architecture. Motte-and-baileys at
Bardsey, Barwick in Elmet, Kimberworth, Laughten-en-le-Morthen have
been omitted but the gazetteer includes Almondbury, Barden, Bolsterstone,
Bolton-by-Bowland, Bradford, Cawood, Farnhill, Harewood, Hazlewood,
Hooton Pagnall, Knaresborough, Newton Kyme, Ripley, Rothwell, Spofforth,
Steeton, Wetherby.

ZOO

In the unscientific sense of a menagerie, a
collection of exhibition animals, castles seem
to have been the first in the field and exotic
animals (particularly if they had heraldic
significance) were an additional
status-symbol. For a long time there was a
menagerie in the Tower, of which the ravens
are a remnant.

Henry III's Elephant

Z-PLAN   see also House of Fence,
L-Plan.

A design for providing flanking fire from
early guns, developed in the 'tower-houses' of Scotland. The house-block,
whether hall or tower, is provided with two corner towers at diametrically
opposite angles. Thus each tower flanked two sides of the main building while
the main building, in turn, covered the towers. An attractive plan on grounds

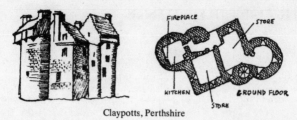

Claypotts, Perthshire

of economy, efficiency and convenience, it was very popular, particularly in Aberdeenshire. There are about seventy survivals in the country as a whole and some variety is given by the towers being both square, both round or one of each. Good examples at Claypotts, Midmar, Noltland, Terpersie.

FURTHER READING

Individual guides to particular castles, especially those of H.M.S.O. The notes on castles in the invaluable and exhaustive volumes of N. Pevsner: *Buildings of England* (1966-76). For royal castles: *The History of the King's Works* (London 1963), Brown, Colwin, Taylor; *English Mediaeval Castles*, R. A. Brown (1954) is an excellent introduction which, for Britain, might be supplemented by *Castles of Great Britain*, S. Toye (1953), and the beautifully illustrated *National Trust Book of British Castles*, P. Johnson (1978). For the earlier castles, *Norman Castles in Britain*, D. Renn, is authoritative. For particular counties: *Castles of Northumberland*, Frank Graham (1976); *Yorkshire's Ruined Castles*, J. L. Illingworth (RP. 1970).

Selected books on background might include: *Military Architecture in England during the Middle Ages*, A. Hamilton Thompson (1912); *Mediaeval Feudalism*, C. Stephenson (1965); *Life in a Mediaeval Castle*, J. & F. Gies (1975); *European Arms and Armour*, C. H. Ashdown (1967); *Shield and Crest*, J. Franklyn (1961).

The *Council for British Archeology's Research Report No. 25* (1978), is a bibliography by J. R. Kenyon of castles, town defences, and artillery fortifications in Britain.

GAZETTEER

OF

Castles in England, Wales and Scotland

The Ruin
(Anglo-Saxon Poem)

'Wondrous is this wall-stone; broken by fate,
The castles have decayed; the work of giants is crumbling.
Roofs are fallen, ruinous are the towers,
Despoiled are the towers with their gates;
Frost is on their cement, broken are the roofs,
cut away, fallen, undermined by age.'

GAZETTEER

Entries are of following form: place, county, map reference, date, classification, access. Figures in parenthesis after entry refer to pages in Glossary (there may be more than one entry).

When a place-name consists of two words of which the first is 'Castle', it is entered under the second word. When the second word is 'Castle', it is omitted from the entry. e.g. Castle Rising, Castle Camps occur under 'Rising' and 'Camps'; Barnard Castle, Bishop's Castle are entered as 'Barnard', 'Bishop's'.

Entries occur according to country, in the order: England, Wales, Scotland.

Because of their historical significance, old counties are retained and ascribed according to Bartholomew's Survey Gazetteer (1966 ed.).

References are four figures according to National Grid omitting first two letters or numerical equivalent.

Dates are of erection (and main surviving remains).

Abbreviations: c.   about
                      C   century
                      d.   demolished
                      lc. licence to crenellate

Classification: A – First rate example, almost complete.
                      B – Very good with substantial and interesting remains.
                      C – Well worth a visit.
                      D – Modest remains.
                      E – Few remains apart from earthworks.

Access: O – Open site (no necessary implication of right of access).
                      DE – In care of Department of the Environment or
                              Scottish Development Department.
                      NT – National Trust.
                      P – Other kind of public or semi-public care.
                      S – In private hands but open at regular times.
                      H – Not generally accessible.
                      W – Accessible by written appointment.

Every effort has been made to give correct information. (Author will be pleased to receive corrections). There is an annual volume called *Historic Houses, Castles and Gardens* (ABC Historic Publications) and DE regularly produces up-dated lists.

ENGLAND

ABINGER, Surrey   1145   c. 1100   d. 1153+   D–E   O   Characteristic early motte-and-bailey. Excavation (1949) proved that such castles were defended by palisades on earth-banks and first keeps were wooden towers (here 12 ft square). (174).

ACRE, Norfolk   8115   C11   C–D   O   Motte and U-shaped bailey covering 15 acres and comprising 'perhaps the grandest earthworks in England'. Motte encircled with revetted shell-keep (160 ft diameter) with foundation of rectangular keep (50 ft × 40 ft) within. More substantial remains of C15 gatehouse. 'Outer bailey' extending to church was probably village enclosure. Rectangular earthwork between church and castle probably siege-work. (128, 134, 159, 177, 181).

ACTON BURNELL, Shropshire   5202   lc. 1284   C–   DE   Fortified manor-house, roughly contemporary with Stokesay. Large windows, no moat or curtain. Keep has become a tower-house. Pleasantly sited. (160).

ALDFORD, Cheshire   4159   C12   E   O   Remains of motte-and-bailey, north of church. (32).

ALDINGBOURNE, Sussex   9025   C12   D   O?   Remains of square limestone keep with plinth, some Caen stone. Originally possessed forebuilding and well. (174).

ALLINGTON, Kent   7557   lc. 1281   A–   S   Former manor-house converted into real castle in C13. In spite of much restoration, very substantial remains. Occupied by Carmelite Friars. (95, 102).

ALMONDBURY, Yorkshire, West Riding   1614   C12   D   O   Mighty Iron Age fortress converted into castle by construction of great ditch to form inner bailey. Had wall and stone keep. (87, 200).

ALNWICK, Northumberland   1912   1096,   C12, 18, 19   C–B   S   Much restored but original gateway and barbican (1310–14). William the Lion of Scotland captured here at siege of 1174. Percy stronghold. Characteristic 'defenders', original gates and some towers. 'One of best barbicans in England'. (9, 13, 20, 22, 47, 51, 67, 72, 84, 130, 134, 145, 160, 161, 166, 171, 187, 190, 194).

ALTON, Staffordshire   0742   c. 1175   D   H   Substantial part of one tower remains of castle originating as motte-and-bailey, separated from later Hospital of St John by 'ravine-like moat'. Stands in forecourt of C19 Gothic castle. (170).

AMBERLEY, Sussex   0313   lc. 1377   B   H   Substantial remains, including imposing gatehouse, of episcopal castle with C16 additions, C18 modification and C20 restoration. (54, 174).

ANSTEY, Hertfordshire   4032   before 1085, d. 1218?   E   O Motte-and-bailey, with possible village enclosure, N of church. (85).

APPLEBY, Westmoreland   6820   C12   B   H   Former Vipont and Clifford castle. Typical late keep of three stages but no cross-wall, 31 ft 6 ins square internally. Other C12 remains include curtain, postern, wall-tower. Visible from road. C17–18 additions and modifications. (31, 36, 80, 81, 82, 195).

ARMATHWAITE, Cumberland   5046   C15?   D   H   Pele-tower with C18 additions in romantic site by R. Eden. (44).

ARNSIDE, Westmoreland   4578   C   O?   Unusually large (48 ft × 33 ft) pele-tower of five storeys with four-storeyed annexe. Cross-wall, hall at third storey, vaulted oven in basement. (195).

ARUNDEL, Sussex   0107   c. 1080, C19   B−   S   Original motte-and-bailey
with much later embellishment including almost complete rebuilding in
C18–19. Fine shell-keep, probably built by Robert of Belleme. (3, 12, 39, 46,
49, 71, 72, 84, 114, 142, 145, 159, 174, 176).

ASHBY, Leicestershire   3516   C12, 15   B−   DE   Lord Hastings received
lc. in 1473 and work stopped after his execution in 1483. Two baileys, remains
of C12 hall, kitchen C14, tower-house and chapel C15, and garden C16. (95,
102, 111, 180, 187).

ASCOTT, Oxfordshire   4336   C11?   E+   O/H   Manor-house is within
former bailey of Ascott Doilly (72) while turf mound at other end of village
marks site of castle of Ascott Earl. (135).

ASHTON, Lancashire   4657   C14, 17, 19   C−   H   Original C14
tower-house, modified in C17 and C19 with substantial additions in 1856.
(100).

ASKERTON, Cumberland   5368   C15, 16, 20 C−   H   Hall with original
roof survives from fortified manor-house of Dacres. Towers at each end added
in C16. (44).

ASTLEY, Warwickshire   3189   lc. 1266   C−   H   Home of Greys with
dubious remains of C13 curtain and gatehouse within C16–17 mansion. (192).

ASTWELL, Northamptonshire   6245   C15   D   H(W)   Fortified
manor-house of which a tower and some walling survives. Large house added
C17. (129).

AUGHTON, Yorkshire, East Riding   7038   C12, 14?   E   O   Two sets of
earthworks are all that remain of a. motte-and-bailey b. moated site of Aske
house. (200).

AYDON, Northumberland   0065   lc. 1305   B+   DE   Picturesquely placed
on strong site above Cor Burn. Inner and outer bailey with hall range.
Probably late C13, with C14 additions, in spite of lc. Excellent example of
well-preserved domestic arrangements. 'The most perfect example of a
fortified manor-house.' (Simpson) (64, 86, 130, 163, 166).

BAGINTON, Warwickshire   3474   C14   D   O   Remains of tower-house
and earlier earthworks formerly belonging to Bagots. (192).

BAMBURGH, Northumberland   1834   C12, 18, 19   B−   S   'Very ideal of
natural fortification', a site occupied for at least fourteen centuries. C12 keep
within three baileys. Barbican and gatehouse (C12), considerable remains of
mediaeval walls. Ruined C12 chapel, collegiate. Keep (69 ft × 61 ft × 35 ft
high) with unusual ground floor entrance, vaulted basement with impressive
well (allegedly C8). (9, 12, 19, 25, 28, 36, 46, 58, 80, 81, 83, 94, 130, 141,
161, 164, 166, 177, 194, 197).

BAMPTON, Oxfordshire   3103   lc. 1315   C−   H   Former Pembroke castle,
absorbed by later domestication. Remains of original gatehouse, curtain.
(135).

BANBURY, Oxfordshire   4540   C11   E−   O   Even site, besides
market-place, of this once important castle is obliterated. (135, 143).

BARDEN TOWER, Yorkshire, West Riding   4045   early C16, 17
C−   O/H   Tower-house, hunting lodge of Cliffords. Restored by
indefatigable Lady Anne, who added chapel. Substantial ruin. (90, 200).

BARNARD, Durham   0516   c. 1100   C+   DE   High precipitous site on
banks of Tees. Originally four wards, remains of two, curtain and gateway and
a good deal of three-storeyed keep. Perhaps first fortress to be provided with
private latrines. (52, 81, 84, 93, 104, 166, 169).

BARNWELL, Northamptonshire   0485   c. 1226   C+   O?   Earliest
examples of movement to replace function of keep by curtain and towers.
Rectangular enclosure with corner towers, gatehouse and postern. Curtain
30 ft high and 12 ft thick. Substantial ruin. (73, 107, 129, 141, 159).

BASING, Hampshire   6652   C11, c. 1600   E   O   Originally ring-work and baileys with C13 masonry. Replaced by fortified manor which was centre of heroic C17 siege of which some earthworks survive. (80).

BEAUDESERT, Warwickshire   1465   before 1141   E   O Motte-and-bailey of de Montforts. Humps on site may cover remains of C13 masonry. (192).

BEDFORD, Bedfordshire   0449   c. 1070   E   O   No remains except base of motte (160 ft in diameter) between Newnham Rd and Castle Walks. But see Sieges (160) also (7, 15, 16, 26, 80, 107, 121, 139, 147, 164, 171, 174).

BEESTON, Cheshire   5358   c. 1220   D+   DE   Scanty remains include those of gatehouse and curtain. Magnificently isolated and precipitous site cut off by man-made ravine 35 ft wide and 30 ft deep hewn through rock. (32) See Peckforton.

BEETHAM, Westmoreland   4979   C14   D   H   C17 hall occupies part of site of fortified manor-house of which curtain, domestic range (including chapel) survive in part. (195).

BELSAY, Northumberland   1078   c. 1340   C   P   Fine example of three-storeyed pele-tower with wings for additional accommodation. Four turrets and tower are machicolated. 'One of most interesting and impressive castles in Northumberland'. (13, 130, 137, 171, 187).

BELVOIR, Leicestershire   8133   C12, 19   E   S   Early motte-and-bailey using natural hillock. Completely rebuilt in C19 Gothic manner. (102, 124).

BENINGTON, Hertfordshire   3023   C12   D   H   Small Norman keep (44 ft × 41 ft) whose 9 ft high remains have received C18 Gothic treatment as part of house called 'The Lordship'. (47, 85).

BERKELEY, Gloucestershire   6899   c. 1070   B   S   Originally FitzOsborn castle with shell-keep. Remains (of curtain, hall, chapel, gatehouse, domestic buildings) mainly C14 but with later and much modified private apartments. Prison in S tower said to be scene of atrocious murder of Edward II. (32, 46, 66, 75, 96, 144, 159).

BERKHAMSTED, Hertfordshire   9908   C11 and after   D+   P   Original motte-and-bailey probably built by Robert de Mortain. Masonry very ruinous but interesting defences included moat encircling both bailey and motte and later ditch with bastions to flank assault. Well in basement of keep. Excellent earthworks. (11, 85, 159, 165, 185, 186).

BERRY POMEROY, Devon   8261   C14, 16   C   H   Gatehouse, tower and part of curtain survive from mediaeval castle. (48, 74, 142).

BERWICK, Northumberland   9953   C12   C+   O/P   Scant remains of castle include fragment of curtain and some underground chambers, (9, 77, 130, 197). The massive and unique town fortifications, begun under Mary and completed under Elizabeth, are earliest example in Northern Europe of the Italian technique of civic fortification by bastions. Scant remains of earlier C13 walls in N of town. (14, 61).

BEVERLEY, Yorkshire, East Riding   0339   C15   C   O   Town Gate (North Bar) of 1409 survives, constructed of 125,000 locally made bricks. 'Nowhere else in England, at so early a date, was brick employed with so much refinement'. (Pevsner). (114, 171, 182, 200).

BEVERSTON, Gloucestershire   8693   c. 1225, C14   C+   H   Remains of C13 gatehouse and W. range, chapel and oratory. (32, 75, 101, 169).

BEWCASTLE, Cumberland   5674   C13?   C   O?   Rectangular enclosure (c. 90 ft square), no corner towers but oblong tower to W. Substantial remains include parts of curtain (30 ft high) on two sides and gatehouse. (44). In neighbourhood are remains of pele-towers at Crew Castle, High Grains, Low Grains, Woodhead.

BEWLEY, Westmoreland   6323   C14?   D   O   Ruins of rectangular

207

enclosure with two projecting towers. (195).

BICKLEIGH, Devon   9407   C12, 15, c. 1600   C   S   Remains of Courtenay stronghold on W bank of Exe. Mighty gatehouse with Norman chapel outside. (48).

BISHOP AUCKLAND, Durham   2029   C12, 17, 18   C−   H   Largely Gothicised episcopal castle but present chapel was once (C13) great hall of mediaeval castle. (53).

BISHOP'S, Shropshire   3288   C12   D   O   Motte-and-bailey behind Castle Hotel had ring-wall, curtain and inturned entrance to bailey. Sparse masonry and earthworks remain. (48, 160).

BISHOPS STORTFORD, Hertfordshire   4821   C12?   D   O   Remains of Waytemore castle across river include motte-and-bailey and foundations of rectangular shell-keep. (49, 85).

BISHOPS WALTHAM, Hampshire   5517   C12   C   DE   Palace-castle of bishops of Winchester with remains of moat, gatehouse, hall, kitchen, tower, chapel and domestic buildings. (30, 78, 80).

BLETCHINGLEY, Surrey   3250   C12 d. 1264   D−   H   Ring-work on edge of scarp with irregular bailey. Sparse remains of rectangular keep with 5 ft thick walls. (126, 174).

BOARSTALL, Buckinghamshire   6214   1312   D−   H   Sole survival is C14 gatehouse much altered in C17. (21).

BODIAM, Sussex   7826   1386–90   A   P   (NT)   Picture book example of C14 castle set within its moat which contains outwork and barbican of square castle with round corner towers and square ones on faces not occupied by gatehouse and postern. Domestic buildings round central courtyard include hall, kitchen, chapel. (2, 12, 17, 34, 43, 52, 68, 77, 100, 105, 106, 109, 131, 134, 138, 140, 174).

BOLINGBROKE, OLD, Lincolnshire   3564   C11   E   O   Motte-and-bailey with water defences. Only traces of earthworks remain above ground. (104).

BOLSOVER, Derbyshire   4770   c. 1070   D–E   H   Site occupied by C17 house with some remains in garden and present 'Little Castle' may stand on foundations of C11 keep. (47, 82).

BOLSTERSTONE, Yorkshire, West Riding   2696   C13?   D   O   Scant remains of gatehouse across road from church. (200).

BOLTON, Yorkshire, North Riding   0391   c. 1379   A–B   S   'A climax of English military architecture' forming an aesthetic balance between domestic and military convenience. Scrope castle guarding Wensleydale, substantially complete apart from NE tower, a casualty of Civil War. (30, 32, 33, 34, 54, 81, 88, 114, 134, 141, 142, 145, 177, 180, 184, 200).

BOLTON BY BOWLAND, Yorkshire, West Riding   7849   C13?   D   H. Hall may contain fragments of fortified house where Henry VI fled after Hexham. The Peel, in spite of its name, appears to be a C17 house. (200).

BORWICK HALL, Lancashire   5273   C14   D   H   Elizabethan mansion which incorporates mediaeval pele-tower. (100).

BOTHAL, Northumberland   2386   lc. 1343   C   H   Smaller version of Dunstanburgh. Keep-gatehou e with umbrella vault, 'defenders' on merlons, display of armorial shields below battlements. Window from Cockle Park pele. (47, 84, 113, 127, 130).

BOURNE, Lincolnshire   0920   C11   E   O   Motte once bearing stone castle with two baileys. Extensive earthworks only survive – even motte has been dug away for gravel. (104).

BOWES, Yorkshire, North Riding   9913   1171   C+   DE   Remarkable in that its masonry buildings never seem to have been more than keep (cost c. £600) of which there are substantial remains. (42, 55, 65, 80, 82, 137, 178, 200).

BRADFORD, Yorkshire, West Riding 1633 C15, 17, 18, 19 C P
Bolling Hall contains remains of mediaeval fortified manor-house, tower and
part of domestic range. (200).

BRADLEY HALL, Durham 0737 lc. 1431, C18 C– H Though partly
Georgianised, remains of quadrilateral castle with moat, sparse traces of
curtain. (53).

BRAMBER, Sussex 1810 before 1073 D P (NT) Motte surmounting
large natural mound with huge fragment of gatehouse-keep. Fragments of
curtain (herringbone). Village enclosure? (85, 126, 174).

BRAMPTON BRYAN, Herefordshire 3672 C14 C– H Only strong
gatehouse and hall remain of original castle whose site now encloses Georgian
hall. (85).

BRANCEPETH, Durham 2238 before 1216 D H Impressive C19
building but masonry of Neville castle is just discernible in curtain and some
towers (C14–15). (52, 166).

BRANDON, Warwickshire 4076 early C12 D– O Rectangular moated
site with concentric enclosure on banks of Avon. Few rubble fragments. (192).

BREDWARDINE, Herefordshire 3344 C12? E O Motte-and-bailey
beside Wye S of church. Had a 78 ft × 45 ft rectangular keep. (85).

BRIDGNORTH, Shropshire 7193 before 1102 D O Remains of square
keep (forebuilding vanished), bailey (curtain disappeared). (30, 160, 166).
Town Walls; thoroughly restored North Gate, bastion in Pound St.

BRIDGWATER, Somerset 3037 1216 D O Water-gate on W quay
survives of C13 castle. Earthwork on road to Cross may be remains of
motte-and-bailey besides Parrett (lc. 1200). (92, 167).

BRIGHTWELL, Berkshire 5790 C11? E O Motte near church. (16).

BRIMPSFIELD, Gloucestershire 9312 C11, 13 D O In field near church
are remains of earthworks of C13 castle with scanty remains of gatehouse. (75)
Motte of earlier castle nearer Ermine St.

BRINKLOW, Warwickshire 4379 before 1130 E O Two baileys with
motte (40 ft high and 60 ft diameter at top). (192).

BRISTOL, Somerset 5872 before 1088 D O/P Remains (early C12) of
keep (110 ft × 95 ft), vaulted chambers (C13?) and traces of watergate. (3,
39, 83, 144, 167). Town walls – two stretches discernible. (141, 182).

BROMWICH, Warwickshire 1489 C12? E O Bailey surrounding small
motte (25 ft high, 25 ft diameter at top). (140, 192).

BRONCROFT, Shropshire 5587 C14 D H Mid C19 except for tower to
right of entrance. (160).

BRONSIL, Herefordshire 7337 lc. 1460 D O Sparse remains, moat and
part of gatehouse tower. (85).

BROUGH, Westmoreland 7914 before 1157 B DE Triangular
enclosure sliced off corner of Roman fort by U-shaped ditch. Herringbone
masonry, keep (c. 1180), Clifford's tower (C13), domestic buildings and
earthworks. (30, 44, 78, 82, 177, 195).

BROUGHAM, Westmoreland 5228 C12–14 B DE Quadrilateral
enclosure, partly ditched. Remains of curtain, keep (c. 1175 with later
forebuilding) remodelled c. 1300. Fine small chapel. (30, 93, 195).

BROUGHTON, Oxfordshire 4030 lc. 1386, 1405 B S Spectacular
moated site. Tudor veneer conceals 'finest and most complete mediaeval house
in county'. Gatehouse, fortified walls, chapel. (31, 135, 169, 177).

BROUGHTON TOWER, Lancashire 2187 C14 D H Substantially C18
house incorporates mediaeval pele-tower. (100).

BRYN AMLWG, Shropshire 1684 C12 D O Ring-work, bank and traces
of wall. (160).

BUCKENHAM, Norfolk 3505 C11, 12, 13 C O Old Buckenham

possesses enclosure of most unusual rectangular shape (C11 or earlier) with no trace of motte.

New Buckenham (c. 1150) built by de Albini, has ring-work with two baileys whose banks rise 40 ft above moat. Outer possibly village enclosure. Keep may be earliest round tower in England. Also remains of gatehouse (c. 1200) and chapel (C12) incorporated in house. (128).

BUCKINGHAM, Buckinghamshire   6933   before 1216   No remains – even motte was flattened in C18 to provide churchyard of SS Peter and Paul. (21).

BUNGAY, Suffolk   3389   C12, lc. 1294   C   O   Hugh Bigod's powerful and troublesome fortress is largely built over but there are some remains of a square keep (70 ft side), traces of massive forebuilding, curtain and remains of gatehouse towers. Unique survival in England of mine-gallery (from siege of 1174) at SW corner of keep. (13, 44, 47, 121, 145, 173, 186).

BURLEY, Rutland,   8710   C11   E   O   No history but excavations in 1935 indicated motte-and-bailey surrounded by U-shaped ditch cut in underlying ironstone. Not completed? (154).

BURWELL, Cambridgeshire   5866   mid C12   E   O   Rectangular flat mound (200 ft × 125 ft) surrounded by wide ditch 9 ft deep. Last masonry disappeared recently. (24).

BUTTERCRAMBE, Yorkshire, North Riding   7358   lc. 1201   E   H Traces of mounds and bank in grounds of Alby Park probably belong to castle of William de Stuteville. (200).

BYTHAM, Lincolnshire   9818   C11   E   O   Impressive earthworks towering above stream. Inner bailey seems to have been defended by double bank. No masonry above ground. (104).

BYWELL, Northumberland   0461   c. 1430   C+   H?   Former Neville fortress of advanced design – a cross between pele-tower and keep-gatehouse. Unusual machicolations, rare English yett, battlements and 'murder-holes' above stairs. (130).

CAISTER, Norfolk   5211   1432–5   B–   S   Built by Sir John Falstolf from booty of French War. Early and fine example of mediaeval brickwork. Substantial remains of tower with oriel and machicolated curtain. Gun-ports. (13, 20, 34, 54, 114, 128, 150, 151, 174).

CALLALY, Northumberland   0509   C13?   C   S   House of C17–19 which conceals a pele-tower in SW angle. (130).

CALUDON, Warwickshire   3579   lc. 1304   D   O   Moat and impressive fragment of hall. (192).

CAMBER, Sussex   9218   c. 1540   B   DE?   Practically complete example of Henrician coastal fort. Tower at core is c. 1512 or earlier. Bastions remodelled later in C16. (9, 174).

CAMBO, Northumberland   0285   C15?   D   S   Pele-tower masquerading as Post Office and shop in picturesque village. (130).

CAMBRIDGE, Cambridgeshire   4658   1068   D–   P   Largely destroyed in C16–17 but remains of motte (40 ft high and 200 ft at largest diameter), bastions and curtain (restored c. 1642). (24, 164, 175, 177).

CAMPS, Cambridgeshire   6242   c. 1070   D   H/O   De Vere castle which once occupied eight acres. Motte-and-bailey with added circular keep and attached hall. Remains; extensive earthworks, moats and wall-fragment. (24).

CANTERBURY, Kent   1557   C11   D+   O   Original castle of Conquest, keep (c. 1080) originally of three storeys with two cross-walls. Little remains except keep standing to half height. (39, 63, 69, 71, 80, 95, 123, 194, 196). City gate (West Gate) c. 1390 with cross-bow loops modified for artillery. (54, 77, 94, 182).

CARISBROOKE, Isle of Wight   4888   before 1080   B–   DE   High motte with two rectangular baileys. Shell-keep (C12) with deep well. Substantial remains of all periods include curtain, towers, domestic buildings and fine gatehouse. (12, 22, 44, 46, 54, 80, 124, 159, 171, 194 197).

CARLISLE, Cumberland 3955 1092 B/C DE/H Triangular site, keep (c. 1150), modified. Two baileys. Remains of curtain, outer gatehouse (C13), inner gatehouse (C14). (52, 80, 177, 187). Traces of city walls (from 1130). (17, 36, 39, 145). Deanery (former Prior's lodging) based on pele-tower and hall (C16). (44, 67).

CARN BREA, Cornwall 6941 C12 D O Fortified site from prehistoric times; remains of iron age fort, traces of Roman occupation, remnants of mediaeval cliff-castle. (38).

CARTINGTON, Northumberland 0304 lc. 1441 D+ H Modified C17 and insensitively 'restored' in C19. Early C14 tower (in spite of lc.), remains of domestic buildings and other towers. (130).

CARTMEL, Lancashire 3778 C14 C− P (NT) Augustinian priory defended by curtain and gatehouse (c. 1335) which is not dissimilar to pele-tower (well restored c. 1930). (100).

CARY, Somerset 6332 C12 E O (Natural) motte with curved enclosure NE of church. Marked site of 78 ft square keep. Starved into surrender 1138, beset by siege castle 1147. (167).

CASTLETHORPE, Buckinghamshire 7944 c. 1157 d. 1215 E O 36 ft high motte with two baileys and outwork. Well-preserved earthworks and ditches up to 60 ft wide. (21).

CASTLETON, Yorkshire, North Riding 6808 C12 E O Horseshoe-shaped mound on Castle Hill had C12 masonry with 13 ft thick walls. (166, 200).

CATTERICK, Yorkshire, North Riding 2397 C12? E O Traces of two motte-and-baileys; a. a reduced motte with deep ditch on W, N of church whose yard probably represents bailey. b. Castle Hills, half mile SW with reduced motte but earthworks still reaching 60 ft at E. (200).

CAUS, Shropshire 3308 C12 D O Motte-and-bailey with complex earthworks. Fragments of shell-keep, foundations of inner curtain, well in ditch between motte and inner bailey. (160).

CAVERSWALL, Staffordshire 9442 lc. 1275 C+ H Roughly oblong enclosure with four polygonal angle-towers. C17 house built into mediaeval castle. (170).

CAWOOD, Yorkshire, West Riding 5737 C15 and earlier D H All that remains of archiepiscopal palace-castle is fine gatehouse. (200).

CAXTON, Cambridgeshire 3058 early C12 E O Wide ditches surrounding rectangular islands, probably result of Stephen's reaction to Essex's rebellion in 1143 (c.f. Burwell, Lydgate, Rampton, Eaton Socon, Weeting). (24).

CHALGRAVE, Bedfordshire 0027 C12 E O Low oval motte and small bailey near church. (15).

CHARTLEY, Staffordshire 0028 c. 1220 D O Motte with two baileys (some earthworks may predate C13). Foundations of round keep and curtain with half-round bastions (originally five). (170).

CHESTER, Cheshire 4066 1070, C12 D P? Much altered motte-and-bailey with remains of C12? tower included in angle of city walls which are unique in preserving complete circuit of about two miles. N and E sides on Roman foundation but mainly late C13 with much subsequent restoration. Interesting spur-work (Water Tower) c.f. Southampton. (32, 39, 83, 91, 143, 169, 183). Walls as such (they lack gates and towers) have been considered finest in England. (181).

CHICHESTER, Sussex 8605 before 1142 d. 1217? E O Damaged motte in Priory Park has, as one of its boundaries, a complete section of city wall. (174).

CHILBURN, Northumberland 9727 before 1313 C− O Neglected ruins

211

of moated Commandery of Knights Hospitaller with remains of walled rectangular courtyard, chapel, domestic buildings. (118, 127).

CHILHAM, Kent 0753 C12 C H Now in private grounds, royal castle of Henry II with keep of rare octagonal plan (c.f. Odiham), standing to nearly full height on motte, remains of curtain and hall. (30, 39, 95, 178).

CHILLINGHAM, Northumberland 0625 lc. 1344 B− H? Characteristic fortress of C14 with square angle-towers at corners of rectangular enclosure. Extensively remodelled C17 and further modifications in C18, 19. (54, 88, 130).

CHIPCHASE, Northumberland 8875 c. 1340 B− H? One of finest English tower-houses. L-plan, unusual in possession of private kitchen. Chapel with piscina, altar and squint. Halls with original fireplaces. Well, turrets, machicolation, portcullis. (13, 31, 130, 137, 146).

CHIPPING ONGAR, Essex 5502 C12 D O Motte-and-bailey within village enclosure. Motte of 230 ft diameter and 48 ft high. Some fragments of wall and tower. (10, 59, 72, 82, 159, 181).

CHRISTCHURCH, Hampshire 1593 C11? C DE Motte-and-bailey with added Norman hall. Substantial remains of latter (including fine window and chimney) with fragments of C14 keep and curtain. (33, 37, 64, 80, 145, 178).

CLARE, Suffolk 7645 before 1090 D O Motte with two baileys (inner one containing railway station). Fragment of shell-wall with wall-walk and hoarding holes, remains of curtain on bailey base. (86, 159, 173).

CLIFFORD, Herefordshire 2445 C12, 13 C O? Clifford/Mortimer stronghold on cliff above Wye consisting of motte and two baileys with remains of polygonal shell-keep, traces of gatehouse and tower. (85). Earthworks of two other early castles at Old Castleton, Newton Tump.

CLIFFORD'S TOWER See YORK.

CLITHEROE, Lancashire 7441 before 1102 C P Natural motte with triangular bailey. Remains of tower keep (smallest) c. 1180? and subsequent additions. (100).

CLUN, Shropshire 3081 C12 or earlier C O Complex earthworks forming motte and two baileys interconnected by causeways with river protection on W and N. Remains of Norman keep, fragments of inner curtain with plinthed bastions (C13). Keep built into side of mound so that two of its four storeys are below level of mound top. (43, 49, 160).

COCKERMOUTH, Cumberland 1230 mid C13, 14, 19 C S Keep and two baileys at confluence of Cocker and Derwent. Remains of curtain, tower, gatehouses, domestic buildings. (44, 84, 96, 126, 134, 145, 187).

COCKLAW, Northumberland 9371 C15? B− S Well preserved pele-tower of excellent masonry. Basement with pointed vault and three superior floors. Considerable remains of mural paintwork in first floor chamber. Machicolation, prison, first floor postern. (130).

COCKLE PARK, Northumberland 4259 c. 1450 C H Magnificent pele-tower converted into farmhouse. Corbelled-out bartizans and machicolations. Some windows C18. Heraldry (130).

CODNOR, Derbyshire 4149 C13–14 D+ O? Visually impressive but not very informative remains of curtain, towers and domestic buildings. (47).

COLCHESTER, Essex 0025 1072? C+ P 'Greatest hall keep in Europe' with destroyed inner and outer baileys. Enormous keep designed on grander scale than tower but possibly never completed. Extremely fine spiral stair. (58, 59, 63, 80, 85, 142, 166, 175, 194, 196).

COMBE, Wiltshire 8477 C11? D O Motte, later crowned with small stone keep (16 ft × 10 ft), with four successive baileys on spur above brook. Remains of earthworks and scant masonry. (195).

COMPTON, Devon 8664 c. 1420 C P (NT) Fortified manor-house

with high wall instead of moat. Vulnerable N wall machicolated. Chapel. Inner court divided by (destroyed) great hall. (48, 166).

CONISBROUGH, Yorkshire, West Riding   5098   c. 1180   B   DE   Single bailey on high natural mound, scarped and ditched. High curtain with bastions. Long narrow barbican (much ruined). Almost intact circular keep 'one of finest surviving pieces of C12 secular architecture in country' – three floors and basement, formerly crowned with two fighting platforms. Beautiful chapel in buttress. (12, 14, 30, 31, 34, 50, 63, 65, 81, 93, 101, 126, 134, 139, 141, 146, 166, 173, 176, 190, 194, 195, 200.

COOLING, Kent   7575   lc. 1381   B−   H?   Two wards, originally separated, inner rectangular enclosure with round towers at angles. Magnificent and well-preserved gatehouse with interesting inscription. (34, 54, 77, 91, 95, 100, 109, 141).

CORBRIDGE, Northumberland   9964   early C14   C   ?   Good example of 'Vicar's pele', three storeyed, embattled and machicolated. Yett, looped and vaulted basement, living-rooms with built-in amenities. (130, 146, 160, 187).

CORBY, Cumberland   4754   C13 or 14   D   H   Mediaeval pele-tower engulfed in mansion of C17–19. (44).

CORFE, Dorset   9681   C11, 13   C+   P   Early motte-and-bailey (Wareham) sited on natural hillock isolated by two streams developed into 'one of strongest castles in all England'. Thoroughly slighted after heroic defence in Civil War but eloquent and impressive ruins. (7, 16, 38, 39, 54, 57, 65, 75, 80, 83, 85, 107, 114, 126, 140, 141, 144, 165, 177–177, 187).

COTHERSTONE, Yorkshire, North Riding   0119   c.1200   D   O   Motte of FitzHervey's castle (no bailey). Fragments of masonry on motte and in neighbouring cottage. (87, 200).

COUPLAND, Northumberland   9331   late C16/early C17   C   H   Original L-shaped tower-house or 'pele' of three storeys with tunnel-vaulted basement and projecting parapet. C19 alterations and additions. (130).

COVENTRY, Warwickshire   3379   C12   D   O   Priory was converted into temporary castle in 1143 and besieged by Earl of Chester. (See also CALUDON). Remains of town walls with two minor gates. (192).

COWTON, Yorkshire, North Riding   2802   C15   C   H   High rectangular tower-house, embattled and turreted. (200).

CRANBOURNE, Dorset   0513   C13, 17, 19   C   S?   Beneath Jacobean disguise of manor are substantial remains of King John's defensible hunting-lodge, indicated by compactness, protruding tower, battlements with looped merlons. (51).

CRASTER, Northumberland   2519   c. 1400   D+   H   (W)   Tower-house or 'pele' with C18 wing and other Gothic embellishments. Modern battlements. (130).

CRAYKE, Yorkshire, North Riding   5670   C15, 18, 19   C   H   Motte-and-bailey site on which bishop of Durham fortified manor c. 1440 to which a tower-house was added later in C15. C18 modifications, C19 additions. Part ruined, part inhabited. (200).

CRESSWELL, Northumberland   2993   C14?   C   ?   Pele-tower with tunnel-vaulted basement and two floors above connected by corner stair ending in roof-turret. (130).

CROFT, Herefordshire   4565   c. 1400   C   S   Basically castle of Bolton type, modified C17, Gothicised C18. (85).

CROPTON, Yorkshire, North Riding   7589   C12?   D   O   Motte (20 ft high, 150 ft diam.) at W point of triangular bailey with traces of foundations of domestic buildings. (200).

CUCKNEY, Nottinghamshire   5771   c. 1150   E   O   Motte west of church. (127).

DACRE, Cumberland 4526 early C14 C/D S? Strong pele-tower with tunnel-vaulted basement, hall with laver, solar above, good battlements. Had a chapel in C14. (44, 101).

DALDEN TOWER, Durham 2908 C15? D+ H Ruins of mediaeval pele in grounds of Dalton Hall. (53).

DALSTON, Cumberland 3750 C16, 17, 19 D H Nucleus is pele-tower built c. 1500 with original yett. (44, 199).

DALTON, Lancashire 2374 C14 D P (NT) Pele-tower probably built by monks of Furness Abbey as refuge against Scots raiders. (100).

DANBY, Yorkshire, North Riding 7107 c. 1300 C S Sir William Latimer's replacement for the old castle at Castleton. Forerunner of Bolton, Sheriff Hutton, Wressle. Angle-towers set out diagonally. Confused through part use as farmstead but substantial remains. (200).

DARTMOUTH, Devon 8751 C14, 15, 16 C DE Tower and bailey castle c. 1380, strengthened towards close of C15. Gun loops in basement, living quarters on first floor. River Dart could be closed by boom from here to Kingswear. (34, 48).

DEAL, Kent 3752 c. 1540 B– DE One of largest artillery forts built for coastal defence in time of Henry VIII. Three tiers on sexfoil plan surrounded by moat originally crossed by drawbridge. (9, 95).

DEDDINGTON, Oxfordshire 4631 C11 d. C14 E O Rectangular ring-work surrounded by strong enclosure within which was added (C12–13) a polygonal inner bailey with curtain, keep, domestic buildings. Only remains; huge mounds S of village. (75, 135).

DEVIZES, Wiltshire 0061 C12 D-E H Oval mound on promontory with two baileys, each protected by double ditch. Outer one formed town enclosure and its shape is perceptible in street line. St. John's may have been castle chapel. Great royal castle with enclosed deer park. Remains pretty thoroughly obliterated by C19 tradesman's mansion. (156, 171, 195).

DILSTON, Northumberland 9763 C15? C H? Tower-house with modifications in C16–17 including addition of chapel. (130).

DONINGTON, Leicestershire 4427 C12 E O Tree-covered mound NE of church marks ring-work abandoned C15. (102).

DONNINGTON, Berkshire 4668 lc. 1386 C H Unusual shape, irregular oblong with round corner towers and square towers in middle of long sides. Third (shorter) side had very strong gatehouse which magnificently survives, fourth side developed towards field in half hexagon. (16, 52, 73, 101).

DOVER, Kent 3141 before 1064, C12, 13 A DE 'Most luxurious of all keeps' dominates 'key of England' on which great expenditure was lavished by successive monarchs. Modified into concentric plan in C12. Constable's gate. (C13) of unique design and one of most imposing in country. (22, 27, 30, 34, 35, 36, 38, 39, 44, 46, 55, 58, 64, 65, 66, 70, 73, 83, 92, 94, 95, 107, 126, 132, 143, 164, 166, 169, 173, 177, 178, 181, 187, 194, 197).

DUDLEY, Worcestershire 9390 C12, 14, 16 C+ P (Zoo) Motte-and-bailey d. 1173. Present remains largely of C14 rebuild in form of tower-house including gatehouse, barbican and chapel. (5, 152, 180).

DUFFIELD, Derbyshire 3443 C12 E ? O Its keep (95 ft × 93 ft and 15 ft thick) once rivalled Tower and Colchester. No remains above ground except motte. (47, 80).

DUNSTANBURGH, Northumberland 2521 lc. 1316 C+ DE Strong coastal site with defence concentrated on most vulnerable approach. Magnificent gatehouse, mural towers and curtain. 'One of most moving sights in Northumberland'. (28, 65, 68, 73, 130, 146, 166, 180).

DUNSTER, Somerset 9943 C11, 13, 15, 18 C S (NT) Original motte-and-bailey centred on scarped hill. Nine centuries of occupation but mediaeval remains include C13 gateway and towers (modified C18), C15 gatehouse. (167, 177).

DUNSTON HALL, Northumberland 4262 C14–15 D H A C17 mansion has been attached to mediaeval pele-tower and altered in C18, 19. (130).

DURHAM, Durham 2742 c. 1080, C12 B+ P (Univ.)
Motte-and-bailey on naturally strong triangular site in loop of Wear. In spite of use as bishop's palace and university college, much original work remains including doorway to Pudey's Hall 'the most magnificent example of late Romanesque art in England'. (8, 13, 20, 30, 49, 52, 58, 66, 78, 79, 96, 124, 159, 166, 183).

EARDISLEY, Herefordshire 3149 C11 E O Motte in corner of square moated bailey with outer bailey or village enclosure. (85).

EARL SHILTON, Leicestershire 4697 C12? E O Only remains the motte W of church. (102).

EARLS BARTON, Northamptonshire 8564 C11 E O A short-lived motte-and-bailey which enclosed the pre-existent Saxon church. (30, 126).

EATON SOCON, Bedfordshire 1658 1221 E+ O Traces of moat and foundations of buildings. (15).

ECCLESHALL, Staffordshire 8329 C13 C H Episcopal moated manor c. 1200, later reconstructed as tower-house whose remains are incorporated in C17 residence. (170).

EDLINGHAM, Northumberland 1108 c. 1350 C O Simple rectangular walled enclosure with square tower at one end (original gateway at other?). Neglected but interesting site. Church has refuge-tower. (65, 130).

EGREMONT, Cumberland 0110 c. 1135 C O? Remains of gatehouse and curtain (both with herringbone), ruined domestic buildings. To N is mound of C11 castle. (44, 72, 84, 114).

ELLESMERE, Shropshire 3934 C12 E O Motte-and-baileys with outwork. (160).

ELMLEY, Worcestershire 9367 before 1216 D H Complex earthworks, rubble remains (of rectangular keep?). (30, 140, 197).

ELSDON, Northumberland 9393 C11 C O/S 'Best example of motte-and-bailey in county.' Vicar's Pele N of church (c. 1400) with armorial shield on exterior, interior reconstructed C18–20. (130, 187).

ELY, Cambridgeshire 5380 C12 or earlier E O Motte (40 ft high, 250 ft diam.) and bailey of 2½ acres. (24, 171).

EMBLETON, Northumberland 2322 1395 C H Vicar's pele, modified C16, 19, still used as vicarage. (130, 187).

ETAL, Northumberland 9339 l.c. 1341 C+ O? Minor castle with rectangular tower crossing simple bailey also protected by gatehouse and small wall-tower. Could contain 100 men for 'assembly'. (130).

EWYAS HAROLD, Herefordshire 3828 C11 E O Motte-and-bailey to which shell-keep and gatehouse were added. Remains of earthworks only W of church. (85).

EXETER, Devon 9292 c. 1068 D+ P 'Rougemont', a royal castle built in angle of Roman wall. Remains of ditch, curtain (with herringbone), towers and keep-gatehouse. Some sections of city walls still visible. (48, 73, 84, 171, 183, 193, 196).

EYNSFORD, Kent 5365 c. 1100 C DE Substantially complete example of early form of masonry castle, polygonal mound surrounded by high flint wall with (vanished) timber tower. (58, 95, 113).

EYE, Suffolk 1473 before 1086 D O Motte-and-bailey, ditched and scarped. Traces of wing-wall. Overgrown. (3, 159, 173).

FARLEIGH HUNGERFORD, Somerset 7957 c. 1375 C+ DE
Characteristic rectangular bailey with circular angle-towers and great gatehouse in centre of curtain. Outer bailey with chapel and barbican (C15). Former in use as parish church. (136, 167).

215

FARNHAM, Surrey 8446 1138? C+ H Motte-and-bailey with D-shaped enclosure. Later shell-keep of 23 sides, impervious to mining, encloses motte. Mediaeval remains of chapel (modified mid. C13), outer curtain (C14), tower (C15). 'Episcopal castle with domestic air.' (30, 31, 49, 96, 159, 174).

FARNHILL, Yorkshire, West Riding 9946 C14 B− H Fortified mansion; rectangular hall with square battlemented turrets at corners. Additions of C15. (200).

FAULKBOURNE, Essex 7917 lc. 1439 C+ S? Most impressive secular brick building in county – half castle, half mansion. (20, 112).

FEATHERSTONE, Northumberland 6761 C13, 14, 19 C− H Original hall-house strengthened by C14 tower with battlements and bartizans. Interior modified greatly and much C19 romanticism. (130).

FILLONGLEY, Warwickshire 2787 C12 D O Well-marked banks and ditches remain of motte-and-bailey with fragment of stone keep. (192).

FLAMBOROUGH, Yorkshire, East Riding 2270 lc. 1351 D O Fortified manor-house of Constables. Remains of keep with traces of vaulted basement. (199).

FLEET, Lincolnshire 3823 C11–12 E− O Only motte, greatly reduced by ploughing. (104).

FOLKESTONE, Kent 2236 C11 E O Ring-work and bailey on spur of N Downs above town. It had well and masonry. (95, 114).

FOLKINHAM, Lincolnshire 0733 C12 E O Site marked by remains of House of Correction. Square moated mound with larger bailey to N. (104).

FORD, Northumberland 9437 lc. 1338 C H/O Nucleus of C14 castle, unusual as square towers seem to have been only masonry buildings within curtain. Largest tower (of five floors) survives, SW exists in isolation, NE overwhelmed by later structures, SE vanished entirely. (Modified in C16, 18, 19). Also remains of vaulted ground floor of Vicar's Pele (Parson's Tower). (130, 187).

FOTHERINGAY, Northamptonshire 0593 c. 1100 E O Both castle and great collegiate church have vanished apart from earthworks of powerful motte-and-bailey in fetterlock shape. (129).

FRAMLINGHAM, Suffolk 2863 C12, 13, 16 B DE Motte-and-bailey on banks of Ure with extensive ditches once supplemented by damming river. Traces of C12 (hall, chapel) but remains mainly work of Roger Bigod (c. 1200). Curtain with 13 flanking towers, merlons with long arrow-loops. Bridge and gatehouse (C16). (13, 33, 44, 47, 64, 71, 75, 81, 84, 107, 126, 146, 173, 190).

GARLINGE, Kent 3669 C16 D+ O/H Fine 'Dent-du-lion' gatehouse alone survives of magnificent mansion. (20, 95, 114).

GATEHOUSE, Northumberland 7988 C14–15? C− O Possesses two characteristic Tynedale pele-towers with a number of others in neighbourhood. (127).

GAWTHORPE, Lancashire 8033 C15? D H Early C17 house encloses mediaeval pele-tower. (100).

GIDLEIGH, Devon 6788 c. 1300 D O Scant remains include part of small keep (22 ft × 13 ft interior). (48).

GILLING, Yorkshire, North Riding 6176 C14 C+ S Exceptionally large tower-house (80 ft square) with substantial additions in late C16 and C18. (138, 200).

GLEASTON, Lancashire 2570 c. 1330 B− ? Unusual plan consisting of irregular rectangle with various angle-towers. NW (keep) projects entirely beyond curtain to flank it and command entrance. Abandoned C15, probably uncompleted. (100).

GODARD'S, Kent 8057 C11? D O Ring-work with bailey on natural spur. Some masonry of curtain, gatehouse and (polygonal?) keep. (95, 121). Just over a mile away is another motte-and-bailey with scant masonry (Binbury).

GOODRICH, Herefordshire 5719 C11, 13 B DE Small Norman keep (29 ft square); C13 work – curtains, hall, towers, oratory and chapel, monumental barbican, asymmetrical gatehouse, fragments of outer bailey, impressive rock-cut moat. 'The most spectacular and best preserved castle in Herefordshire.' (23, 35, 85, 93, 101, 141, 144, 169, 170).

GOXHILL, Lincolnshire 1021 C12 C H The house calling itself a priory may contain the C14 hall of castle. Motte-and-bailey at Barrow End. (104).

GREASLEY, Nottinghamshire 4847 c. 1341 D– H Typical rectangular enclosure with square angle-towers. Remains of moat and masonry incorporated in farmhouse. (130).

GREAT ASBY, Westmoreland 6813 C14 D H Remains of Vicar's Pele incorporated in present rectory. (195).

GREAT CANFIELD, Essex 5917 C12 E O Fine motte (275 ft diam. 45 ft high) with two baileys. Ditch originally flooded from Roding. (59).

GREAT CHALFIELD, Wiltshire 8663 c. 1480 C+ P (NT) Well-preserved example of late mediaeval domestic building (moated manor) showing arrangement of domestic quarters. Hall can be overlooked from chamber above by squints through hollow masks decorating its ceiling. (169, 195).

GREAT EASTON, Essex 6125 C11? E H Motte (21 ft high, 130 ft diam.) and bailey with 45 ft wide ditch. (59).

GREENHALGH, Lancashire 3935 lc. 1490 D O 25 ft high ruins of pele-tower. (100).

GRESGARTH, Lancashire 5363 C15? D– H C18–19 house built round core of mediaeval pele-tower. (100).

GREY'S COURT, Oxfordshire 7282 lc. 1347, C16–18 C– P (NT) Built from spoils of Crecy, much modified through continuous occupation but retains great tower and three others. Well-house, 200 ft deep well and great donkey-wheel. (135).

GREYSTOKE, Cumberland 4330 1353 D+ H Original great pele just discernible amid C18 and C19 accretions. (44).

GRIMSTHORPE, Lincolnshire 0423 C13, 17, 18, 19 C H In spite of C16 enlargement and further work in C17, 18, 19, nucleus survives; courtyard with curtain and rectangular towers of varying size. (104).

GROBY, Leicestershire 5207 C12 d. 1176 D O/H 20 ft mound covers rubble-walled building and obliterates 50 ft wide ditches. Some masonry may be incorporated in manor-house. (47, 102).

GUILDFORD, Surrey 0049 C11, 12 C P Motte-and-bailey, crowned with shell-wall (C12) and later tower keep (c. 1170), 47 ft square and 63 ft high. Chapel on first floor. (43, 46, 65, 85, 132, 146, 174).

HADDON HALL, Derbyshire 2366 lc. 1195, C14–16 A S 'The English castle 'par excellence'... none other so complete and convincing.' (Pevsner). Perfect domestic arrangements, chapel with murals and mediaeval glass, hall, kitchen, parlour, solar. Gatehouse tower (c. 1530). (47, 61. 138).

HADLEIGH, Essex 8087 c. 1232 C DE Once most important castle in county. Rebuilt C14 in irregular oblong. Much obliterated by landslide but remains of curtain, towers, barbican. (59).

HALTON, Cheshire 5381 Mid C12 D O Fine site, neglected and in danger from Runcorn New Town. Some masonry. (32).

HALTON, Northumberland 9967 C14, 15, 17 B H Very fine pele-tower of cannibalised Roman masonry with battlements and bartizans. Later additions well composed. (130).

HAMPTON COURT, Herefordshire 5152 lc. 1434 C– H C15 gatehouse and chapel. Rest mainly C18–19. (85).

HANWELL, Oxfordshire   4343   late C16   C–   H   More a decorated manor-house than castle. Largely demolished in C18 and converted into farm-house. (135).

HARBOTTLE, Northumberland   9304   c. 1157   D+   O   'Finest mediaeval earthwork in county.' Motte-and-bailey beside Coquet, traces of curtain, tower, gatehouse, barbican. Original shell-keep reconstructed as gun-tower (1541). (130).

HAREWOOD, Yorkshire, West Riding   4344   lc. 1367   C+   H Rectangular structure, similar to Nunney, but with unique features e.g. kitchen projection. Tower-house sited on steep slope of hill. (101, 166, 200).

HARLSEY, Yorkshire, North Riding   4299   C12?   D   O Rectangular outer bailey with 30 ft deep ditch on three sides, inner enclosure with basement of stone keep (?) (200).

HARTLEBURY, Worcestershire   8470   1255, lc. 1268, C15, 17, 18   C H/S   Episcopal residence with few traces of its militant past. Mainly C17–18 but moat, part of tower and great hall are mediaeval. (48, 194).

HASTINGS, Sussex   8009   c. 1070   C+   P   Complex earthworks largely destroyed by erosion. Motte and two baileys. Scant remains of curtain and collegiate church (C11), wing-wall on motte, gatehouse (C13), fragment of wall-walk, tower. So called 'dungeons' probably storerooms. (30, 53, 85, 174, 177).

HAUGHLEY, Suffolk   0262   c. 1100 d. 1173   D+   O   Motte (80 ft high and 210 ft diam.) and bailey (rectangular with moat and outer enclosure). Impressive earthworks. (159, 173).

HAUGHTON, Northumberland   9172   C14   B   H   Typical tower-house but with additional tower in centre of front supported on five arches (c.f. Southampton walls). Umbrella vault in SW tower. Much altered in C19. (130).

HAWKESTONE, Shropshire   5829   1228   D+   O/H   Motte-and-bailey perched on two natural escarpments divided by deep glen. Remains of towers and fragments of curtain used as vista for C18 mansion. (160).

HAYTON, Cumberland   1041   C15, C11   a. C:H   b. E:O   a. A C17–18 mansion containing a very substantial mediaeval structure. b. Site of previous castle, N of village, with remains of great motte with double rampart and ditch (44).

HAZELSLACK, Westmoreland   4578   C14   D   0?   Pele-tower with subsequent annexe on E. Remains of tower, cross-walled with tunnel-vaulted ground floor. (195).

HAZLEWOOD, Yorkshire, West Riding   4439   lc. 1290   C   S Largely C18 but original (C13) chapel survives as does much modified hall. (200).

HEDINGHAM, Essex   3193   C12   B–   S   Motte-and-bailey of de Vere. Perhaps most magnificent and best preserved of English tower keeps (c. 1140). Scant remains of other structures. (42, 59, 63, 65, 70, 93, 177).

HEIGHLEY, Staffordshire   7647   C13   D   O   Spectacular rocky site with overgrown remains of two sections of walling, one arcaded. (170).

HELMSLEY, Yorkshire, North Riding   6183   c. 1190, C13, 14   B–   DE Very substantial remains: earthworks of de Roos, curtain and shattered D-shaped keep still standing to 100 ft, drawbridge-pit, foundations of domestic buildings and large chapel. (29, 53, 73, 93, 134, 143, 153, 155, 166, 172, 200).

HEMYOCK, Devon   1313   C12?   D   O   Confused remains of masonry including recognisable gateway. (48).

HEREFORD, Herefordshire   5040   C12   E   O   Motte-and-bailey with subsequent keep. Only remains of bailey rampart survive above moat (Castle Pool). (48, 56, 83, 85, 166, 177).

Some remains of town walls (c. 1300) including two bastions.

HERSTMONCEUX, Sussex   6410   lc. 1440   B   P/H   Rectangular enclosure with octagonal corner-towers and semi-octagonal ones along sides. Counterpoise drawbridge and impressive gatehouse. Early use of brick in ostentatious mansion rather than serious military work. Restored C20. Home of Royal Observatory. (20, 34, 52, 58, 77, 84, 100, 114, 131, 151, 174, 187).

HERTFORD, Hertfordshire   3212   C12, 15   D+   H   Motte-and-bailey beside river. Ditches filled in, remains of motte, curtain wall, tower, C15 gatehouse. (85).

HEXHAM, Northumberland   9364   C14   B   P   Moot Hall, former tower-house and courtroom of Archbishop of York (now library). Manor Office, associated prison built from cannibalised Roman stones. Sheer parallelogram with corbels for machicolation. Interior modified for contemporary use. (130).

HEVER, Kent   4744   lc. 1384   C   S   'Semi-fortified house par excellence.' Fortification mainly in impressive gatehouse with portcullis and machicolations. The square house is substantially C14 apart from fenestration and C16 gables and chimneys. (95, 111, 141).

HIGHAM FERRERS, Northamptonshire   9669   C11–15   E   O   Only slight ditches remain to indicate moat of great castle which once stood north of church. (30, 126).

HINCKLEY, Leicestershire   4294   Mid C12?   E   O   No remains except ring-work E of church. (102).

HINTON WALDRIST, Berkshire   3799   C11   E   H   (Conical) motte-and-bailey site now occupied by house. (16).

HOGHTON, Lancashire   6125   C16–17   C   S   Fortified manor-house ('tower') of late C16 with later additions on dramatic hilltop site. (100).

HOLDGATE, Shropshire   5589   C13–14   D   H   One semi-circular tower remains behind farmhouse. (160).

HOLLINSIDE, Durham   2061   C13   D+   O?   Fortified manor-house in picturesque site. Remains of hall, great entrance tower and other masonry. (53).

HOLT, Worcestershire   8262   C14   C+   S   Four-storeyed tower-house to which detached hall-range was added in C15. They were joined together in C18. (198).

HOOTON PAGNELL, Yorkshire, West Riding   4808   C14, 19   D+   H   Hall covers remains of fortified manor-house of which C14 gatehouse remains. (200).

HOPTON, Shropshire   5926   C12   D   O?   Substantial remains of Norman tower-keep, modified C14. (160).

HORNBY, Lancashire   5868   C11   C−   H   Motte-and-bailey, later impressive pele-tower (C13 with early C16 additions including oriel). Lost in massive castellated mansion (C19). (100).

HORNBY, Yorkshire, North Riding   3605   C15   C   H   Late Georgian house enfolds remains of tower-house and associated domestic range. (197, 200).

HORSFORD, Norfolk   1915   C12?   E   O   'Castle Hill' is site of substantial (natural) motte with bailey. (128).

HOUGHTON, Cumberland   4159   C13, 15   C   H   'Drawdykes' has mediaeval pele-tower incorporated in C17 house. Linstock possesses characteristic pele and hall which marks site of Bishop of Carlisle's residence C12–13. (44).

HUNTINGDON, Huntingdonshire   2371   1068   E   O   Low motte-and-bailey on bank of Ouse with second mound, possibly siege-work. (90, 165).

HYLTON, Durham   3558   c. 1400   C+   H   Oblong tower-house with square angle-turrets and towers at entrance. Bartizans and 'defenders'. Detached C15 chapel. (47, 52, 180).

IGHTAM MOTE, Kent 5956 C14, 16, B S Moated manor-house in idyllic setting. Most complete in county. Excellent C14 hall. C16 chapel with undercroft, squint from solar and priest's room. Gatehouse. C16 armorial glass. (95).

IRTON, Cumberland 1000 C14 D H C19 mansion incorporating mediaeval pele-tower. (44).

KENDAL, Westmoreland 5192 C12, 14 D+ O Ring-work on natural motte with outwork along ridge. Deep ditch, fragments of curtain and towers (C12) with tunnel-vaulted remains of C14 range. (166, 195).

KENILWORTH, Warwickshire 2875 C12–17 B DE 'One of grandest ruins in England.' Sited on natural knoll with extensive earthworks and water defences. Massive keep (1170–80), curtain (C13) with a self-contained wall-chamber, gatehouses, towers, foundations of chapel, domestic buildings include hall which rivalled Westminster. (12, 14, 15, 22, 29, 31, 39, 43, 55, 65, 66, 76, 78, 79, 81, 83, 84, 94, 96, 107, 126, 130, 131, 141, 146, 147, 155, 163, 165, 170, 177, 181, 190, 191, 193, 194).

KENTCHURCH, Herefordshire 4125 C14 C S Gateway, modified NW tower and domestic quarters survive within Nash mansion. (85).

KILPECK, Herefordshire 4430 C11–12 D O Small motte, surmounted by remains of polygonal shell-keep, and kidney-shaped bailey. Outer baileys and village enclosure containing one of the best small Norman churches in country. (85).

KILTON, Yorkshire, North Riding, 6918 C12 C– O Narrow natural site on ridge above beck, isolated by ditch. Remains of towers obscured by encroaching woods. (200).

KIMBOLTON, Huntingdonshire 0967 C12? E– S C18 house occupies site which was successively occupied by mediaeval castle and houses of C16 and C17. (90).

KINETON, Warwickshire 3351 C12? D O Remains of large motte-and-bailey with some masonry. (192).

KINGSBURY, Warwickshire 2196 C14? C H Remains of fortified manor-house, separated from village by ravine, include fragments of curtain, tower and arch. (192).

KINGSWEAR, Devon 8851 1491–4 C ? Built to match Dartmouth and close Dart to hostile shipping. Much restored and modified. (48).

KIRBY MUXLOE, Leicestershire 5104 lc. 1474 B– DE Fortified manor in brick of Lord Hastings on symmetrical pattern. Substantial remains of rectangular moat, gatehouse, W tower and curtain. Gun-loops among earliest in England. (13, 25, 31, 77, 100, 102, 111, 131, 171).

KIRKANDREWS, Cumberland 3558 C12, C16 D+ H/O Tower is early C16 pele showing Scottish influence. (44).
Liddell Strength, half mile away, has motte and double-bailey (before 1174).

KIRKBY FLEETHAM, Yorkshire, North Riding 2894 D O Two castles: one near Post Office (lc. 1314) with remains of moat and curtain; other at Killerby with damaged motte, impressive ditch and bailey. (200).

KIRKOSWALD, Cumberland 5541 1201 D+ O Motte with rectangular bailey. Remains of moat, towers and fragments of gatehouse. (44, 92).
'The College' (C17) incorporates defensive pele-tower and walls of mediaeval college of priests.

KNARESBOROUGH, Yorkshire, West Riding 3557 C14 C P Royal castle beautifully sited above Nidd. Remains of curtain, towers and substantial part of keep which is interesting for its design. (39, 68, 81, 90, 93, 145, 166, 177, 187, 200).

KNEPP, Sussex 1620 C11? d. 1215? D O? Motte-and-bailey with added stone keep of which there are some remains. (143, 175, 193).

KNOCKIN, Shropshire 3322 C12 or earlier D O Motte-and-bailey with fragments of rubble wall, E of church. (160).

LAMBTON, Durham 2952 C19 Picturesque Gothic extravaganza on fine site. 'Nothing of the building is, in fact, genuine except the solid, beautifully biscuit-coloured stone.' (53).

LAMMERSIDE, Cumberland 7704 C14 C O Pele-tower of rectangular plan with cross-wall and tunnel-vaulted lower storey. (44).

LANCASTER, Lancashire 4761 C11 etc. C+ P Splendidly sited above Lune. Mostly C18, 19 but mediaeval remains: keep (apart from top storey), inner gatehouse (C11), monumental outer one (c. 1400), parts of walls and towers are C13. (39, 42, 49, 68, 73, 80, 93, 100, 147, 166).

LANGLEY, Northumberland 3856 c. 1350 B S Interesting tower-house of unusual plan. Square angle-towers are set close together to provide single room on each of four floors. Forebuilding added to guard entry. Lavish provision of privies. Large windows and battlements not original but latter may be good imitations. (88, 130, 146).

LAUNCESTON, Cornwall 3384 C11, 13 C P Motte-and-bailey with interesting shell-keep and inserted tower of C13. Remains of gates, curtain and ruins of domestic buildings. (38, 52, 159, 165).

LAVENDON, Buckinghamshire 9153 C12 E O Motte (d. 1944) and three rectangular baileys. (21).

LEA, Shropshire 3589 C14 D H High fragment of C14 keep attached to house (C19?). (160).

LEAVINGTON, Yorkshire, North Riding 4309 C11 E+ O Large Norman motte, completely surrounded by ditch, sited above Leven. No bailey. Earth breastwork on summit of motte has inner platform with entrance at S. (200).

LECONFIELD, Yorkshire, East Riding 0143 lc. 1308 E O Nothing remains above ground of large Percy castle except traces of moat. (111, 200).

LEEDS, Kent 8353 C12, 13, 16 B+ S 'Fulfills the imagined picture of what a castle should be.' Set on three islands in artificial lake which provide location for bailey, barbican and keep (Gloriette). Much restored but many interesting original features. (14, 19, 30, 34, 36, 54, 95, 120, 177, 193).

LEICESTER, Leicestershire 5904 C11 B P Motte-and-bailey beside Soar. Second bailey (Newarke) added C14. Remains of decapitated mound, gateway (C15), great hall (in Courthouse), gatehouse and chapel (still in use). (30, 46, 49, 69, 102).

LEVENS, Westmoreland 4886 C15? D S Hall may enclose mediaeval pele and domestic range but substantially it is C17–18 with C19 additions. (195).

LEWES, Sussex 4110 C11, 12, 14 C+ P Pre-conquest castle with two mounds within long oval bailey. Remains of shell-keep (c. 1180), curtain, tower, barbican (C14), gatehouse (C11). (12, 13, 73, 87). Sections of town-walls (C13–14) survive and fragment of Westgate. (174).

LEYBOURNE, Kent 6858 C14? D H Parts of castle (gatehouse, tower, fragment of curtain) incorporated in C20 house. (73, 95, 109, 159).

LICHFIELD, Staffordshire 1209 C12 No remains of castle which probably stood in Ware/Frog St. area. (67).

LIDGATE, Suffolk 7258 C12 D O Rectangular mound with three baileys, one containing church. Remains of ditch and fragment of rubble wall. (173).

LINCOLN, Lincolnshire 9771 C11, 13, 14 B− P 166 Saxon houses were destroyed to make room for Norman castle. Two mottes, one with polygonal shell-keep, other with square tower. Prominent ditches and massive earthworks, remains of towers and fine gates. (1, 13, 27, 31, 67, 83, 85, 91,

104, 159, 164, 165, 166, 177, 181, 182, 187).

LITTLE WENHAM, Suffolk 0838 c. 1270–80 C+ H Ranks with Acton Burnell and Stokesay in transition from castle to house. L-shaped fortified manor with first-floor entrance, vaulted basement, hall and chapel, solar or guard-room. One of earliest uses of English brick. (173).

LLANCILLO, Herefordshire 3625 C12? D O Motte-and-bailey with traces of (c. 50 ft diameter) shell-keep. (85).

LOCKINGTON, Yorkshire, East Riding 9947 C11? E O Low motte with bailey, both moated. (199).

LONDON, Middlesex 3079 1078 A DE White Tower is one of finest and best preserved structures of its kind in Europe. Palace-fortress and prison continuously added to until it was concentric with three baileys, numerous towers and gates and water-defences. Castles also at Baynard's and Mountfitchet. (1, 7, 10, 21, 22, 28, 30, 35, 37, 39, 43, 46, 54, 56, 63, 74, 83, 86, 92, 101, 102, 113, 114, 118, 127, 133, 141, 142, 144, 145, 151, 155, 164, 166, 177, 181, 183, 187, 193, 195, 200).

LONG CRENDON, Buckinghamshire 6908 C15 C H House includes elements of fortified manor-house, including gateway. (21).

LONGTHORPE, Northamptonshire 1698 c. 1300 C DE Tower added to earlier hall. Important for the remains of wall-paintings. (46, 90, 127, 129).

LONGTOWN, Herefordshire 3228 C11, 12 C+ P Motte with baileys and outwork on spur site overlooking Monmow. Remains of keep, curtain and gatehouse. (85, 181, 196).

LUDGERSHALL, Wiltshire 2650 C11, 12 D+ DE Ring-work with double ditch, elaborated as popular royal hunting-lodge. Remains of extensive earthworks and scant masonry. (96, 195).

LUDLOW, Shropshire 5175 1085, C11–16 B+ DE 'One of most powerful and complete examples of military architecture in Great Britain.' Site above river, isolated by rock-cut ditches. C11 keep, curtain and wall-towers; outer bailey with curtain and gate (C12). Fine range of domestic buildings (C13–14), unique chapel (C12). (22, 30, 44, 46, 68, 73, 76, 78, 79, 94, 96, 134, 143, 146, 160, 166, 179, 190).

LUDWORTH, Durham 3641 lc. 1422 D O Fragmentary remains, divided by road, of Cardinal Langley's tower. (53).

LULLINGSTONE, Kent 5763 C16 D+ S fortified manor with moat and two gatehouses. (20, 95, 114).

LUMLEY, Durham 2851 lc. 1389 B S In spite of C16 and C18 improvements substantially survives as a fine example of a typical C14 castle. (52, 88, 180).

LYDFORD, Devon 5084 C− P? Fortified Saxon promontory site to which motte-and-bailey were added (1087?). Present keep (1195) built in side of motte expressly to house prisoners. (48, 144).

LYMPNE, Kent 1235 C15 C S Fortified manor formerly belonging to Archdeacons of Canterbury. (95).

LYONSHALL, Herefordshire 3356 C12–13? D O Ring-work within rectangular enclosure. Remains of curtain and fragments of keep within polygonal projection. (85).

MACKWORTH, Derbyshire 3137 C15 D O Only remains are ruins of gatehouse (1495). (47).

MARKENFIELD, Yorkshire, North Riding C14–16 B S Fine example of moated manor-house. (111, 200).

MARLBOROUGH, Wiltshire 1869 C12 E S Of royal castle in use up to C14 nothing survives above ground except a 60 ft high mound in College grounds. (3, 39, 46, 83, 96, 152, 195).

MARSHWOOD, Dorset 3899 C13 D O Low motte in moated enclosure with further outer enclosure to SW. Stump of oblong tower. Fortified manor rather than castle? (51).

MAXSTOKE, Warwickshire   2386   lc. 1346   B   S?   Characteristic rectangular enclosure with angle-towers and gatehouse in one long side. Transitional between Harlech and Bolton. C16–17 modifications but mediaeval remains include: moat, gatehouse, polygonal towers, curtain, domestic range. (52, 68, 100, 111, 131, 160, 192).

MERDON, Hampshire   4226   1138   D   O   Circular ring-work sub-divided to provide bailey or barbican. On site of Iron Age fort? Remains of curtain and tower. (80).

METTINGHAM, Suffolk   3689   lc. 1342   C−   H?   Site occupied by mediaeval college before end C14 and by house in C19. Remains of gatehouse, fragments of barbican, traces of curtain. (52, 100, 173).

MIDDLEHAM, Yorkshire, North Riding   1287   C12–15   B   DE   Favourite castle of Richard III whose heir was born here. Unique plan with one of largest keeps in England and remains of curtain walls and towers, gatehouse, earthworks. (30, 35, 42, 65, 68, 76, 80, 87, 120, 146, 166, 193, 200). 500 yards SW are remains of earlier castle; 40 ft high motte with kidney-shaped bailey and formidable ditch.

MIDDLETON, Norfolk   6616   C12, 15   D   H   'Towers' is C19 house incorporating C15 gatehouse. The Mount, about 400 yards away, may be damaged motte of C12 castle. (128).

MIDDLETON STONEY, Oxfordshire   5323   C12   d. 1216   E   O Motte-and-bailey E of church. (135).

MIDHURST, Sussex   8821   C12?   E   O   On St. Anne's Hill are vague remains of triangular mound with ditch and bailey – all that remains of castle with shell-keep, curtain, chapel. (175).

MILEHAM, Norfolk   9119   C12   D   O?   'The Hall Yards'' contain circular motte with foundations of small keep, remains of two baileys. (128).

MILLOM, Cumberland   1780   1335   C+   H   Pele-tower and hall with domestic buildings, now much intermingled with farm. (44).

MITFORD, Northumberland   1685   C12, 13   D+   O   Improved natural site on bank of Wansbeck. Oval enclosure with motte, curtain and (unique?) pentagonal keep (C13). Curtain and outer bailey (C12) with undefended courtyard beyond. (93, 130, 166).

MIXBURY, Oxfordshire   6033   c. 1100   E   O   Originally called 'Beaumont'. Remains: mounds in field near church. (135).

MORE, Shropshire   3491   C11   E   O   Immediately post-Conquest ring-work overlaid by more elaborate castle consisting of motte with two square baileys in echelon, flanked by marsh. (160).

MORETON CORBET, Shropshire   5523   C12, 13, 16   C   S?   'Magnificent ruin' of roughly triangular enclosure, keep (c. 1200) with fine fireplace, gatehouse (C13 altered C16), fragments of curtain (C13?), Elizabethan domestic range. (160).

MORPETH, Northumberland   2085   C12, 15   C   S?   Original motte-and-bailey on natural site on spur above Wansbeck d. 1215. New castle built in bailey of old, mainly gatehouse-keep which substantially exists with portions of adjoining curtain. (130, 177).

MORTHAM, Yorkshire, North Riding   0814   mid C14?   C−   H Tower-house or pele with tourelles and unique (?) battlements. Hall added C15 and remodelling in C17 and C18. (61, 200).

MULGRAVE, Yorkshire, North Riding   8412   1214   D+   H/O Natural (?) motte with remains of small square keep (c. 1215 with modifications of C14). Polygonal bailey with fragments of curtain. In grounds of Mulgrave Castle. (200).

MUNCASTER, Cumberland   1096   C15, 19   D   S   C19 mansion on superb site enveloping remains of pele-tower. (44).

NAFFERTON, Northumberland 0863 1217 D+ O 'Lonkins Hall'.
Scanty remains due to cannibalisation in bridging Whittle Dean but example of
adulterine castle whose building was stopped by writ of Henry III. Its
unfinished state gave rise to rich harvest of legend and song. Planned as keep
with inner and outer baileys. (19, 130, 143).

NAPPA, Yorkshire, North Riding 9490 c. 1460 C+ H Fortified
manor-house: two unequal towers with hall between. Wing of C17. (200).

NAWORTH, Cumberland 5662 1335, C16-19 C H Dacre fortified
mansion, restored mid C19. Yett, timber ceiling from Kirkoswald, parts of
screen from Lanercost. (44, 199).

NEROCHE, Somerset 1618 C11, 12 E+ O Natural spur isolated by
bank and ditch. Inner square enclosure added followed by outer bank and
ditch. 'A prodigious structure'. (167).

NETHER STOWEY, Somerset 1939 C12 D O Motte with foundations
of square keep and two baileys. Probably FitzOdo castle captured by torches
being thrown through tower loops. (167).

NEWARK, Nottinghamshire 7953 C12, 13, 15 C+ P Trapezoidal site
on cliff above Trent. Remains of biggest and most elaborate gateway of its
period (c. 1170) with first-floor chapel, C12 angle-tower and crypt, wall and
hexagonal towers (C13), hall with oriel (C15), watergate. (13, 31, 69, 73, 78,
130, 133, 166, 171, 172, 177, 193).

NEWCASTLE, Northumberland 2464 C12, 13 B P Site at confluence of
Tyne and Lort Burn isolated by ditch. One of greatest citadels in country
disintegrated by railway. Massive keep, with polygonal turret at most exposed
angle, entered at third storey (C12), gatehouse (c. 1247), base of square tower,
S postern, fragments of curtain among railway yards. (19, 29, 30 38, 43, 56,
58, 59, 62, 63, 64, 65, 66, 70, 73, 82, 83, 93, 94, 103, 126, 127, 130, 143, 146,
164, 166, 177, 178, 193, 194).
Scattered remains of town walls with towers and turrets. No gates survive. (47,
141, 183).

NEWCASTLE, Staffordshire 8445 C12 D O Of royal castle there are
remains of motte-and-bailey and fragments of curtain in Queen Elizabeth
Gardens. (3, 127, 143, 170).

NEWTON KYME, Yorkshire, West Riding 4644 C13 D H Scant
masonry remains of domestic buildings (?) in garden of hall. (200).

NEWTON ST LOE, Somerset 7064 C13, 15, 16 C P In grounds of
Newton Park are remains of much restored keep (C13), gatehouse (C15),
domestic range (remodelled C16). (167).

NORHAM, Northumberland 9047 C12, 14-16 B DE Chief Northern
stronghold of Prince-bishops of Durham. Originated in square ring-work and
bailey (c. 1121). Masonry remains include great keep (C12, 15), curtain walls
and towers, gatehouse with drawbridge pit, casemates for cannon and
gun-ports. (39, 58, 65, 80, 82, 86, 94, 99, 104, 130, 166, 177).

NORTHAMPTON, Northamptonshire 7561 C11 E+ O Nothing
remains of one of most famous Norman castles except minor archway (not in
situ). (16, 129, 141, 164).

NORTHBOROUGH, Huntingdonshire 1508 c. 1335, C17 B− S Hall
and gatehouse (C14) of major defensible manor-house. (90, 129).

NORTH ELMHAM, Norfolk 9820 c. 1050 lc. 1388 C DE C14
conversion of former Saxon cathedral into fortified hunting-lodge by
Despenser. Abandoned uncompleted 1406. Rectangular moated enclosure
containing modified cathedral within inner moat. Outer bailey. (128).

NORWICH, Norfolk 2308 C11, 12, 19 C+ P Two baileys and motte
which was flattened to seat enormous keep (c. 1160). Magnificent in spite of
C19 refacing, gutting of interior and demolition of forebuilding. (27, 35, 37,
58, 67, 70, 71, 80, 95, 102, 128, 177, 180, 183, 191).

NOTTINGHAM, Nottinghamshire   5740   1068, C17   D+   P   Danish stronghold in C9, motte-and-bailey elaborated during Middle Ages but nothing remains except drastically restored outer gate. Underground passages. Site occupied by Cavendish palace. (3, 38, 50, 69, 83, 106, 130, 133, 141, 166, 173, 187).

NUNNEY, Somerset   7345   lc. 1373   B−   DE   'Aesthetically the most impressive in Somerset'. Tower-house built from French loot and probably inspired by French models. More status symbol than serious defensive work. Interesting details: fireplace, well, chapel (with original piscina and altar). (31, 54, 68, 100, 109, 111, 131, 151, 167, 180).

OAKHAM, Rutland   8509   C11, 13   C+   S   Traces of motte within square bailey with ditch. Of masonry only hall survives (1180–90). Earliest and magnificent example : aisled with excellent carving on corbels and capitals. (78, 154).

ODIHAM, Hampshire   7350   c. 1210   D   O   Trapezoidal moated site in bend of Whitewater. Complex earthworks and remains of rare octagonal keep with Caen facing. (39, 49, 71, 80, 173, 178).

OGLE, Northumberland   1378   lc. 1341   C   H   L-shaped tower-house with original fireplaces and beams, incorporated in later manor-house. (130).

OKEHAMPTON, Devon   5895   C12?   C   DE   Motte-and-bailey beside river. Remains of rectangular keep, curtain, gate, barbican, domestic quarters. One of largest Devon castles in picturesque situation. (48, 79, 177).

OLD SARUM, Wiltshire   1332   c. 1075   C+ DE   Magnificent site shared by castle and cathedral C11–13 until conflict led clergy to new site in valley. Ring-work with complex banks and ditches. Remains of C12 curtain, gatehouse, tower, curious keep, postern and domestic buildings. 'Greatest motte-and-bailey in Europe'. (45, 46, 48, 49, 126, 144, 147, 172, 173, 177, 180, 187, 191, 195).

OLD WARDOUR, See WARDOUR.

ONGAR, See CHIPPING.

ORFORD, Suffolk   4250   1165–73   B−   DE   Bailey and keep of revolutionary design : 18 sides with three rectangular turrets. Interesting interior arrangements include three-sided chapel over entrance and cistern on top of W turret. (13, 14, 30, 38, 49, 71, 82, 93, 114, 173, 177, 178).

OSWESTRY, Shropshire   2829   C12   D   O   Motte with rubble fragments of shell-wall. (27, 60).

OTTERBURN, Northumberland   8893   C14?   D   H   Remains of pele-tower incorporated in mansion of C18–19, now hotel. (130).

OVERSLEY, Warwickshire   0755   C12?   E−   H   C19 tower with attached C20 house. In grounds vague traces of angular motte and triangular bailey. (192).

OWSTON FERRY, Lincolnshire   8000   C11   d. 1176   E   O   Motte with evidence of deliberate slighting and bailey containing church. (47, 104).

OXBURGH HALL, Norfolk   7401   lc. 1482, C18, 19   C+   P   (NT) Moated house with superb unaltered gatehouse possessing unique (?) brick spiral stair. (128).

OXFORD, Oxfordshire   5106   1071   D+   Prison   Large motte with bailey beside river. Masonry remains of chapel crypt, well-chamber and tower which served both church and curtain.
Early C13 fragments of city walls with open-gorged towers. (43, 46, 95, 135, 151, 179, 183).

PAULL HOLME, Yorkshire, East Riding   1823   C15   C   H   Brick tower-house or pele with characteristic tunnel-vaulted basement. (197).

PECKFORTON, Cheshire   5356   c. 1850   A   H   Salvin's masterpiece – 'the only fully deceptive of all the English C19 castles'. (32).

PEMBRIDGE, Herefordshire   3858   C12, 13 etc.   B−   S   Well preserved small castle in spite of C16–17 additions. Mediaeval remains include tower (C12?), curtain (C13), impressive gatehouse (C13+) and chapel undercroft. (85).

PENDENNIS, Cornwall   8231   1544–6   C   DE   Henrician coastal castle: circular keep within two rings of fortification. (9, 38).

PENDRAGON, Westmoreland   7802   C12   C–   O   Characteristic example of N country pele-tower, somewhat elaborated: buttress developed into turret, vaulted mural chambers. Ruinous. (195).

PENGERSICK, Cornwall   5829   C15?   C   H   Battlemented and gun-looped, two towers. Carving and murals. (38).

PENRITH, Cumberland   5130   lc. 1397   C   O   Uncharacteristic Cumbrian castle of unified form: high rectangular curtain with two defensive towers. (44).

PENSHURST, Kent   5243   lc. 1341, C16, 19   B   S   C14 manor-house with later additions. Unfortified house surrounded by complete system of defensive walls and towers. Magnificent hall, with traces of wall-painting, preserved entire except for louvre. (54, 95, 169).

PENYARD, Herefordshire   6323   C13?   D   O   Converted into farm-house (collapsed). Remains: gable-end and undercroft. (85).

PEVENSEY, Sussex   6405   c. 1100   B   DE   In corner of Roman fort whose walls form outer bailey. Inner bailey enclosed with bank and ditch. Remains of rectangular keep, C13 curtain and gatehouse, semi-circular wall-towers. (35, 36, 44, 72, 80, 87, 114, 161, 166, 174, 177, 185, 190, 193, 194, 197).

PEVERIL, Derbyshire   1482   C11   C   P?   'Only castle of importance in county'. Strong natural site with remains of curtain (herringbone), square keep (1176), ruins of gatehouse, foundations of chapel and hall. (30, 47, 82, 85, 90, 138, 146, 166, 177).

PICKERING, Yorkshire, North Riding   7983   C12–14   B   DE   Fine motte, unusually enclosed by bailey. Remains of shell-keep, traces of hall with 'seat of honour', curtain walls, towers. Situated on edge of moor and popular with hunting kings. (7, 11, 19, 31, 36, 39, 53, 69, 85, 90, 114, 123, 134, 143, 145, 151, 159, 165, 166, 169, 179, 185, 186, 189, 194, 197, 200).

PIEL, Lancashire   2363   lc. 1327   B–?   Island site S of Barrow with substantial ruins of tower-house keep, curtain and towers of inner bailey, gatehouse. Less of outer bailey but discernible towers and chapel. (100).

PILLATON, Staffordshire   3664   C15   C   ?   Remains of large brick fortified mansion with gatehouse and chapel. (170).

PLESHEY, Essex   6614   C12   E   O   Large motte with kidney-shaped bailey to which another was added to form figure-of-eight. All within village enclosure. (59, 181).

PLYMPTON, Devon   5356   c. 1100   D   O   Motte and rectangular bailey. Fragments of shell-keep and remains of curtain. (48, 159).

PONTEFRACT, Yorkshire, West Riding   4522   C12 etc.   D+   P   Once 'the Troy of England', now scattered and obscured by slighting, new road and commercial and recreational abuse. Probably most powerful castle in England and some evidence that its keep was the greatest tower in Britain. Extensive underground works beneath keep and bailey. (25, 30, 46, 61, 74, 78, 87, 124, 134, 141, 143, 144, 145, 151, 165, 166, 170, 185, 187, 200).

PONTELAND, Northumberland   1672   C14, 17   C–   S   C14 pele-tower incorporated into C17 manor-house and whole now handsomely used as inn. Ruins of vicar's pele in gardens of nearby rectory. (130, 187).

PONTESBURY, Shropshire   3905   C11?   E+   O   Ring-work with traces of bailey and village enclosure (?). (160).

PORTCHESTER, Hampshire   6105   C3, 12, 14   B   DE   Rectangular bailey with two sides formed by Roman walls. Curtain, keep, SE tower and gatehouse (C12). Improvements including domestic buildings of C14. (12, 30, 42, 44, 46

54, 63, 64, 65, 66, 68, 73, 80, 93, 94, 114, 126, 146, 166, 177, 190, 196).

PORTLAND, Dorset   6972   c. 1540   C+   DE   Perhaps best preserved of Henrician channel forts. (9, 51).

POWDERHAM, Devon   9784   C14, 16, 18, 19   C   S   Some mediaeval towers survive subsequent rebuilding and additions. (48).

PRUDHOE, Northumberland   0962   C12, 19   C+   S   Keep and bailey on strong natural site. Remains of keep, tower and gatehouse ('one of most rewarding in county'), chapel with corbelled-out sanctuary in 'earliest oriel in England'. (30, 35, 46, 130, 133, 138, 166).

PULFORD, Cheshire   3758   before 1190   E   O   Motte-and-bailey beside Alyn. (32).

QUEENBOROUGH, Kent   1361   No remains of this castle on Sheppey but mentioned for its unique circular and concentric plan, attributed to Henry Yevele. (54, 95, 159).

RABY, Durham   1321   lc. 1378   B+   S   In spite of C18–19 alterations, substantially of C14. 'Largest mediaeval castle in county and one of most impressive in North of England.' (4, 47, 52, 68, 88, 96, 180).

RADCLIFFE TOWER, Lancashire   7806   C15   D   O   Only fortified building in S Lancashire. Scanty remains of pele or tower-house. (100).

RAVENSWORTH, Yorkshire, North Riding   2359   C14 or earlier   D+   O   Extensive castle but sparse remains above ground: gatehouse and masonry fragments. (46, 87, 91, 200).

RAYLEIGH, Essex   8090   Pre-conquest   E   P   (NT)   High motte with small bailey to which another was later added (as village enclosure?). Domesday mentions a vineyard here. (59, 124).

READING, Berkshire   7272   c. 1140   d. 1151   E   O   Much altered mound in Forbury Gardens may be remains of Stephen's castle. (16, 103).

REIGATE, Surrey   2550   before 1157   D–   O   Oval ring-work within wide, deep ditch which extended over present Tunnel Rd to form bailey. Ring-work now rose garden with C18 gatehouse fabricated from castle masonry. (114, 174).

RESTORMEL, Cornwall   1059   c. 1100, C12, 13   B   DE   'The most perfect example of military architecture in Cornwall'. Motte-and-bailey on strong natural site, remains of gate, keep, curtain, domestic buildings. (38, 126, 159).

RICHMOND, Yorkshire, North Riding   1701   1071, C12, 14   B   DE   Triangular enclosure on cliff above Swale. Uniquely situated and substantially complete keep (1150–80), curtain walls with mural towers (C11+), well-chamber, remarkable number of posterns, domestic apartments include earliest stone hall in country. (20, 31, 43, 44, 46, 57, 58, 68, 73, 78, 85, 86, 87, 94, 104, 111, 126, 143, 166, 177, 189, 191, 193, 195, 200).

RIPLEY, Yorkshire, West Riding   2860   C15, 16, 18   C   S   Remains of fortified manor-house consisting of gatehouse and tower block. Rest later. (200).

RISING, Norfolk   6624   c. 1150   B   DE   Albini castle possibly modelled on Norwich. Massive rectangular earthwork enclosing 12 acres. Large central ring-work. Magnificent hall-keep with impressive fore-building, remains of chapel and gatehouse. (30, 31, 42, 53, 64, 65, 66, 72, 80, 81, 126, 128, 145, 177).

ROCHESTER, Kent   7467   c. 1128   B   DE   Archiepiscopal castle of lozenge-plan divided into two baileys. Gatehouse and large portion of curtain vanished but keep remains and 'few keeps can be named in the same breath as this'. (10, 21, 39, 42, 44, 52, 54, 64, 65, 67, 70, 93, 95, 104, 121, 141, 142, 145, 147, 153, 155, 163, 164, 166, 173, 174, 180, 191, 194).

ROCKINGHAM, Northamptonshire   8691   Pre-Conquest?, C13, 19   C   S   Motte-and-bailey with later masonry of which remains a magnificent gatehouse, part of curtain and some of hall. Rest mainly C19. (73, 129).

ROSE, Cumberland 5746 C13–15 etc. C– H Episcopal palace with nucleus formed of pele-tower (c. 1300), another tower of C15 and some mediaeval walling. (44).

ROTHERFIELD GREYS, Oxfordshire See GREY'S COURT.

ROTHWELL, Yorkshire, West Riding 3428 C13? D– O Odd fragments of wall, SW of church. (200).

RUDGWICK, Surrey 0934 C12? E O 'Ring-work in Broomhall copse, 90 ft across' (Renn). (174).

RUFUS, Dorset 6971 before 1142 D H/O Also called 'Bow and Arrow', above Church Ope Cove in Isle of Portland. Pentagonal tower with gun-loops on earlier building, entrance gateway. (51, 77).

RUYTON, Shropshire 3922 C14 D O Ruins of small keep near church. Built by Earl of Arundel who created borough out of eleven small townships. (160).

RYE, Sussex 9220 mid C13 C+ P Ypres (Baddings) Tower was town castle in Middle Ages and town prison from 1518 to C19. Two-storeyed rectangle with round corner towers, remains of machicolation. Attached to part of C14 town wall of which there are other fragments, including gates (especially Landgate). C19 Martello tower. (174, 182, 183).

SAFFRON WALDEN, Essex 5438 C11? D O Motte-and-bailey levelled but some streets mark ditch line. Fragments (with herringbone) of C11 keep. (1, 59).

ST BRIAVELS, Gloucestershire 5504 C12, 13 B S Royal hunting-lodge and administrative centre for Forest of Dean. Splendid keep-gatehouse (C13), remains of curtain, chapel, hall range (now Youth Hostel). (33, 73, 75, 120, 142).

ST JOHNS JERUSALEM, Kent 2343 C13, 17 D+ P (NT) Formerly Commandery of Knights Hospitallers. After Dissolution a secular house was built on moated site but chapel survives. (95, 120).

ST MAWES, Cornwall 8433 1540–3 C+ DE Perhaps best of Henrician artillery forts. (9, 38).

SALISBURY, See OLD SARUM.

SALTWOOD, Kent 1536 C11, 12, 14 etc. B S Former archiepiscopal castle: large oval ring-work with ditch and triangular bailey. Masonry remains: curtain towers of inner bailey (C12?), outer bailey (C13), impressive gatehouse (c. 1390) with Courtenay arms, well, domestic range with (unusually) two halls. (22, 47, 73, 77, 95, 192).

SANDAL, Yorkshire, West Riding 3418 C11, 12 D O Remarkable plan: circular outer bailey, inner ditch round barbican tower connected to shell-keep on motte by two attached towers, one semi-circular, the other polygonal. Major mediaeval castle, besieged in Civil War. Remains only of earthworks and scant masonry of keep. (159, 166, 200).

SANDGATE, Kent 2035 1539–40 C– P? Henrician coastal fort, converted into Martello tower (1806). (9, 95).

SANDWICH, Kent 3358 C14 C– O Brick gateway and earthen banks survive of town fortifications. (181).

SCALEBY, Cumberland 4563 lc. 1307 C H In spite of C17 modifications and C19 additions, mediaeval remains of gatehouse (C14) polygonal tower, rectangular pele and first storey of associated hall (C15). (44, 141).

SCARBOROUGH, Yorkshire, North Riding 0388 C12, 13 B– DE Royal castle from Henry II on magnificent peninsular site. Remains of impressive curtain with postern, extensive barbican and high ruins of shattered keep. (12, 33, 34, 39, 42, 65, 66, 82, 83, 93, 94, 141, 143, 166, 171, 174, 177, 178, 194, 200).

SCARGILL, Yorkshire, North Riding 0510 C15 or earlier D+ H

Fragments of masonry and substantial remains of gatehouse incorporated in farm. (200).

SCOTNEY, Kent 7035 C14, 16 etc. C S (Gdns.) House fortified with moat, curtain and towers of which there are substantial remains in spite of much later modification and rebuilding. (54, 95).

SEDGWICK, Sussex 5186 lc. 1258 D H Neglected site in grounds of park with fragmentary masonry is all that remains of C13 castle of advanced design. (141).

SHERBORNE, Dorset 6316 c. 1120 C+ DE Originally episcopal, taken by Crown. Unique plan: rectangle with chamfered corners within wide ditch and bank, defended by towers and gatehouse. Rectangular keep. In spite of Raleigh's development and Fairfax's slighting, interesting remains in fine ashlar. (49, 51, 72, 78, 80, 171).

SHERIFF HUTTON, Yorkshire, North Riding 6566 lc. 1382 C S Built by Neville of Raby, similar to Bolton but much more ruinous. (54, 200). Square mound S of church may represent Bulmer castle of c. 1140. (54, 88, 200).

SHIRBURN, Oxfordshire ʹ995 lc. 1377 C18, 19 C H Originated as typical C14 castle: moated rectangular site, round angle-towers, gatehouse in front of curtain. Earliest Oxfordshire use of brick. Drastically remodelled C18, 19. (68, 135, 177).

SHRAWARDINE, Shropshire 3915 C12 D O Motte-and-bailey beside Severn: masonry fragments of square keep. (160).

SHREWSBURY, Shropshire 4912 C11, 12 C P? Motte-and-bailey at bottleneck in Severn loop. Royal from 1102. Masonry remains: gateway (C12–13), postern (rebuilt C16), hall (C13, 17), inner bailey curtain (C12). (11, 27, 46, 83, 160, 171, 197).

SIGSTON, Yorkshire, North Riding 4194 C12? E O Lozenge-shaped enclosure of c. 2½ acres with good ditch. Central square ring-work (100 ft × 6 ft high) which supported wooden tower. (200).

SINNINGTON, Yorkshire, North Riding 7485 C12 D+ H Barn, N of church, belonging to hall was originally great hall of fortified manor-house or castle. C12 windows and remains of screens. (200).

SIZERGH, Westmoreland 4886 C14 etc. C+ P (NT) 'Most impressive house of its type in Westmoreland.' Great pele-tower with latrine and staircase turrets. Attached hall may be C15 in substance. (195).

SKELTON, Yorkshire, North Riding 5656 C12, 18, 19 D H Late mansion on site of castle much used by John as prison. Traces of extremely wide moat enclosing rhomboid area of 5½ acres. Some mediaeval masonry and fenestration (of chapel) survives in house. (166, 200).

SKIPSEA, Yorkshire, East Riding 1665 1086 E+ O Motte separated by marsh from long narrow bailey. 'Extensive and monumental earthworks.' (166, 192, 199).

SKIPTON, Yorkshire, West Riding 9851 C14, 17 B− S Clifford castle on cliff above beck. Magnificent gatehouse and towers, curtain and early C16 domestic range. (46, 96, 120, 150, 193, 200).

SNAPE, Yorkshire, North Riding 2684 C15, 16 C− H C16 rebuilding of Bolton-type castle. Chapel remains though much altered in C17. (67, 200).

SNODHILL, Herefordshire 3140 C11 D+ ? Complex earthworks covering 10 acres, motte which had polygonal keep (c. 1200). Remains of curtain and towers (C14?). (85).

SOMERIES, Bedfordshire 0821 mid C15 D+ O? Episcopal fortified mansion with remains of gatehouse, chapel, wall. Earliest use of brick in county. (15).

SOMERTON, Lincolnshire 9558 lc. 1281 C S? Tower-house of bishop Bek of Durham surrounded by complex earthworks and moats. One tower survives with remains of two others and curtain. Late C16 wing added. (104, 141).

SOUTHAMPTON, Hampshire   4212   C12 or earlier   C   O
Motte-and-bailey largely obliterated by later building. Scant masonry remains include fragments of curtain, watergate and vault for storing materials landed at castle quay. (54, 161, 173).
Town walls among finest in England. The long rows of arched recesses are notable though their purpose is obscure. (Perhaps economical). Several gates of which Bargate is most monumental. (80, 141, 169, 181, 183, 190).

SOUTH KYME, Lincolnshire   1749   C14   C−   H   Tower-house of four storeys with battlements and stair-turret. (104).

SOUTH MORETON, Berkshire   5688   C11?   E   O   Motte-and-bailey of which motte survives near church. (15).

SOUTH WINGFIELD, Derbyshire   3755   1440–1460   C   S?   Dramatic and picturesque ruins of very large fortified manor-house. (47).

SOUTHWICK, Northamptonshire   0192   C14 etc.   C   H   Small tower-house with Elizabethan and C18 additions. May have been fortified manor-house but never a castle. (129).

SOWERBY, Cumberland   3638   C12   E   O   If hill fort of Castle How is to be identified with Vaux castle of 1170s, then this is a rare example of Norman occupation of earlier fortified sites. (44).

SPOFFORTH, Yorkshire, West Riding   3650   lc. 1308   C   DE
Fortified manor of Percies. Substantial remains of 'hall-keep' with undercroft, chamber and chapel, polygonal stair turret. (78, 88, 111, 200).

STAFFORD, Staffordshire   9223   lc. 1348   D   O?   Remains of typical C14 castle incorporated in C19 mansion, largely demolished. There was an earlier royal castle (C11–12) on motte-and-bailey site (Tenter Banks) SW of town. (68, 101, 170).

STAMFORD, Lincolnshire   0207   C12   E   O   Motte with triangular bailey whose last remains, apart from trace of C13 masonry, were destroyed in 1933 to accommodate car-park. Traces of town walls with bastions and posterns. (104).

STANSTED MOUNTFITCHET, Essex   5124   C12?   E   O   Motte (perhaps with stone keep) and two small baileys. (59).

STAWARD PELE, Northumberland   3755   C14   D+   O   Rather uninteresting and neglected ruin on superb site. Scant remains of gatehouse, tower, wall. (130).

STEBBING, Essex   6624   C11?   E   O   Motte-and-bailey. High motte survives N of Town Mill. (59).

STEETON, Yorkshire, West Riding   0344   C14   C   O   Gatehouse (c. 1360) survives complete and some masonry (including chapel?) remains in later hall. (200).

STOGURSEY, Somerset   2042   C13–14   C   O?   Castle of de Courcy. Neglected remains of moat, curtain and bases of gatehouse towers. (167).

STOKESAY, Shropshire   4381   lc. 1202   B   S   One of earliest fortified houses in England with very interesting original domestic arrangements. Tower of unique shape, enclosing well. Great hall (c. 1250), gatehouse, hall range and another tower of curious plan. (30, 78, 111, 159, 160, 169).

STOWEY, Somerset   5959   C14   C   H   Sutton Court (C16, 19) preserves tower, later hall and section of wall of mediaeval castle. (167).

STURMINSTER NEWTON, Dorset   7813   before 1208   D   O
Motte-and-bailey (?) inserted in Iron Age fort to which manor-house was added C14. (51).

SUDELEY, Gloucestershire   0327   C14–16, 19   B   S   Begun by Ralph Boteler, became property of Richard III. Mediaeval remains of wall, towers, gateway, barn and church together with royal apartments of Richard. (4, 75).

SUTTON VALENCE, Kent   8150   C12   D   O   Remains of small keep, splendidly situated on escarpment commanding Weald. Other masonry possibly among vegetation. (95).

SWERFORD, Oxfordshire   3731   C12   E   O   Motte-and-bailey (now cut into by churchyard) with further oval enclosure. (135).

SWINESHEAD, Lincolnshire   2340   C12   E   O   Oval enclosure, largely occupied by low mound. Defences seem to have relied more on water than earthworks. (Edge of Fens). (104).

TAMWORTH, Staffordshire   2004   C11, 12   C–   P   Large motte-and-bailey on banks of Tame. Masonry remains include: polygonal shell-keep with square wall-tower (C12?), wing-wall with herringbone (C11), postern. Shell filled with C16–18 buildings. (85, 159, 170).

TATTERSHALL, Lincolnshire   2157   C13, 15   B   P   (NT)   In inner bailey of earlier castle stands great brick tower which substantially is all that remains. 'Unquestionably the most imposing and elegant building of its kind and period in the kingdom.' (13, 20, 61, 81, 84, 104, 111, 114, 177, 180).

TAUNTON, Somerset   2324   C12 etc.   C   P   Castle of bishops of Winchester, much confused by re-use and additions. Mediaeval remains of modified C13 gateway, parts of C12 ranges (altered C13, 18), C13 tower (restored C18). (78, 167).

THETFORD, Norfolk   8783   C11   E+   O   Castle Hill with very large motte within Iron Age banks and ditches. Red Castle – ring-work, enclosing original town (?). (47, 53, 124, 128).

THIRLWALL, Northumberland   6566   C14   D+   O   Picturesque ruin above stream, largely from Roman materials. (130).

THISTLEWOOD, Cumberland   5845   C15, 16   D   H   Mediaeval pele-tower with C16 additions. (44).

THORNBURY, Gloucestershire   6590   C12, 16, 18, 19   C   H   Original castle rebuilt by Stafford, Duke of Buckingham, (c. 1511). 'Perhaps the last great baronial house to be built in the old castellated style.' (75, 106, 111).

THORNTON, Lincolnshire   2467   lc. 1382   D+   DE   Abbey ruins include largest gatehouse in England, apparently designed as fortified residence for abbot (barbican added C15). (67, 104).

THURNHAM, Kent   see GODARD'S.

TICKHILL, Yorkshire, West Ridings   5892   C12 etc.   C   H   Motte-and-bailey with early stone improvements. Remains of shell-keep, curtain and most interesting gatehouse. (73, 107, 142, 166, 200).

TINTAGEL, Cornwall   0588   C12–13   D+   DE   Three wards on strong natural site. Remains confusing and not very rewarding but situation unforgettable. (38, 54, 166, 177, 187).

TIVERTON, Devon   9512   C13–15   C–   S   Courtenay castle whose substantial remains include two corner towers of quadrangular ward with walls and foundations of domestic range. (48).

TONBRIDGE, Kent   5845   C12–13+   C   P   Impressive motte-and-bailey covering Medway ford. Traces of shell-keep and curtain. Massively fortified keep-gatehouse (c. 1300) with portcullis, machicolations, two gates, 'the most formidable in Britain'. Hall above gateway. (73, 95, 124, 127, 159, 177).

TONGE, Kent   9364   C12?   E   O   Motte and trapezoidal bailey, adjoining mill-pond (water defence). (95).

TOPCLIFFE, Yorkshire, North Riding   3976   C11   E+   O   Motte-and-bailey by ford at junction of Swale and Cod Beck. Well-preserved motte, horseshoe-shaped bailey with ditches. Original home of Percys. (53, 200).

TOTNES, Devon   8060   C11   C–   DE   Motte with circular bailey. Masonry remains of shell-keep which may have had a tower inside. (48, 159).

TOTTERNOE, Bedfordshire   9921   C12?   E   O   Small motte with three baileys. 'Once the strongest of the early castles of Bedfordshire.' (15).

TOWER, London   see LONDON.

TREAGO, Herefordshire   4924   C14   D   H   Mansion may absorb remains of earlier castle but earliest incorporations seem to be of C15 with considerable modifications C17–19. (85).

TREMATON, Cornwall   3959   C11, 19   C+   S   One of most extensive castles of Cornwall on superb site. Remains include curtain of inner bailey, very fine gatehouse, well-preserved shell-keep. (38, 54, 107, 159).

TRIERMAIN, Cumberland   6366   lc. 1340   D–   O   Probably similar plan to Penrith but almost nothing remains except fragment of tower. (44).

TURTON TOWER, Lancashire   7315   C15, 16, 19   D   H   Mediaeval pele-tower incorporated in house of C16 and 19. (100).

TUTBURY, Staffordshire   2129   C12, 14, 15, 18   C+   S   Motte (partly natural) and bailey. Mediaeval masonry of double S tower and N tower (C15), gateway (C14–15), remains of C12 chapel. Fine site. (60, 124, 159, 170).

TYNEMOUTH, Northumberland   3468   lc. 1296   C–   DE   Priory position made it as much a fortress as religious house and it was protected by curtain walls and towers at end C13. A massive gatehouse keep with barbican was added c. 1400. Its fortress function continued and increased after Dissolution. (67, 130).

UPNOR, Kent   7569   1559–67, C17   C   DE   Henrician fort to guard Chatham harbour which it signally failed to do on first test 1667, consequently rebuilt. (9, 95).

WALLINGFORD, Berkshire   6089   before 1142   D   H   Motte-and-bailey with some masonry. Siege work remains in grounds of St Peter's. (28, 165, 177).

WALMER, Kent   3750   c. 1539   C   DE   Henrician coastal fort modified C18 and 19 as residence for Warden of Cinque Ports. (9, 95).

WARBLINGTON, Hampshire   7205   early C16   D   H   Remains of gatehouse are all that survive of Margaret Pole's fortified manor-house. (80).

WARDOUR, Wiltshire   9226   lc. 1393   B–   DE   Tower-house of unique near-hexagonal plan with one side turned into rectangular projection for gatehouse. Small central hexagonal court. (54, 111, 195).

WAREHAM, Dorset   9287   C12   E   O   No remains above ground but site of royal castle discernible. (37, 51).

WARK, Northumberland   8576   C12   D   O   Motte-and-bailey covering ford over Tweed with traces of village enclosure to S and E. Alleged scene of traditional incident leading to foundation of Order of Garter (1350). Substantial earthworks and rubble core of some walls only remain of one of strongest and most important of Border castles. (16, 36, 39, 72, 82, 127, 130, 164).

WARKWORTH, Northumberland   2306   C12–14   B+   DE   Motte-and-bailey in loop of Coquet with room for village enclosure. Continuous development culminating in tower-house keep, 'rare case of military engineer being a great architect'. Unique plan difficult to describe and internal disposition of rooms show both intelligence and imagination. (9, 20, 22, 30, 36, 42, 46, 52, 68, 72, 82, 84, 93, 96, 107, 108, 113, 115, 130, 131, 142, 145, 155, 166, 171, 180, 187, 191).

WARWICK, Warwickshire   2865   1068, C12–18   B   S   Original motte-and-bailey with early masonry added. Substantially rebuilt in C14. Magnificent remains including unique towers, gatehouse, curtain, domestic range. (2, 3, 9, 12, 14, 30, 41, 43, 46, 57, 65, 68, 79, 81, 109, 117, 127, 133, 145, 159, 160, 166, 167, 179, 186, 190, 192).
Two quite impressive town gates with remains of wall and bastion near one (North Gate) of C14. (182).

WATTLESBOROUGH, Shropshire   3513   C12   C–   H   Considerable remains of small square keep with mediaeval wing forming part of C18 farmhouse. (160).

WEETING, Norfolk 7788 C12 C+ DE Rectangular moated enclosure with large mound. Masonry remains of oblong keep and domestic buildings. (128).

WELBOURN, Lincolnshire 9654 C12 E O Remains of large ring-work which probably had wet ditches. (104).

WELL, Yorkshire, North Riding 2682 C13, 18 C− H Later rebuilding and C18 decoration conceal nucleus of fortified manor-house. (200).

WELLS, Somerset 5445 lc. 1341, C14, 18, 19 B− H/S Most memorable of episcopal palace-castles. Much modern work but gatehouse, moat, chapel, some domestic buildings, undercrofts and ruined great hall are mediaeval. (49, 67, 167).

WEOBLEY, Herefordshire 4051 before 1138 E O Much altered ring-work and bailey S of church. Nothing remains of later stonework of de Lacey castle. (85).

WEOLEY, Warwickshire 0787 lc. 1264 Under corporation housing estate are remains of rectangular castle with six towers, surrounded by deep moat. (95, 192).

WEST MALLING, Kent 6857 c. 1100 C− O St Leonard's Tower, attributed to Gundulph builder of Rochester. Is it a keep or fortified church tower or both? (61, 65, 95, 179).

WESTON TURVILLE, Buckinghamshire 8511 before 1126 E H Motte and two baileys remain in grounds of manor-house. (21, 47).

WEST TANFIELD, Yorkshire, North Riding 2778 C15 D+ H Only fine Marmion gatehouse survives of castle on bank of Ure. (200).

WETHERBY, Yorkshire, West Riding 4048 C13 D− O Scanty remains by Wharfe close to mediaeval bridge. (200).

WHITCHURCH, Buckinghamshire 8020 before 1147 E O Motte-and-bailey (with tradition of masonry keep) NW of church. (21, 126).

WHITE TOWER, see LONDON.

WHITTON, Northumberland 0501 C14 C− H Tower-house incorporated in Children's Home. Originally Vicar's Pele and, unusually seems to have been tunnel-vaulted in two, if not three, storeys. (130, 180, 187).

WHORLTON, Yorkshire, North Riding 4802 before 1216 C? O Angular ring-work, 2½ acre bailey, 60 ft wide ditch, village enclosure to E. Some C14 masonry remains of gatehouse keep and cellars. (122, 200).

WIGMORE, Herefordshire 4169 C11 D+ O Ring-work with trapezoidal bailey and outer village enclosure. Some masonry, including part of shell-keep. (85, 105, 181).

WILTON, Herefordshire 5824 c. 1300, C16 C H Remains of typical C14 castle (rectangular with angle-towers) attached to Elizabethan house developed from its domestic range. Remains of part of curtain and one tower. (85).

WINCHELSEA, Sussex 9017 C13 C O 'Bastide' f. 1283. No castle in spite of 'Castle St.', remains of three mediaeval gates, town ditch. (128, 174, 182).

WINCHESTER, Hampshire 4829 C11, 12, 13 C P Long ovoid enclosure protected by 100 ft wide ditch. Amid plethora of modern offices are traces of C12 masonry and much abused great hall (1222–6) 'the finest mediaeval hall after Westminster', contains Round Table (C14?). (3, 4, 11, 32, 38, 39, 46, 50, 54, 78, 83, 123, 132, 133, 169, 177). See also Wolvesey.
Some remains of town walls and impressive Westgate (C13+). (77, 80, 183).

WINDSOR, Berkshire 9676 1068, C11–14, 19 A S Largest British castle on (natural) motte and double bailey plan. Shell-keep (1175) 'one of most perfect in existence' in spite of C19 remodelling. Always remained in royal hands and therefore subject to continuous alteration or improvement. Extensive work in 1175 and C14 when present chapel replaced older one. (5, 16, 27, 30, 33, 36, 38, 39, 46, 48, 50, 71, 83, 114, 144, 145, 153, 159, 164, 194).

WINGFIELD, Suffolk 2276 lc. 1384 C+ H? Impressive C14 gatehouse of three storeys and a good deal of main castle is incorporated in C16 mansion. (60, 111, 173).

WITTON-LE-WEAR, Durham 1431 lc. 1410, C15, 18, 19 C H Alterations and additions in modern times obscure mediaeval elements which include tower-house, curtain and turrets (with 'defenders'). (52).

WOLVESEY, Hampshire 4829 C12 C H Fortress-palace of bishops of Winchester within cathedral precinct. Ruins include remains of curtain, keep, tower (c. 1135), domestic range including traces of 140 ft long great hall. (49, 78, 80).

WOODCROFT, Northamptonshire 1306 C13 C H Typical late C13 castle: rectangular enclosure with round angle-towers, gateway in centre of front. Some remains survive later alterations and additions including one corner tower, gateway, some of wall and windows with 'Caernarvon arches'. (87, 129).

WOODSFORD, Dorset 7690 lc. 1335 C− H Thatched house with tower remains of rectangular castle with angle towers, gatehouse, machicolated battlements, two halls and chapel. (51, 101).

WORMEGAY, Norfolk 6611 C12? E+ O Village isolated in marsh has its approach commanded by motte-and-bailey castle of unusual size. (128).

WRAY, Lancashire 3700 1840–7 H Extravagant and formidable essay in Gothic Revivalism with battlements, machicolations, towers and turrets everywhere. (100).

WRAYSHOLME TOWER, Lancashire 3675 late C15?, 19 D H Rectangular pele-tower attached to farmhouse. (100).

WRESSLE, Yorkshire, East Riding 7031 c. 1389 C ? Substantial and impressive fragment of the only important castle ruins in ER. Bolton type. Remains of S side: two towers, intermediate hall-range and fragment of entrance. Crucifix in hall basement and angel-corbel which once supported oriel. (54, 88, 199).

YANWATH, Westmoreland 5127 C14–16 etc. B− H Characteristic C14 pele-tower with later attached hall (C15) and Elizabethan and later modifications. (61, 195).

YELDEN, Bedfordshire 0268 before 1174 E+ O Considerable earthworks E of village S of river: unusual oblong mound (130 ft × 90 ft at platform), two large baileys and subsidiary enclosure. (15).

YORK, Yorkshire 6052 1068, C12, 13 C DE/P First castle was motte-and-bailey on W bank of Ouse (Old Baile). Second built (1069) across river. Clifford's tower (C13) crowning motte is of unusual quatrefoil design. Bailey occupied by modern buildings and mediaeval defences largely obliterated but remains of curtain, bastion etc. (10, 26, 39, 53, 83, 94, 124, 159, 166, 177, 181, 195, 197, 199).

City walls and gates are finest in England, substantially complete with magnificent gatehouses, one still retaining barbican and some with 'defenders'. (12, 13, 47, 63, 74, 117, 126, 142, 160, 181, 182, 183, 190).

WALES

ABERGAVENNY, Monmouthshire   2914   C11   D   O   Triangular site at junction of streams isolated by ditch and bank. Motte-and-bailey with some masonry incorporated in Museum. (17, 123, 181).

ABER LLEINIOG, Anglesey   6280   C11   D   O   Motte-and-bailey of Earl of Chester (c. 1088–90), taken by Welsh 1094. Some masonry. Well-preserved earthworks hidden in trees. (5).

ABERYSTWYTH, Cardiganshire   5881   C13   D   P   Concentric, diamond-shaped moat and two baileys inside with towers at three of points and gatehouse at Eastern one. Few and scattered remains. On ridge, one mile S are remains of Aberrheidol (1110, rebuilt end C12): ring-work and bailey. (9, 25, 50, 133).

BEAUMARIS, Anglesey   6076   1287-90, 1316-20   DE
Culmination of concentric plan. Substantially complete: square inner bailey with six towers and two opposing gatehouses, wall and mural gallery. Outer bailey with 15 towers, two gates, watergate and fortified dock. 'No other Edwardian castle presents such a perfectly scientific system of defence.' (2, 5, 6, 12, 34, 35, 39, 54, 72, 73, 100, 112, 120, 127, 130, 134, 142, 145, 155, 171, 174, 188, 190).

BLAEN LLYNFI, Brecknock   8788   C12   D   O   Remains (overgrown) of rectangular moat, curtain and foundations. (20).

BRECON, Brecknock   0428   C11   D   O   At confluence of Usk and Honddu. Motte-and-bailey with remains of polygonal keep. (20, 48, 159). Some fragments of town walls. (181).

BRIDGEND, Glamorganshire   see NEWCASTLE.

BRONLLYS, Brecknock   1435   C12   D+   H   Motte and two baileys, outer rectangular. Remains of round keep on motte and other masonry incorporated in stables. (20).

BUILTH, Brecknock   0351   C11, 13   E   O   Motte-and-bailey, razed by Llewelyn, re-established by Edward. Nothing above ground. (20).

CAERGWRLE, Flintshire   3057   C13   E+   O   Sparse remains but splendid site with good views. (64).

CAERNARVON, Caernarvonshire   4862   c. 1090, 1283–1330   A   DE   'As fair a castle as man ever saw.' A fortress-palace in most advanced military style, incomplete though half a century in building. Magnificent and extremely substantial remains include stupendous curtain with wall galleries, many great towers and gates. (2, 3, 5, 6, 13, 24, 33, 34, 36, 39, 42, 47, 52, 54, 56, 59, 60, 67, 72, 73, 74, 96, 108, 117, 126, 127, 128, 136, 141, 144, 145, 171, 177, 181, 182, 183, 184, 186, 188, 190, 192, 198).

CAERPHILLY, Glamorganshire   1587   1271–   A   DE   Second largest castle in Europe, built by Gilbert de Clare. Antedated Edwardian fortresses which it may have inspired. Powerful concentric plan supported by extensive and unique system of water defences. Magnificent interesting remains. (12, 13, 21, 35, 54, 68, 69, 74, 78, 109, 134, 147, 155, 171, 177, 190, 193).

CALDICOT, Monmouthshire   4888   before 1216   C+   P
Motte-and-bailey carrying round tower (c. 1190?) of four storeys. Besides keep, remains include curtain, gateways and towers. Beam-holes for brattices below parapet crenels. (22, 73, 93, 123).

CARDIFF, Glamorganshire   1877   1081   C−   P   Motte inside square bailey formed by walls of Roman fort. Entrance through C15 tower. Modern buildings incorporate part of mediaeval domestic arrangments. (74, 96, 159, 181).

CARDIGAN, Cardiganshire 1846 1093 D+ O Original promontory site at Castle Farm. Transferred to present site mid C12: traces in Castle Green. (25).

CAREW, Pembrokeshire 0403 C13, 15 B− P Sited on inlet of Milford Haven. Quadrilateral enclosure with plinthed angle-towers. Additions demonstrate transition from castle to mansion in C15–16. (68, 138, 143, 172, 191).

CARMARTHEN, Carmarthenshire 4120 C12? C− O Original site possibly at Rhyd-y-Gors (no remains). Town site has remodelled motte-and-bailey and remains of walls. (25, 159).

CARREG CENNEN, Carmarthenshire 6421 C12–14 B DE Originally native stronghold but remains are largely English C13. Unusual plan, great gatehouse, long barbican passage, unique water supply, mysterious cave. Substantial remains in spite of C15 demolition. 'Most theatrical of British castles.' (25, 34, 166, 177, 194).

CASTELL COCH, Glamorganshire 1486 C13, 19 D+ DE Ruins of C13 transmogrified into Victorian phantasy with highly imaginative decoration. At least gives impression of colour and splendour which once enlivened all great castles.

CASTELL-Y-BERE, Merionethshire 6708 C11–13 C DE Native Welsh castle, captured and strengthened by Edward I but apparently d. 1294. Remains of irregular bailey and two D-shaped towers on magnificent and hardly accessible site. (116).

CHEPSTOW, Monmouthshire 5393 c. 1070, C13 B DE FitzOsbern castle on promontory between Wye and ravine. Keep (C11) on narrowest point between two baileys. Much rebuilding and addition in C13 including lower bailey and domestic buildings. (22, 47, 49, 64, 65, 71, 72, 78, 79, 93, 123, 155, 169, 177, 182, 183, 190, 192).

CHIRK, Denbighshire 2638 1310, C17 etc. C− S (NT) Characteristic C14 rectangular courtyard with round angle-towers. Additional tower to protect entrance. Impressive exterior. Motte above stream near church may represent site of C12–13 castle. (47, 68).

CILGERRAN, Pembrokeshire 1943 C12? C− DE Promontory site above gorge isolated by two rock-cut ditches. Substantial remains of walls and tower. (138).

COITY, Glamorganshire 9281 C11 C+ DE Ring-work with banks and later masonry including square keep. Ovoid tower (C13), outer bailey added and other rebuilding. Domestic buildings ruinous but interesting site. (74, 146, 190).

CONWAY, Caernarvonshire 7777 1283–92 B+ DE Long narrow site on rock bank of river. Two unequal baileys divided by cross-wall, enclosed by eight round towers, two gateways with barbicans. Fine example of climactic castle-building with associated bastide. (2, 3, 6, 24, 31, 33, 34, 36, 39, 40, 54, 64, 72, 74, 78, 96, 115, 127, 136, 146, 171, 177).
Town is a kind of bailey of which castle is keep. Walls nearly complete with remains of nearly 30 open-gorged towers. (13, 40, 67, 128, 146, 160, 181, 182, 183, 188, 190).

CRICCIETH, Caernarvonshire 4938 Mid C13 C DE Natural site on rocky promontory. Outer ward Welsh (1200–40), inner lozenge-shaped bailey English (1285–92). Much damaged by Glendower to whom it surrendered in 1404. Remains of curtain, strong gatehouse, three rectangular towers. (34, 44, 56, 72, 185).

DEGANWY, Caernarvonshire 7779 1088, C13 d. 1263 D O Two conical hills joined by earthworks to form double motte-and-bailey. Stone building in C13 but subsequent robbery has left but few scattered fragments of former powerful castle. (24).

DENBIGH, Denbighshire 0566 C12, 13 B− DE Early motte-and-bailey probably occupied town site known as the Mount. C13 castle built on present site. Interesting strong keep-gatehouse (c. 1280) formed of three towers about a central hall. (13, 46, 47, 54, 68, 73, 114, 126, 145, 155, 169, 183).

DINAS EMRYS, Caernarvonshire 2736 Prehistoric, C12 D O Legendary site of Vortigern's palace, rich in fable, sited on small hill above lake. (24).

DINBAUD, Radnorshire 0975 Prehistoric, C12 D O Impressive earthworks and fragments of stone tower. (149).

DINEFWR, Carmarthenshire 6121 C12, 15, 18 C H? Pentagonal enclosure on bluff. In Dynevor Park are remains of keep, curtain, entrance. (25).

DINGESTOW, Monmouthshire 4510 1182 E O Motte-and-bailey between church and river. (123).

DIXTON, Monmouthshire 5114 C12 E O Motte NE of church. (123).

DOLBADARN, Caernarvonshire 5760 c. 1220 d. 1284 C− DE Isolated round tower within small elliptical bailey. Native castle to guard pass of Llanberis. (24).

DOLFORWYN, Montgomeryshire 1496 1273 E+ DE Built by Llewelyn the Last. Captured by English in 1277. (123).

DOLWYDDELAN, Caernarvonshire 7352 C12 and later C− DE Rectangular keep of two storeys within polygonal curtain. Nearby mound has traces of square tower (25 ft sides). Traditional birthplace of Llywelyn Fawr. (24).

EWLOE, Flintshire 3066 c. 1257 C DE Native Welsh castle in position of great natural strength. U-shaped keep and two baileys. Remains of keep, curtain, tower, well. (44, 64).

FLINT, Flintshire 2472 1277 C+ DE Site protected by marsh. Unique cylindrical keep (inspired by Aigues Mortes where Edward stayed in 1270), rectangular inner bailey with three curtain towers, moat, well. (21, 23, 34, 39, 54, 64, 93, 115, 128, 133, 181).

FONMON, Glamorganshire 1172 C12 D H/S Later 'castle' encases what may have been great hall of Norman castle. (74).

GROSMONT, Monmouthshire 4024 c. 1150 C DE One of famous 'three castles of Gwent' along with Llantilo (White) and Skenfrith. Remains include earthworks, curtain and interesting hall. (33, 56, 83, 123).

HARLECH, Merionethshire 5831 1283–90 B+ DE Magnificent hill site overlooking sea. Remains of three concentric rectangular baileys, gatehouse-keep, artillery platforms, posterns, prisons. Represent culmination of mediaeval military architecture. (2, 6, 9, 30, 36, 39, 54, 56, 72, 96, 112, 116, 127, 133, 134, 147, 174, 186, 190, 193).

HAVERFORDWEST, Pembrokeshire 9515 C12, 19 D P Much altered remains, mainly due to modern use as prison. (138).

HAWARDEN, Flintshire 3165 c. 1285? C P Motte-and-bailey with remains of round keep, hall and barbican. (64).

HAY, Brecknock 2342 C12? C− O Two sets of earthworks: motte-and-bailey and ring-work. Besides earthworks, masonry remains of tower and associated curtain. (20).

HOLT, Denbighshire 4053 C12? c. 1300 D O Unusual plan: single pentagonal ward on mound by river. Scant remains due to cannibalisation to build Eaton Hall. (47).

KENFIG, Glamorganshire 8081 C12 E O Motte with large bailey which may have provided village enclosure. No remains above ground of later masonry. (74).

KIDWELLY, Carmarthenshire 4106 before 1114 B DE Early motte-and-bailey, remodelled C13, 14. Inner ward with four angle-towers (1280–1300), great curtain of outer bailey and gatehouse (C14). Substantial remains of these together with chapel and domestic buildings. Impressive earthworks. (2, 13, 25, 29, 31, 32, 49, 54, 73, 109, 141, 155, 159, 166, 197).

LAUGHARNE, Carmarthenshire 3011 before 1189 C P Strategic site at mouth of Taf. Remains of late C13, chiefly of round keep which unusually is vaulted in all three storeys. (25).

LLANDOVERY, Carmarthenshire 7634 before 1116 C P Motte-and-bailey beside river. Masonry remains of curtain, tower and gatehouse. (25).

LLANSTEPHAN, Carmarthenshire 3511 before 1146 B– DE Remains of de Chamville castle include earthworks, substantial part of inner curtain (C12), gate, outer curtain with flanking towers, great gatehouse (C13). (25, 68, 73, 106, 166, 180).

LLAWHADEN, Pembrokeshire 0717 before 1175 d. 1193 C DE Former episcopal castle. Oval ring-work with masonry remains: foundations of round towers (C12), rather more of C14 rebuilding. (138).

MANORBIER, Pembrokeshire 0698 C12, 13 B S Moated fortress with two baileys. Little survives of outer ward, but much of inner with nucleus of gatehouse, hall and chapel (unique). Birthplace of Giraldus Cambrensis. (2, 33, 52, 68, 78, 138, 146, 190).

MOLD, Flintshire 2363 C12 E O Motte-and-bailey with subsequent development. Only earthworks survive above ground on Bailey Hill. (64).

MONMOUTH, Monmouthshire 5113 C11, 12 C DE Triangular site at junction of Wye and Monmow. Motte and square town enclosure. Remains of keep and curtain. (123).
Unique fortified bridge (C13) over Monmow. (20, 181).

MONTGOMERY, Montgomeryshire 2296 before 1085, 1223–5 D+ DE Motte-and-bailey. Remains of impressive earthworks and fragments of masonry. (83, 123, 180).

NARBERTH, Pembrokeshire 1411 C12, 13 D O Earlier castle (d. 1116) probably represented by motte called 'Sentence Hill'. Scant remains of C13 castle. (138).

NEATH, Glamorganshire 7597 C12, 13 C– P? Nothing much remains except great gatehouse (C13). (74).

NEWCASTLE (Bridgend), Glamorganshire 9079 late C11, early C12 C DE Remains of polygonal curtain and two square towers, all with plinths, and doorway. (74).

NEWCASTLE EMLYN, Carmarthenshire 3040 C13? D O Sparse masonry fragments. The 'old castle' of Emlyn may be represented by large mound SW of church at Cenarth Fawr. (25).

NEWPORT, Monmouthshire 3197 C12, 13 C P No remains of C12 castle but of that c. 1300 there is the former E front of rectangular bailey on bank of Usk with towers, curtain and most interesting water-gate. (123, 171).

NEWPORT, Pembrokeshire 0639 c. 1200? D H/S Ring-work overlaid by later masonry and incorporated in private house. (138).

OGMORE, Glamorganshire 8877 1106? C DE Ring-work with outer ward. Masonry remains of rectangular keep, curtain. Good fireplace. (74).

OYSTERMOUTH, Glamorganshire 5386 C12, 13–14 C P? Sited above shore at Mumbles, C13 or 14 replacement of earlier castle burnt down in 1215. (74).

PEMBROKE, Pembrokeshire 9901 C12, 13 B+ DE Promontory site at junction of river and stream. Massive circular keep, two baileys: inner (c. 1190–1200), outer (early C13) joined to town walls. Very substantial remains, including unique cavern (Wogan). (17, 33, 65, 74, 93, 107, 127, 138, 151, 166, 172, 180, 193, 196).

PENARD, Glamorganshire   5785   C12   D   O   Scant remains of earthworks with some masonry. (74).

PENHOW, Monmouthshire   4191   C12, 15, 17   C   S   'Oldest inhabited castle in Wales.' Keep and great hall (C15). (123).

PENRICE, Glamorganshire   4988   c. 1190   C   H   (W)   Isolated site on W side of Gower. Single rectangular bailey, considerably ruined but interesting remains of gateway, curtain, towers and two-storeyed keep with chemise. (74).

PICTON, Pembrokeshire   0113   C12   C   S   Remains of castle incorporated in private residence occupied from C13. (138).

POWIS, Montgomeryshire   2106   C13, 14, 17, 18   C   P   (NT)   General aspect of C13–14 (apart from fenestration) though reconstructed C17. Spectacular site. (123).
Fine C14 gateway. Amazing interior.

RADNOR, (NEW), Radnorshire   2161   1096, C13   C–   P   Remains of characteristic C13 castle – square plan with massive corner towers (two smaller to SE). Entire garrison of 60 massacred by Owen Glendower. (149, 181).

RAGLAN, Monmouthshire   4107   C15   B–   DE   Very considerable remains of walled enclosure divided by hall, gateways and moated keep. Heavily machicolated. Fine example of period with touch of nostalgia. (3, 76, 100, 109, 111, 123, 131, 179, 190).

RHUDDLAN, Flintshire   0277   c. 1280   B   DE   Edwardian castle on similar plan to Aberystwyth but substantial remains: inner bailey, two strong towers, high battered curtain. Outer bailey largely destroyed. (3, 17, 39, 54, 64, 72, 73, 86, 133, 136, 145, 181, 188, 192).

ROCHE, Pembrokeshire   8821   C13   C   H   Tower-house altered to meet more domestic requirements. (138).

RUTHIN, Denbighshire   1257   1277   C   P/H   Edwardian castle with moat, curtain with round towers. Considerable remains in grounds of mansion now used as hospital. (47, 68).

ST CLEARS, Carmarthenshire   2716   C12–13   E   O   Coastal castle of which only moated mound survives. (25).

ST DONATS, Glamorganshire   9368   C13, 14, 20   C–   S?   'One of most perfect old baronial halls of Wales' (!). Mediaeval castle of concentric plan, continuously inhabited and extensively reconditioned by Hearst. Now Atlantic College. (74).

ST FAGANS, Glamorganshire   1177   C13   D   P   Only curtain wall survives around C16 house, now Folk Museum. (74).

SKENFRITH, Monmouthshire   4520   C12, 13   B   P   (NT)   Early motte-and-bailey remodelled c. 1203 by Hubert de Burgh. Excellent example of period: round keep on motte within quadrangular curtain with round corner towers. 45 ft wide moat on three sides, rover on other. (44, 56, 94, 107, 123, 145, 196).

TENBY, Pembrokeshire   1300   C12, 13   C   P   No remains of the castle of 1153 but there is some masonry of the later (C13) building. (138).
Some sections survive of town walls. (182, 183).

TOMEN Y MUR, Merionethshire   7139   c. 1090   D–   O   Motte, with some ashlar on its top, built within earthworks of Roman camp reduced by cross-ditch on line of motte. (116).

TOMEN Y RHODWYDD, Flintshire   0942   f. 1149   E   O   Text-book example of motte-and-bailey, guarding head of pass. Well preserved. (47).

TRETOWER, Brecknock   1821   C12, 13   C+   DE   Motte-and-bailey, former with L-shaped building into which a great circular tower was built (c. 1240?) – a unique modification. Substantial remains of keep, curtain, kitchen. Foundations of gatehouse. (20, 159).

UPTON, Pembrokeshire 0105 C12–13 D+ ? By creek in Milford Haven, facing Carew. Fine C13 gatehouse. (138).

USK, Monmouthshire 3701 C12 D+ H? Mound with traces of other earthworks and ruins of keep attaining three storeys in part. Picturesque site, much overgrown. (123).

WEOBLEY, Glamorganshire 4893 before 1306 C+ DE Considerable remains of irregular 'courtyard' castle: tower, chapel, domestic buildings. (30, 45, 82, 112, 137). The original (C12) fortification is probably represented by the ring-work at nearby Bishopston. (101).

WHITE, Monmouthshire 3217 C12 or earlier C+ DE Large, low mound with outwork and bailey. Foundations of rectangular keep, remains of curtain with round flanking towers (C12) and some later masonry including gatehouse. Moat. (44, 56, 123).

WISTON, Pembrokeshire 0218 C12 D O Bailey and motte crowned with polygonal shell-keep of which some masonry survives. (138).

SCOTLAND

ABERCORN, W Lothian 0878 C12 E O Only motte remains. (194). In neighbourhood is Blackness (q.v.).

ABERDOUR, Fife 1885 C14, 15, 16, etc. C+ DE Mediaeval tower-house, rebuilt C15, extended C16, 17, abandoned 1725. (61).

ALYTH, Perthshire 2448 C15? C O? In neighbourhood are ruins of Bamff, a former Ramsay stronghold. (139).

ANNAN, Dumfriesshire 1966 C12 E O Remains of motte-and-bailey. Head of Bruce barony. (52, 129).

BALVENIE, Banffshire 3242 C13, 15, 16 C+ DE Originally quadrangular enclosure with salient towers at W and N (possibly also E) — replaced by large round tower (C16). Formidable mass on well-chosen site. (10).

BANFF, Banffshire 6863 C12, 18 E O/H? C18 building occupies site of C12 royal castle on plateau overlooking sea. (10).

BEAULY, Inverness 5246 c. 1400 d. 1746 C H Original Fraser-Dounie castle now a ruin in terraced garden of Beaufort (C19, 20) (91).

BLACKNESS, W Lothian 0579 C15, 16, 17 C+ DE Tower on promontory site, enclosed with walls in C16 with an added massive tower. Converted for artillery later. Impressive and unusual ship-shaped structure. (194).

BLAIR ATHOLL, Perthshire 8865 C13 etc. C S Seat of Duke who still has 'retinue' or private army. Much rebuilding and additions due to continuous habitation. (139).

BORTHWICK, Midlothian 3659 lc. 1430 B+ S? 'By far the finest Scottish tower-house' sited at junction of two streams. Rectangular with two wings, four stone-vaulted storeys, machicolated parapet, free-standing within bailey. (115, 118, 157).

BOTHWELL, Lanarkshire 7058 1242, C14 B DE 'Largest and finest stone castle in Scotland.' Rocky promontory site with scarped banks. Keep on motte in pentagonal bailey. Rebuilt to reduced plan after damage in early C14. Substantial remains of curtain, postern, several towers, foundations of domestic range, hall, cellars. (57, 100, 157).

BRODICK, Buteshire   0236   C14, 17, 19   C   P   (NT)   Former Hamilton castle on island of Arran. Associations with Bruce. (23).

BRODIE, Moray   9857   C15–17, 19   C   S   Nucleus formed of C15 tower-house, other remains from C16. Rebuilt mid C17 with C19 additions. (123).

BROUGHTY, Angus   4630   C15   C   P?   Ruins of mediaeval castle on sea-shore site. (5).

BURNTISLAND, Fife   2585   C12, 14, 16   C+   P?   Substantial remains of Rossend, originally palace-castle of abbots of Dunfermline. Associations with Mary, Queen of Scots. (61).

CAERLAVEROCK, Dumfriesshire   0265   1230, C14   B   DE   Triangular moated site with gatehouse at one corner, round towers at others. Twice rebuilt in C14. Remains of magnificent gatehouse (c. 1390), much of curtain, foundations of domestic buildings. (52, 157).

CAIRSTON, Orkney   2611   C12   D+   H   Farmstead incorporates remains of square curtain wall with small square tower in NW angle. (133).

CAIRNBULG, Aberdeenshire   0163   c. 1260, C14, 16, 19   C   H   Comyn stronghold, destroyed by Bruce, rebuilt by Fraser. In spite of considerable rebuilding there are mediaeval remains in keep and round tower of C16. (1).

CAMPBELL, Clackmannonshire   9699   C15, 16, 17   B–   DE   Replacement of motte-and-bailey (C12) by pele and barmkin (C15), elaborated and extended later. Pit-prison. Third floor barrel-vaulted, interesting grotesques. (34).

CARDONESS, Kirkcudbrightshire   5653   C15   C   DE   Substantial remains of rectangular tower-house (c. 1450), of ground floor and entresol with three upper storeys. Gun-loops, murder-hole (?), double prison, handsome fireplace. (95, 180).

CARDROSS, Dunbartonshire   3477   C13–14   C   P   (NT)   Site of former Douglas castle with Bruce associations. (52).

CARNASSERIE, Argyll   8399   late C16   C   DE   More a 'pele-tower' than a castle proper. Square fortified tower with attached house and barmkin. (7).

CARSLUITH, Kirkcudbrightshire   4578   C15, 16   C   DE   L-plan tower-house on promontory overlooking Wigtown Bay. Wing added to rectangular tower in C16. Two floors and basement. Curious salt-box in hall, together with laver and aumbry. (95).

CARNWATH, Lanarkshire   9846   C15?   C   ?   Ruins of Cowthally, castle of Somervilles, with royal associations. (100).

CARY, Stirlingshire   7878   C15   C   H   (W)   Typical tower-house, using material from nearby Roman fort, C17 hall wing. (172).

CAWDOR, Nairnshire   8450   lc. 1454, C14, 15, 17   B–   S   Rectangular structure on stream bank, ditched on other three sides. Originated as four-storeyed tower-house with C15 additions and improvements, including domestic range. Drawbridge, yett. (128, 157, 199).

CLACKMANNAN, Clackmannanshire   9191   C14, 17   C   DE   Tower-house occupies site of royal hunting lodge. (34, 180).

CLAYPOTTS, Angus   4631   late C16   B   DE   One of best preserved Z-plan tower-houses of striking aspect. Small vaulted basement, gun-loops including one through kitchen fire-back, cylindrical towers corbelled out to carry unique square garrets. Barmkin obliterated by encroaching housing scheme. (138, 180, 201).

COLMONELL, Ayrshire   1586   C   O   Ruins of several castles in vicinity: Craigneil (fragment of C13 tower), Knockdolian (ruined tower of C14?), Kirkhill (C16). (10).

CONON BRIDGE, Ross and Cromarty   5455   C15   C   H   Kinkell is site of former Mackenzie castle, an unaltered T-plan tower-house. Unoccupied. (153).

COSHIEVILLE, Perthshire   7948   C14   C   O/H   In neighbourhood are ruins of Comrie, former Menzies castle (C14+) and the restored and occupied Garth of about the same original date. (139).

COXTON, Moray   2263   C17   C+   H?   Coxton Tower, 2 miles SE of Elgin, is interesting in that, although built in 1644, it is mediaeval and practical in all its defensive details: gun-loops, machicolations, yett. Well preserved. (123).

CRAIGIE, Ayrshire   4232   C13   D   O   Mound with remains of curtain and hall. Overgrown. (10).

CRAIGIEVAR, Aberdeenshire   5609   C17   B−   P   (NT)   Described both as 'a fairy-tale castle' and as 'a testimony of taste'. L-plan tower-house (c. 1626) built by nostalgic speculator. (1).

CRAIGMILLAR, Midlothian   2871   C14–16   B   DE   Nucleus is tower on cliff-edge (1374) 'among finest and best-preserved of its type'. Bailey added c. 1430 and later, its buildings and outer court. Ingeniously defended entrance. Magnificent remains. (118, 157).

CRAIGNETHAN, Lanarkshire   8844   mainly early C16   C+   H?   Large tower-house of unusual design (Hamilton), with well preserved outer walls and towers. Large retainer's fore-court. (100).

CRAIL, Fife   6107   C12   D   O   Scant remains on site above harbour on Forth estuary. (61).

CRATHES, Kincardineshire   7396   C16   C   P   (NT)   L-plan tower-house of Burnetts. Continuously inhabited. Interesting C17 decoration. (95).

CRICHTON, Midlothian   3862   C14–17   C+   DE   Well-situated river site. Nucleus of extensive later building is characteristic mediaeval tower-house with interesting prison. (118).

CROOKSTON, Renfrewshire   5864   C12, 14   C+   P   (NT)   No trace of C12 but remains of Stewart castle (c. 1340). Much modified through continuous occupation. (150).

CUBBIE ROO'S, Orkney   4264   C12   C   O   At Wyre are remains of ring-work with banks and ditch around small square keep with forebuilding and cistern. (133, 158).

CULLEN, Banffshire   5166   C16 etc.   C−   S   Fortified house on rocky outcrop. Some remains of mediaeval work but extensive additions and alterations. (10).

DALHOUSIE, Midlothian   2924   C15   C−   P?   Former baronial seat, converted into school. Interesting prison. Vicinity of colliery. (118).

DELGATTIE, Aberdeenshire   7550   see TURRIFF.

DIRLETON, E Lothian   5183   early C13, 14–16   B   DE   Originated in (natural) motte with bailey, rebuilt in stone as rectangular enclosure with group of three towers at SW angle. Keep remains of this period. Massive development in C14 including great hall, dais-chamber, chapel and prison (C15) together with formidable gateway. Substantial remains. (53, 148).

DOON LOCH, Ayrshire   5098   C14   C−   O   Remains transferred from island to mainland to avoid inundation resulting from hydro-electric scheme. (10).

DOUNE, Perthshire   7301   C13, 14   B   DE   Rectangular site at junction of Teith and Ardoch Water. Considerable remains of Moray stronghold include domestic buildings (with two halls characteristic of livery and maintenance castle). Mighty gatehouse with prison and well-chamber. Yett. (138, 157, 199).

DRUM, Aberdeenshire   7900   C13, 17   C   S   Tower-house of C13, rectangular with rounded corners with added C17 mansion. (1).

DRUMCOLTRAN, Kirkudbrightshire   8668   C16?   C−   DE   L-plan tower-house, probably developed from simple rectangle. (91, 95, 108).

DRUMMINOR, Aberdeenshire   4927   1440   B   S   Forbes stronghold, restored 1966. (1).

DUFFUS, Moray   1668   1151, C14, 15   C+   ?   DE   Great Norman mound with oval bailey. Later masonry of keep and curtain (C14), domestic buildings (C15). Exemplifies danger of erecting heavy stone structure on earth – both tower and part of bailey have slipped down bank, but masonry has held! (123, 125, 129).

DUMBARTON, Dunbartonshire   4075   C5+, 17, 18   D+   DE Magnificent site on volcanic basalt plug. 'Longest recorded history as a stronghold in Britain.' Little mediaeval apart from 'portcullis arch' and line of curtain. (52, 166).

DUMFRIES, Dumfriesshire   9776   C12   E   O   Beside Nith are remains of two mottes: Castle Dykes and other within Dumfries Academy. (52).

DUNBAR, E Lothian   6878   before 1216, C14   C   O   Ruins of castle d. C16. Associations with Mary, Queen of Scots. (53).

DUNDONALD, Ayrshire   3634   C14   C   O?   Ruins of royal castle, including remains of Edwardian gatehouse, where both Robert II and Robert III died. (10).

DUNNOTTAR, Kincardineshire   8883   before 1209, C14, 16, 17   B   S Formidable natural site on promontory into North Sea, accessible by narrow defended causeway. Remains of C14 curtain, gateway, postern to beach, interesting L-plan keep (c. 1390?). Residential additions of C16, 17. (95, 157).

DUNOLLIE, Argyll   8532   C13 etc.   C   S?   Precipitous site overlooking sea. Remains of MacDougall castle include parts of curtain, postern, gateway, three-storeyed keep. (7).

DUNS, Berwickshire   7855   C14   D+   H?   Moray castle incorporates tower of 1320. (16).

DUNSCAITH, Invernesshire   5040   C13?   C   O   Remains of ruined castle of Barons of Sleat, on Isle of Skye. Sited on rocky promontory approached across deep ditch, strewn with sharp stones, via two arches and (former) drawbridge. (91, 166).

DUNSCATH, Ross and Cromarty   8269   1179   E   O   Only motte remains of William the Lion's castle in Ross. (153).

DUNSTAFFNAGE, Argyll   8935   early C13, 17, 19   C   O?   Base for driving Norse from Hebrides. Promontory site, royal then Campbell castle. Mediaeval remains of curtain, tower (including keep), gatehouse, chapel. (7).

DUNTREATH, Stirlingshire   5380   C15   C   S?   Substantial remains of mediaeval building. Prison. (172).

DUNVEGAN, Invernesshire   2549   C9?, 15–19   B   S   Impressive seat of Macleods on Isle of Skye. Fundamentally rectangular with wings. Mediaeval portions include moat, towers, bartizans, prison. (91).

EDINBURGH, Midlothian   2571   C11 etc.   C+   DE   First mentioned 1093 as 'castle of the maidens'. Magnificent promontory site, isolated by moat and three gates. Much altered, especially in C18–19 but retains St Margaret's chapel (c. 1100), east curtain, basement of C14 tower and some C15 work in palace. See also CRAIGMILLAR. (25, 118).

EDZELL, Angus   5968   C16, 17   C+   DE   Stirling, then Lindsay castle consisting of early C16 tower with added mansion (C16–17) and Renaissance garden. Unique display of heraldic and symbolic decoration on garden wall. (5).

EILEAN DONAN, Ross and Cromarty   8925   C14? etc.   C   S   Island site linked to shore by causeway. Castle of Mackenzie, MacRae. Scant remains of rock-based keep, more of mediaeval walls. Thoroughly restored C20. (153).

ELCHO, Perthshire   1620   C16   B–   DE   'Among most perfect and well preserved of late tower-houses.' Rectangular with two wings and projecting round towers. Four storeys with battlements and bartizans. Widely splayed gun-loops along all sides of base, machicolated entrance. (138).

ELGIN, Moray 2162 C12? D+ O Motte at W end of burgh supporting rectangular tower. See also *Coxton.* (123).

FALKLAND, Fife 2507 C15–16 C S (NT) Courtyard palace-castle. Stewart hunting-lodge used by James III, IV, V. Occupies earlier fortified site. (61).

FINDOCHTY, Banffshire 4667 C16 D O Ruins of rectangular tower-house with small oblong tower attached on N. (10).

FINLAGGAN, LOCH, Argyll 3868 C14–15 D ? On Islay, Hebrides. Ruins of Macdonald palace-castle on island site. (7).

FINTRY, Stirlingshire 6286 C16, 17 C H In neighbourhood is Culchreuch, a tower-house of C16 with C17 additions. (172).

FORRES, Moray 0358 C12? E O Motte which once supported seven-sided shell-wall about summit. Royal associations. (123).

FRASER, see MONYMUSK.

FYVIE, Aberdeenshire 7637 c. 1400, C17 C H Nucleus in tower-house paid for by Percy ransom. Developed into what has been called 'crowning glory of Scottish baronial architecture'. (1).

GARLIESTON, Wigtownshire 4746 C15–16 C− O? In neighbourhood are two ruined castles on cliff-edge sites: Eggerness (C15?), Cruggleton (C15–16). (195).

GLAMIS, Angus 3848 C17, 19 C− S Difficult to exclude but little to interest the authentic castle explorer. The site is ancient and parts of the rectangular tower-house at the centre of the modern building are late C14. The curious may find it interesting that the newel of C17 staircase is hollow and contains the cords and weights of turret clock. (5).

GLENBUCHAT, Aberdeenshire 3815 1590 C+ DE One of finest examples of Z-plan tower-house. Had interesting inscription over entrance. Complete. Unusual support of stair-turrets on 'trompes' (squinches) instead of corbels. (1, 180).

GLEN COVA, Angus 3073 C15? C− O Ruins of Ogilvie castle in village. (5).

GLENLIVET, Banffshire 2126 There are two ruins in the vicinity: Castle Drumin with remains of C14(?) keep; Blairfindy, the former 'hunting tower' of the earls of Huntly (DE?). (10).

GRANDTULLY, Perthshire 8951 C16? etc. C H Family seat of Stewarts with nucleus of tower-house and gatehouse (with prison) of C16 or earlier. (139).

GREENKNOWE, Berwickshire 6443 1581 C+ DE Fine example (ruined) of L-plan tower-house with characteristic bartizans and crow-stepped gables. Yett of typical Scottish design. (16, 108, 180).

GUTHRIE, Angus 5650 C15, 19 C S Remains of altered late mediaeval tower-house containing traces of contemporary mural paintings. (5).

HAILES, E Lothian 5877 C13, 14, 15 C+ DE Rare Scottish remains of C13 masonry in curtain and tower (with prison); tower (with prison and massive wall) (C14); bakehouse and chapel (C15), postern, well. (53).

HALKIRK, Caithness 1359 C14 C− O In vicinity are ruins of Braal castle, the site of the burning of the bishop of Caithness (1222). (24).

HAWICK, Roxburghshire 5014 C12 E O Remains of motte-and-bailey on spur between Teviot and Slitrig. (153).

HERMITAGE, Roxburghshire 2253 C14 B− DE Rectangular enclosure of four great towers linked by curtain. Bothwell castle much visited by Mary, Queen of Scots. Impressive pile with considerable remains. (153). Nearby at Liddesdale is motte-and-bailey of original de Soulis castle.

HODDOM, Dumfriesshire 1573 C16 C+ S? Massive tower-house, ancestral home of Johnstones. (52).

HUNTINGTOWER, Perthshire 0924 C15, 16 B DE Great castellated house on site above Almond, ancestral home of Ruthvens. Considerable remains. Fine painted ceilings. (138).

HUNTLY, Aberdeenshire 5339 1600 B DE Gordon castle replacing mediaeval one at Strathbogie nearby. Site has been described as 'an epitome of the development of Scottish castles from the earliest Norman fortress to the palace of the 17th century'. Remains of motte, keep. (1).

INNELLAN, Argyll 1470 C15? C− P Knockarmillie castle, a former Campbell stronghold, sited above sea. (7).

INSCH, Aberdeenshire 6327 1260 C+ P? The ruined remains of Dunnideer castle represent the earliest authenticated tower-house on Scottish mainland. Built by John de Balliol on conical hill within prehistoric ramparts (two lines of different periods). (1).

INVERBERVIE, Kincardineshire 8372 C15, 17 C− H Two nearby castles: Benholm, C15 stronghold of Keiths with C20 additions; Allardyce of C17 with interesting corbelling. (95).

INVERLOCHIE, Invernesshire 1376 c. 1270 C− P? Former castle of Comyns: a quadrangular enclosure with looped round towers at corners. Outer bailey (C15) largely destroyed but remains of battlemented towers including SW (keep). (91, 157).

INVERURIE, Aberdeenshire 7721 C12 E O Traces of modified motte-and-bailey in churchyard (Bass and Little Bass). Associations with Robert Bruce. (1. 129).

KEITH, Banffshire 4350 C15 D P Milton Tower, a stronghold of the Ogilvies was built in 1480. (10).

KELLIE, Angus 6340 1170, C17 C S Originally Mowbray castle, thence Bruce and Stewart. Substantially rebuilt in 1679. (5).

KILCHURN, Argyll 1327 C15, 16, 17 C+ S 'One of finest baronial ruins.' A Campbell castle on what was originally an island site, begun 1440, much altered and extended. Ruins include mediaeval work. (7, 166).

KILDRUMMY, Aberdeenshire 4617 c. 1240, C14 B− DE Best surviving example of a C13 castle of enceinte in Scotland. Palace-castle of bishop of Caithness with chapel thrust through curtain for orientation. Rough pentagon with gatehouse at most salient angle, towers at others – one of which is keep. Postern with tunnel to stream. Substantial remains. (1, 161).

KILLIN, Perthshire 5732 C14? C O Near village are ruins of Campbell castle of Finlarig with traditional location of associated 'pit and gallows'. (139).

KILLOCHAN, Ayrshire 2200 c. 1586 C S Remarkably unchanged tower-house of Cathcarts. (10).

KILRAVOCK, Nairnshire 8149 C15, 17 C H Seat of chief of Clan Rose. Original tower-house (1460+) remains amid later building. Royal associations. (128).

KINCARDINE, Kincardineshire 6775 C13, d. 1646 C P? Ruins of former royal castle, built before 1212, on island in marsh. Remains of rectangular curtain, gate-towers, domestic buildings. (95).

KINCLAVEN, Perthshire 1538 C13 C+ O Remains of royal castle, consisting of rectangular enclosure with angle-towers. Postern with 'dog-leg'. Neglected and overgrown. (138).

KINNAIRDS, Aberdeenshire 6357 1574 D+ O? Remains of Fraser stronghold on sea-cliff, consisting of square machicolated tower of four storeys. (1).

KINTORE, Aberdeenshire 7916 C14 C+ O? Hall forest has the precarious ruin of a castle resembling Drum. Remains of a four-storeyed rectangular keep, two floors vaulted. (1).

KIRKCALDY, Fife 2791 c. 1460, C16, 17 C+ DE Ravenscraig was built for James II's queen on a bold and exposed site. Remains of curtain, towers, well-defended entrance, domestic offices. Gunports. (61).

KIRKCUDBRIGHT, Kirkcudbrightshire 6851 1583 C+ P? On site dominating harbour are imposing ruins of rectangular McLellan castle. Substantial remains, largely to roof height. (95, 166).
Half a mile S is mound of C13 castle (Castle Dykes).

KIRKLISTON, W Lothian 1274 C O Had a preceptory of the Knights Templar and in the neighbourhood are the ruins of Niddrie where Mary, Queen of Scots spent the night after escaping from Loch Leven. (194).

KIRKWALL, Orkney 4410 C12 D DE Remains of the hall belonging to the former episcopal palace-castle. (133).

KISIMUL, Invernesshire 6698 C13, 15 B− O Relatively small but formidable, sited on rock off Castlebay, Barra. Remains of curtain, remarkable keep, gateway, well, foundations of domestic buildings in barmkin or bailey. (91, 157).

LAUDER, Berwickshire 5347 C17 D H House on site of castle of 1590. There was a C12 castle which might have occupied any of four sites in neighbourhood (two of earthworks only and two with additional scant masonry). (16).

LINLITHGOW, W Lothian 9977 C12, 15, 17 C DE Royal palace-castle, birthplace of Mary, Queen of Scots. Magnificent C15 hall with vault over dais. (142, 194).
In the vicinity is 'The Binns', a tower-house of C17(?) with later additions (C−, P[NT]). The most important secular building in Lothian. External aspect of a greatly enlarged tower-house.

LOCH LEVEN, Kinrosshire 1401 C14−15 B− DE Island site with ruins (substantial) of castle from which Mary, Queen of Scots, escaped. Tower (C14), part of curtain (C13?), rest mainly C16. (95, 180).

LOCHMABEN, Dumfriesshire 0882 C12−14 B− P? Interesting ruins with long and eventful history including many sieges of which the last was in 1588. Associations with Bruce and Edward I. In the neighbourhood are early C17 tower-houses at Elshieshields (inhabited), Amisfield and Spedlin's (both uninhabited); all interesting. (52, 129).

LUFFNESS, Midlothian 4780 C13, 16 C H (W) Allegedly Norse site. C13 keep and earlier earthworks. Mainly C16 buildings. (118).

LUMSDEN, Aberdeenshire 4722 Two sites in neighbourhood: Motte of Auchindour (C12?) and Craig Castle (C16). L-plan tower-house with gun-loops, yett etc. (1).

McLELLAN'S, see KIRKCUDBRIGHT.

MIDMAR, Aberdeenshire 7005 C16? B− H Z-plan tower-house, with square and round turrets. 'One of most original and distinctive.' (1, 201).

MINGARY, Argyll 5164 C13, 17, 18 C+ O? Originated as castle of enceinte belonging to McIans. Rocky coastal site. Substantial remains include towers and curtain. (7).

MINNIGAFF, Kirkcudbrightshire 4166 C15−18 C O? In neighbourhood are ruins of Garlies, a Stewart seat. Its nucleus is a tower-house (C15−16), with considerable extensions in C17.

MOFFAT, Dumfriesshire 0805 C11−12 E O A 'fine motte-and-bailey' attributed by E. S. Armitage to the Bruces on whose demesne land it was built. (52, 129).

MONIKIE, Angus 4938 C15 B− S? Affleck is an L-plan machicolated tower-house in good condition. Solar and chapel. (5, 108).

MONYMUSK, Aberdeenshire 6815 C15, 16 etc. C S Nucleus is L-plan tower-house on site of dissolved priory (of which one defensive tower survives).
Nearby is spectacular Castle Fraser (C15, 17) a developed Z-plan tower-house with the interesting facility of 'the Laird's Lug'. (1, 166).

MORTON, Dumfriesshire 8900 C12, 13 B? O? No remains of earlier castle but there is rare Scottish example of lightly fortified manor-house which is substantially complete apart from roof. 'A very striking ruin.' (52).

MOTHERWELL, Lanarkshire 7557 C15, 17 C H Dalzell House, now boys' school, has C15 pele-tower as its nucleus with C17 additions. (100).

MOULIN, Perthshire 7735 c. 1320 C O Ruins of Black Castle (Campbell). Site originally surrounded by water and approached by causeway. (139).

MUNESS, Shetland 6009 1598 C+ DE On island of Unst, most northerly castle in British Isles. Ruins of Z-plan tower-house, substantially complete apart from top storey. Interesting inscription. (91, 160).

NAIRN, Nairnshire 8756 C15 C+ O? In neighbourhood is Rait, substantially complete ruin of tower-house, unusual in having a circular plan. (c.f. Orchardton). (128).

NEWARK, see PORT GLASGOW.

NOLTLAND, Orkney 4348 C16 B DE On island of Westray is Gilbert Balfour's bolt-hole: 'the most formidable castle on Z-plan.' It was not completed but considerable remains of great hall with square flanking towers with prodigious provision of gun-loops. (59, 91, 133, 197, 201).

ORCHARDTON, Kircudbrightshire 8052 mid C15 C DE Pele-tower and barmkin. The arrangement of the tower-house is typical but highly untypical in that is built on a circular plan. Vaulted basement and three superior storeys, quaint cap-house leading to parapet. Remains of enclosing walls and vaulted cellar in court. (95, 180).

ORKNEY, see CAIRSTON, CUBBIE ROO'S, KIRKWALL, NOLTLAND.

OYNE, Aberdeenshire 7625

Two castles: Harthill (1601) ruined Z-plan with barmkin. C O
        Westhall (C16) occupied L-plan. (1) C H

PEEBLES, Peebles 2540 C12 E O Site of Norman castle at junction of Tweed and Eddleston Water, motte now occupied by church. Royal castle. At neighbouring Neidpath is a former Fraser castle (C14–15 etc.) C H (137).

PENICUIK, Midlothian 2359 C15? C O? In neighbourhood are the impressive remains of ruined Brunstane, sited on bank of Esk. (118).

PITCAPLE, Aberdeenshire 7225 C15, 19 C S Occupied Z-plan tower-house with later wing. Associations with royalty and Cant. (1).

PORT GLASGOW, Renfrewshire 3274 C15–17 C+ DE Between two shipyards stands Newark. Nucleus is rectangular tower-house (c. 1480) with a detached gatehouse. These elements were united by a mansion in late C16 – early C17. Partly inhabited. (150).

RAVENSCRAIG, see KIRKCALDY.

ROSEHEARTY, Aberdeenshire 9367 C15 etc. C — Remains at Pitsligo include ruins of massive keep (1424) of three storeys, two vaulted, each holding a single room. (1).

ROSLIN (Rosslyn), Midlothian 2663 C14–16 B– P Impressive cliff site above Esk. Substantial remains of walls and towers (C14) and keep (restored c. 1580). Associated collegiate chapel with 'prentice pillar' (C15), incomplete. (118).

ROSYTH, Fife 1183 C15–17 C+ DE Originally tower with unusually lofty barmkin, turnpike wing added and later rectangular enclosure. Substantially complete remains of tower and fragments of enclosure. (61).

ROTHESAY, Buteshire 0864 C11, 13, 14 B DE 'One of most remarkable mediaeval castles in Scotland.' Ovoid enclosure on square island in pentagonal moat. High curtain wall, four projecting drum towers, great forework (keep-gatehouse of C16), chapel. (23, 28, 157).

ROXBURGH, Roxburghshire 6930 C12, 13 D O Sited on narrow

triangular mound between Teviot and Tweed. Scant remains of much fought-over royal castle. (153).

ROY, Invernesshire 0021 c. 1200? C– O Diamond-shaped enclosure beside Spey. Remains of ditch, curtain, square tower, privy. (91).

RUTHWELL, Dumfriesshire 1067 C15 C+ H? Neighbouring Comlongon is basically a simple tower-house of rectangular plan with amenities built into thickness of walls. (52).

ST ANDREWS, Fife 5016 C14, 16 C+ P Similar to Tantallon both in site and plan. Remains: substantially those of rebuilding c. 1390, including gatehouse-keep. C. 1570 this gatehouse was blocked and new gateway opened in curtain to W Mine and counter-mine of siege (1546–7). (61, 121, 134, 157).

ST MARYS LOCH, Selkirkshire 2422 C15? C ? N of loch is Dryhope, a strong pele-tower or tower-house. (159).

SCALLOWAY, Shetland 4039 1600 C DE L-plan tower-house of four storeys built by Patrick, earl of Orkney. Corbelled turrets, shot-holes, gun-ports, well in kitchen. (108, 160).

SCOTSTARVIT, Fife 3711 c. 1570 C DE Tower-house with barmkin of which latter has disappeared. Simple rectangular tower of four storeys with stair wing crowned with cap-house. Parapet angles with gun-loops. (61).

SCRABSTER, Caithness 1070 C13? C– O Ruins of palace-castle of bishops of Caithness. (24).

SMAILHOLM, Roxburghshire 6436 early C16, 17 C– DE Splendidly sited tower-house with barmkin. Oblong masonry survives through all five storeys. Crow-stepped gables. (153).

SELKIRK, Selkirkshire 4728 C12 E O Motte and angular bailey on N shore of Loch Haining. (159).

STIRLING, Stirlingshire 7993 C15 etc. C+ DE Precipitous hill site approached by causeway cut by two ditches. Two baileys. Much altered but parts of curtain survive and remains of domestic buildings (C15–16) including much mutilated great hall. Palace (mainly C16) of little military significance. (133, 171, 173, 185).

STRANRAER, Wigtownshire 0660 C16 C P Substantial remains though much modified as gaol in C18, 19.
Nearby is Craigcaffie Tower (1570), a well-preserved tower-house. C H (195).

STRATHAVON, Lanarkshire 7044 C15 C ? Avondale is a Z-plan tower-house (ruined) on natural defensive site: lofty isolated mound nearly surrounded by burn. (100).

SWEEN, Argyll 7178 c. 1220, d. 1647 B– ? Perhaps the earliest stone castle in Scotland consisting of two-storeyed rectangular keep, curtain and towers. Great rectangular tower-house and drum tower added later. Fine natural site on side of loch at its narrowest. (7, 158).

TANTALLON, E Lothian 5985 C14, 15 B DE Sited on precipitous promontory into North Sea. Landward side defended by two baileys, ravelin, three lines of ditches. Inner bailey defended by massive curtain from cliff-edge to cliff-edge with central gatehouse and drum towers at each end. Very substantial remains include keep-gatehouse (c. 1370), curtain. (53, 126, 157).

TARVES, see TOLQUHON.

TERPERSIE, Aberdeenshire 5420 1561 C– O? Ruins of Z-plan tower-house with gun-ports. (1, 201).

THREAVE, Kirkcudbrightshire 7362 c. 1380, C15 C+ DE On edge of island in Dee, other three sides protected by ditch and outwork. Five-storeyed tower-house of Black Douglas. Basement with well and prison, vaulted second floor, curtain looped for fire-arms. Remains of what may be earliest extant artillery works in Europe. Mons Meg used against it in siege. (1455). (95, 139, 180).

THURSO, Caithness 1168 C12, 15? C P? May occupy site of castle d.
1196 by William the Lion but existing roofless ruin (Sinclair) is much later.
(24).

TIBBERS, Dumfriesshire 1298 D+ O? Remains of castle built by
English knight in service of Edward I. (52).

TIORAM (TIRRIM), Invernesshire 6772 C13 C+ S? Macdonald castle
in splendid location on rocky hill projecting into Loch Moidart, islanded at
high tide. Great curtain, domestic buildings (c. 1600). (91).

TOLQUHON, Aberdeenshire 8631 c. 1420, late C16 B− DE Unusual
rectangular block, enclosing a courtyard (1584–9) but incorporating earlier
tower with added square and round salient towers to produce a large Z-plan,
guard-room looking on to large forecourt with outbuildings. (1).

TORPHICHEN, W Lothian 9672 C15 C P Interesting remains of the
Scottish H.Q. of the Knights of St John of Jerusalem – tower and vaulted
transepts of preceptory. (120, 194).

TORTHORWALD, Dumfriesshire 0378 C13, 15, 18 C− O? Brow of
brae fortified from prehistoric times, castle stands within mediaeval
earthworks. Remains of C15 tower-house. (52).

TOWARD, Argyll 1368 C15, 16 d. 1646 C− O? W of Toward Point
are ruins of late mediaeval castle, once seat of Lamonts, destroyed by
Campbells. (7).

TRAQUAIR, Peebles 3334 C14, 17 etc. C S One of several 'oldest
inhabited houses' in Scotland. Nucleus is impressive tower-house, rectangular
with bartizans. Various additions, particularly in C17. (137).

TULLIALLAN, Fife 9388 C14, 16 C− ? Ruins of Blackadder
hall-house above Forth. Splendid undercroft. (61).

TURNBERRY, Ayrshire 2007 C13 D O Remains of Robert Bruce's
ancestral castle on promontory above sea. (10).

TURRIFF, Aberdeenshire 7249 Two castles in vicinity: Delgatie:
rectangular tower (C13?) of Hays, converted into L-plan tower-house (C16).
Interesting decoration. (108). C S
Towie Barclay: tower-house, expressing late C16 mediaevalism, originally of
four storeys, savagely truncated in C18. Fine hall. (1). C P?

UDNY, Aberdeenshire 8726 C16–17 C S Great rectangular
tower-house of five storeys. Fine hall, secret passage and privy stair. (1).

URQUHART, Invernesshire 5328 C12, 14, 16, 17 C+ DE Scarped
motte on promontory site on shores of Loch Ness. Remains include: two
walled baileys, gatehouse, C16 tower, foundations of chapel, substantial
elements of domestic and ancillary buildings. Summarises development of
Scottish castle from motte to tower-house. (51, 91, 103, 157, 192).

URR, Kircudbrightshire 8165 C12 E O Motte-and-bailey on mound
between old and new channels of Urr Water. V-shaped ditch. Archaeology
revealed wooden defensive system. (95).

WHITEHILLS, Banffshire 6565 C17? C O? In vicinity is Boyne,
rectangular, of four storeys, drum towers at corners, front defended by ditch
with causeway and barbican. An atavistic reconstruction of a C14 castle with
provision for fire-arms. (10).

WICK, Caithness 3650 C+ O Along coast are ruins of several castles,
including Oliphant (C14), Girnigoe, Sinclair and Bucholly. (24).

WYRE, Orkney see Cubbie Roo's.

YARROW, Selkirkshire 3527 C15 C O In neighbourhood are ruins of
Newark, hunting lodge with royal arms on W side. (159).

YESTER, E Lothian 5667 C13 C+ S Remains of castle in grounds of
C18 house include curtain, postern and remarkable 'Goblin Hall', unique
vaulted underground chamber with well and postern. (53).